Vergil's
Aeneid

Vergil's Aeneid

Selected Readings
from Books 1, 2, 4, and 6

by Barbara Weiden Boyd

Bolchazy-Carducci Publishers, Inc.
Mundelein, Illinois USA

General Editor: Bridget Buchholz
Contributing Editor: D. Scott Van Horn
Cover Design & Typography: Adam Phillip Velez
Cover Illustration: Detail from "Inside the gate" by Thom Kapheim

Vergil's *Aeneid*
Selected Readings from Books 1, 2, 4, and 6

Barbara Weiden Boyd

The selections and notes from Books 1, 2, 4, and 6 are revised from *Vergil's Aeneid, Books I–VI*, by Clyde Pharr (Bolchazy-Carducci Publishers, 1998).

The Latin text is from *P. Vergili Maronis Opera* (Oxford, 1969; repr. with corrections, 1972) R. A. B. Mynors, ed., by permission of Oxford University Press.

AP is a registered trademark of the College Entrance Examination Board, which was not involved in the production of, and does not endorse, this product.

Bolchazy-Carducci Publishers, Inc.
1570 Baskin Road
Mundelein, Illinois 60060
www.bolchazy.com

Printed in the United States of America
2012
by Edwards Brothers

Paperback: ISBN 978-0-86516-764-3
Hardbound: ISBN 978-0-86516-765-0

Library of Congress Cataloging-in-Publication Data

Virgil.
[Aeneid. Selections]
Vergil's Aeneid : selected readings from books 1, 2, 4, and 6 / by Barbara Weiden Boyd.
pages. cm.
Includes bibliographical references.
ISBN 978-0-86516-764-3 (paperback/perfect bound : alkaline paper) -- ISBN 978-0-86516-765-0 (hardbound : alkaline paper)
1. Aeneas (Legendary character)--Poetry. 2. Latin language--Readers--Poetry. 3. Epic poetry, Latin. 4. Virgil. I. Boyd, Barbara Weiden, 1952- II. Title.
PA6801.A45B69 2012
873'.01--dc23

2012001685

CONTENTS

List of Illustrations

—— Preface and Introductory Notes ——

This edition of selections from Books 1, 2, 4, and 6 of Vergil's *Aeneid* is aimed primarily at two audiences: high school students preparing for the Advanced Placement Latin examination; and college students reading selections from the *Aeneid* for the first time in a fourth through sixth semester of college Latin. High school students not preparing for the Advanced Placement examination but prepared to read Vergil should also find this textbook accessible and helpful. The widespread popularity of Clyde Pharr's school edition of the first six books of the *Aeneid* in their entirety (*Vergil's Aeneid Books 1–6* [Lexington, MA: D.C. Heath, 1930; repr. 1964]; now available from Bolchazy-Carducci) in Latin courses at both of these levels has in recent years been qualified at least a little by the implicit definition of Pharr's ideal reader as someone with little need—or taste—for literary subtlety *per se* in the notes. At the same time, its user-friendly layout, with text, vocabulary, and notes neatly arranged on the same page, has made it seem sensible to me to emulate the format and particular virtues of Pharr's edition in the preparation of this revision of the AP selections. I shall indicate more precisely under the separate headings below those features of Pharr's textbook I have adapted for use here, as well as those places where I diverge.

Pharr's text has survived and thrived among several generations of American readers at least in part because, whatever its particular format and technical characteristics, the original editor's devotion to his poet is patent in the book's laborious—and useful—details. I have aimed to emulate this devotion myself, not so much out of a desire to keep the spirit of Pharr alive (although I confess to some residual fondness for the book, remembering as I do my own first acquaintance with it in high school), but because of the gift I have been given in being taught, enabled, and empowered to read, many times over now, Vergil's great poem. I wish for my readers as rewarding an introduction to the *Aeneid* as I myself once experienced.

While it is inevitable that in a book of this sort undetected misprints and occasional opaque comments will survive even the most alert reader's eye, clarity and accuracy remain desirable goals. The preparation of a revised edition gives me the opportunity to extend my thanks to the many readers who have contacted me with their suggestions, observations, and corrections. I offer my gratitude in particular to Katherine Bradley, Margaret Brucia, Darryl Phillips, Ronnie Ancona, Seth Knowles, and Charles Fornara, Jr., *primi inter pares*, for their attentiveness and scholarly *amicitia*. They have helped to make this a better book.

BARBARA WEIDEN BOYD
Bowdoin College

Introduction

I have provided an entirely new Introduction to Vergil and the *Aeneid* to replace Pharr's venerable but dated contribution. Writing with the aim of serving the needs of modern teachers and students, I have drawn on many years of teaching and reading Vergil myself. The focus of this essay is primarily literary, locating Vergil and his work in the intellectual and historical matrices of the late Republic and early Principate. The Introduction's narrative is complemented by a timeline of political and literary events and monumental constructions marking significant occasions in Vergil's lifetime, and by a brief bibliography of recent general works on the period and our poet.

Text

The text used here is that printed in R. A. B. Mynors' 1969 edition of the Oxford Classical Text of Vergil. I have made a few cosmetic alterations to make this text more congenial to the intermediate or AP Latin student: the initial letters of words beginning a new sentence are printed in the upper case; and third-declension accusative plural nouns ending in -**is** are here printed as ending in -**es**.

Orthography

In keeping with contemporary usage (as well as with the format followed by Pharr), I have printed consonantal **u** as **v**. Consonantal **i**, however, remains **i** throughout the text and notes. Thus, the Latin names of the king and queen of the gods appear as **Iuppiter** and **Iuno**.

Vocabulary Lists

An alphabetical list of all vocabulary glossed appears at the end of the text. In determining what vocabulary is to be glossed, I have used Pharr's general Word List as a guide and have not glossed the words on this list. Like Pharr, I have distinguished between glossed and unglossed vocabulary in the text by printing all glossed vocabulary in Roman font, and all unglossed vocabulary in italic.

Macrons

The Latin text in the selections from Books 1, 2, 4, and 6 and relevant running vocabulary lists and notes is printed with macrons to indicate long syllables. Students should nonetheless be encouraged to realize that the Romans did not write with macrons (nor do ancient manuscripts generally feature word division, punctuation, or a distinction between upper- and lower-case letters). They should also be encouraged to practice scansion on a text without macrons. Macrons are also included in the alphabetical vocabulary listing at the end of the book, and so provide to teachers and students alike a point of reference.

Grammatical Appendix

Pharr's grammatical appendix, now available online (www.bolchazy.com/extras/vergilgrammaticalappendix.pdf) remains unchanged, although some readers may find a few of his explanations somewhat dated; other good Latin grammars are available to remedy this situation. The two concluding sections of Pharr's appendix, on the dactylic hexameter and on figures of speech, have been fully revised, and the changes are detailed below.

Dactylic Hexameter

In providing a brief description and discussion of Vergilian hexameter, I have updated Pharr's discussion to make it more accessible to contemporary students and teachers. I have also tried to suggest that Vergilian hexameter is not an "add-on" to the plot, but an essential component in the rich texture of the poetry of the *Aeneid*.

Rhetorical Terms, Figures of Speech, and Metrical Devices

I have included a glossary of the rhetorical terms, figures of speech, and metrical devices mentioned in the notes. In most cases, I have adapted Pharr's original definitions to examples chosen from the selections in this textbook; some terms, however, are new additions, and a few have been redefined. I have also attempted to suggest that many metrical features of the poem are poetic devices in their own right.

Abbreviations

I have kept abbreviations in the vocabulary and notes to a minimum, and have attempted to avoid any potential for confusion. See p. xxxiii for a full list of signs and abbreviations used in the notes.

In the vocabulary lists, I have usually abbreviated only the second principal part of verbs (first conjugation verbs are indicated by a (1) in place of a full listing of principal parts). The genitive forms of third-declension nouns, when abbreviated, are intended to show students the root of a given word.

Grammatical and Syntactical Terminology

In the teaching of Latin in the schools, a wide variety of terminology for grammatical and syntactical constructions is current. Thus, for example, the subject-accusative + infinitive construction with verbs of knowing, saying, thinking, etc., is more commonly learned in American schools as "indirect discourse" or "indirect statement" (and also, albeit much less frequently, as "oratio obliqua"). In choosing to call this construction "indirect statement" in the notes, I am not endorsing a particular method or otherwise attempting to offer a value judgment on the available terminology; rather, I am attempting to represent to the best of my ability, based on many years of college teaching and nine years with the Advanced Placement Latin Test Development Committee, the terminology most likely to be familiar to students reading at this level. The real test of a commentary of this sort is the degree to which it allows students to read Latin independently; I hope that my commentary can make this possible in as unobtrusive a manner as possible.

Teachers and students should also note that I frequently offer two possible interpretations for a given construction (e.g., on 4.202, I comment on the nouns **solum** and **līmina**, "take either as obj. of **sacrāverat** (202), like **ignem**, or supply **erant**"). My purpose in offering these alternatives is not to cause confusion, but to suggest to students that their instincts are often right when they are puzzled by the ambiguity of a particular construction. This occasion also offers teachers an opportunity to remind their students that terms such as "abl. of cause" and "dat. of agent" are artificial constructs—no Roman reader would have needed, or understood, these categories.

Interpretive Comments

While I have not engaged in lengthy discussions of the interpretation of a given passage or subsection, I have on occasion permitted myself to comment on features of Vergil's style that repay close examination. I have attempted to make these comments in an "open," that is, suggestive, manner, rather than as "closed" and definitive statements of Vergil's purpose. I hope that these comments will offer to teachers and students the opportunity for rewarding discussion of the complexities of Vergil's poem.

Introduction

The Life of Vergil

Vergil's literary pre-eminence since antiquity has made not only his work but also his life the subjects of intense study for two millennia. Reliable information about Vergil's life, however, can be gleaned from our ancient sources only with difficulty or not at all. Contemporary (or nearly so) evidence is limited to a few passing references in other writers (e.g., an allusion by the contemporary elegist Propertius, at 2.34.65–66, to the forthcoming *Aeneid*) which tend to tell us something about the work rather than the person. Allusions to Vergil's friendships with Varius Rufus (see Quintilian 10.3.8) and Horace (*Odes* 1.3.6, 1.24.10, and perhaps 4.12.13), for example, do little more than confirm what we would be able to surmise without them, that is, that he was part of a generation of writers who frequented the highest social and intellectual circles. The most reliable tidbit of information is also the most recent to come to light: that is the mention of Vergil among four poets named by the Greek philosopher-poet Philodemus in one of the newly accessible Herculaneum papyri. Vergil's poems themselves contain numerous mentions of historical characters, places, and events, all of which have been used repeatedly by scholars in attempts to reconstruct a biography of Vergil; but their presence in works not of historical data-collecting but of reflective imagination and intertextual richness compromises, to say the least, their reliability as evidence for anything other than Vergil's poetic genius.

Both as a result and perpetuating cause of Vergil's almost overnight inclusion in the Roman school curriculum and speedy ascension to "classic" status in Roman literary tradition, posthumous stories about *Vergilius noster* quickly accumulated and were transmitted, and elaborated upon, through the centuries. The popular historian and celebrity biographer **Suetonius** (c. 70–130 CE) included much of this material in his (now fragmentary) *De poetis*; this in turn provided the basis for the *Vita Donati*, attributed to the fourth-century Vergilian commentator **Aelius Donatus**. Donatus was the teacher of both **Servius**, the Vergilian commentator whose surviving work is one of our greatest repositories of both valuable fact and wildly unreliable (dis)information about Vergil's world, and **St. Jerome**, who collected and translated sources on ancient chronology. Donatus' *Vita Vergilii* is the source of most of the "facts" we think we know about Vergil's life, from his shy and retiring nature and sexual preferences, to the loss of his family's lands during the confiscations after Philippi in 41 BCE, the effect of his recitation of *Aeneid* 6 on Marcellus' mother Octavia, and his deathbed wish that the not-yet-perfect *Aeneid* be burned. In fact, these anecdotes and others are far more likely to be based on (mis)readings of Vergil's works than on any historical reality, and bear witness to the velocity with which Vergil became a secular "saint" long before his "Christianization" in late antiquity and the early middle ages.

What we are left with, then, is little more than a skeleton of fact—itself not provable by any scientific means, but agreed upon by most scholars as offering a reliable framework upon which to hang Vergil's work and experience. He was born on October 15, 70 BCE, in or near Mantua (modern Mantova) in what was then Cisalpine Gaul. He traveled through the northern Italian cities of Cremona and Milan before coming to Rome; he spent time in and around the Bay of Naples as well. He died on September 21, 19 BCE, at Brundisium, and was buried in Naples.

The Works of Vergil

Three separate poems or collections of poems are ascribed to Vergil, all composed in dactylic hexameter: the *Eclogues*, a collection of ten primarily bucolic poems; the *Georgics*, a didactic poem in four books; and the *Aeneid*, an epic poem in twelve books. A fourth collection, the so-called *Appendix Vergiliana*, consisting of a wide variety of poems, has been ascribed to Vergil since antiquity, but most scholars now agree that the works in this compendium are by and large the efforts of Vergilian imitators, rather than authentic juvenilia from the poet's hand. Ranging from epigrams and Catullan-style short lyrics to the mock-epic epyllia (the term "epyllion," meaning "little epic," is a modern convenience, not an ancient category) *Culex* and *Moretum*, the poems in the *Appendix* open a window onto the poetic aspirations of numerous now-anonymous poets working in Vergil's shadow; they also serve as ample evidence of the degree to which the works of Vergil, especially but not exclusively the *Aeneid*, served as a central component in the "core curriculum" offered to elite youth in the centuries following Vergil's death. Like the Vergilian anecdotes transmitted by Suetonius and Donatus, these poems are evidence not so much of Vergil's career as of the power of the myth of Vergil.

The *Eclogues*, on the other hand, provide valuable insight into the formative influences shaping the young Vergil's literary aspirations. Attributed to the years immediately following the redistribution of land following the battle of Philippi—an event for which the *Eclogues* are in fact major "evidence" (see above)—these poems bear powerful witness to the political and social turbulence of the late 40s and early 30s BCE. Their formal model is the collection of *Idyls* by **Theocritus**, one of the great Alexandrian court poets of the third century BCE. Together with **Callimachus** and **Apollonius** (see below), Theocritus articulated a new attitude towards poetry as a mode of communication: unlike the writers of earlier centuries, these men composed in a self-consciously literary, and literate, fashion for a self-consciously literary, and literate, audience. Their readers were by and large elite men, with both the education and the leisure time to enjoy learned texts. It is certainly possible that some at least of this poetry could be performed as well as read—certainly some of the *Idyls*, as well as e.g. Callimachus' *Hymns*, lend themselves to performance. Nonetheless, enjoyment of this kind of poetry was clearly, and intentionally, most accessible to those who could recognize and be entertained by learned allusion: Apollonius' clever deployment of a Homeric *hapax legomenon* in a novel context, or Theocritus' "prequel" to the Homeric Cyclops in his romantic portrayal of Polyphemus. The *Eclogues* too appeal to the reader first and foremost—especially the reader already familiar with the Hellenistic poets, as well as the work of the "new" poets in Rome, like Catullus, Cinna, Varro Atacinus, and Calvus. Aside from Theocritus himself, however, the single greatest influence upon the shape taken by the *Eclogues* is likely to have been exerted by **Gaius Cornelius Gallus**, a contemporary of Vergil whose elegiac *Amores* (and perhaps other works) are known to us not directly (a bare ten lines survive), but through Vergil himself, who makes a fictionalized Gallus the central character in *Eclogue* 10 and whose learning and elegant style are likely to be reflected in the so-called Aristaeus epyllion of *Georgics* 4 (see below).

The dominant themes of the *Eclogues* combine escapist fantasy and nostalgia on the one hand with realistic Italian landscape on the other. Many scholars—this one included—have been tempted to see in the *Eclogues* a desperate, even self-delusive, attempt to replace the harsh realities of the 30s BCE with a better, simpler, and more promising picture of Italy and its inhabitants. *Eclogue* 4 in particular has attracted attention because of its self-fulfilling prophecy of the Golden Age renewed; like the contemporaneous *Epode* 16 of Horace, this *Eclogue* locates at an impossible distance the very escape from the here and now that it imagines. Some readers have found Vergil's love for Italy to be the dominant thematic key to the *Eclogues*, while others have argued that this love itself is compromised by the harsh reality that occasionally intrudes. Whatever the prevailing interpretation of the *Eclogues*, however, one thing remains clear: though these may well be the first formally published work of a young poet (Vergil was 35 in 35 BCE), they reveal a writer already at the top of his form, capable of a delicacy and vividness of expression and a sensitivity to language and rhythm rarely matched in his day—or any other.

To the modern reader, the *Georgics* may well seem an odd second project —a versified handbook of agricultural lore and advice seems hardly the best means to assert one's claim to major literary status. The tradition of didactic poetry is indeed one which has not translated well into the twentieth- and twenty-first century literary vernacular; for us, didacticism is the stuff of tedious textbooks, while the intimate expression of the self we associate with poetry presumes a density of an entirely different sort. For us, the language of poetry and the language of instruction rarely intersect; mnemonic doggerel (e.g., "Thirty days hath September, …"; "After *si, nisi, num*, and *ne*, …") is the only modern approximation, that is, it is no equivalent at all. The ancient world, however, provides a very different context for didactic poetry: second only to the Homeric poems in both temporal roots and cultural impact are the compositions of **Hesiod** (fl. 700 BCE), in particular, the *Works and Days*, combining farming advice, seasonal and meteorological lore, and popular morality in a hexameter poem that challenges the boundaries of genre even as it invents didactic. Hesiod's work, and in particular the richness of his didactic voice, were rediscovered in the Hellenistic era, when the scholarly revolution enabled poets to combine the inspiration of the Muses with their own abstruse researches. The impact of Hesiod is visible everywhere in Hellenistic poetry; only the most obvious index of this is the didactic fashion that gave us everything from the *Phaenomena* of **Aratus** (c. 315–240 BCE), a hexameter poem on the constellations and heavens, to the appropriation of the teacher's role by **Nicander** (fl. 130 BCE). His extant poems the *Theriaca* (on poisonous insects and snakes, and remedies for their toxins) and the *Alexipharmaca* (on antidotes found in nature to various toxins) suggest simply by their titles the extremes to which this tradition was prone. We know, furthermore, of many other no-longer-extant poems that trod similar ground, collecting arcane lore of one sort or another; and scholars have now amply demonstrated the role played by all of these influences in Vergil's poetic instruction.

Vergil looks to a native form of didacticism in shaping his didactic voice in the *Georgics*, too. Prose handbooks of agricultural instruction, written primarily for those elite readers who would eventually end up managing vast estates of their own, synthesized centuries of agricultural knowledge and tradition, covering everything from the proper clothing for slaves to the limits of intra-species grafting. Two of these handbooks survive, in whole or in part: **Cato the Elder's** *De agri cultura* (usually dated to 160 BCE) and **Varro's** *De re rustica* (usually dated to 37 BCE). Especially the latter of these, written in Vergil's own lifetime, exerted a great influence on Vergil; scholars have drawn increasing attention in recent years to the way in which Vergil transforms technical prose into Vergilian hexameters.

What is Vergil's own gift, however, is the ability he demonstrates in the *Georgics* (probably completed in 29 BCE) to transform even the most mundane details of a farmer's life into a powerful poetic lesson about the nature of life, especially human life, itself. The hierarchical organization of the poem, with its four books treating crops and vines, trees and shrubs, domestic animals, and bees, respectively, has long been understood to represent the gradual and continuing process by which man brings order to nature, and in the process creates a place for himself within it. Does the *Georgics* present us with a depiction of human interaction with the natural world as a happy cooperation enabled in the first place by the arts of civilization, or as a constant struggle for survival in a hostile universe? This is the fundamental question that has been asked by the poem's readers over the centuries; and this question is further complicated when we look at the world in which Vergil wrote this poem, a world marked by both the supreme accomplishments of human civilization and the chaos of war.

Similar concerns preoccupy both Vergil and his readers when we turn to the *Aeneid*. In undertaking an epic, Vergil appropriates not only the style and subject matter of the genre established by Homer but also its concern with empire and its symbols. The story Vergil tells—of how Aeneas, escaped from Troy, struggles to bring his people and traditions from Troy to a new home in Italy and there to create a new life for himself and them among the native (at least relatively speaking) peoples of Italy—deals with themes of both national and individual identity, of both personal responsibility and fate, of both the power of desire and the destructiveness of passion. I shall describe more fully below some of the central features of the poem as well as the many literary traditions that informed its creation; here I note simply that there is some evidence to suggest that, having begun the *Aeneid* in 29 BCE, Vergil died ten years later with it not quite complete. The numerous half-lines found throughout the poem (but not found in the *Eclogues* and *Georgics*) are the most frequently cited indication of the poem's incompleteness; it may be noted, therefore, that at least some of these incomplete hexameters occur at moments of high intensity in the poem, and they can therefore at least be argued to serve the poet's intention in their current state. More subtle indications of the lack of final authorial revision have been detected in studies focusing closely on the technicalities of Vergil's diction and meter. For the purposes of this discussion and throughout my notes, however, I shall speak of the *Aeneid* as a complete poem, bearing ample evidence of its maker's careful fashioning. Perhaps most important from a practical point of view, furthermore, I shall use the poem's allegedly unfinished state only as a last resort to explain away difficulties in the text.

The First Century BCE *and the Principate of Augustus*

The social, intellectual, and political turmoil and its consequences that came increasingly to dominate life in the Roman world after the third Punic War are at the heart of a story both too complex and too familiar to allow full discussion here. Readers are encouraged, therefore, to consult any of a number of up-to-date histories of the late Republic and early Principate; I provide a list of suggested titles at the end of this Introduction, noting as I do so the increasing, and therefore increasingly valuable, appearance of studies that synthesize various aspects of life in this period rather than focusing only on, for example, Rome's great military leaders or battle outcomes. It is possible, to be sure, to read the *Aeneid* in a cultural vacuum, equipped with little more than a cast of characters and a list of ablative constructions. Such a reading, however, necessarily entails treating the poem as a fiction rather than as both beneficiary and shaper of the defining issues of its day and indeed of Roman culture generally. In order to help my readers make at least a beginning at seeing the *Aeneid* as part of a larger cultural matrix, I have also located at the end of this Introduction a timeline that is meant to illustrate the relative chronology of several landmarks—physical, intellectual, and/or historical—during Vergil's lifetime.

The AENEID

MODELS

The epic ancestors of the *Aeneid* have been known since antiquity, yet they continue to provide rich new insights into both the methods and the meanings of Vergil's work. The twelve-book design of the poem, clearly divided into two halves (the Wandering and the War), both acknowledges and inverts the narrative sequence of the **Homeric epics**. This structural principle is echoed on countless occasions in the smallest details of the poem, beginning with the opening two words, *arma virumque*, evoking the central concerns of the *Iliad* (*arma*) and the *Odyssey* (*virum*). The movement back and forth between divine and human perspectives—as well as the occasional confluence or clash of the two—is also a central feature of Homeric narrative. Other Homeric features of Vergil's work will be observed in my notes on the poem.

A second prominent model for Vergil's epic is the **Argonautica of Apollonius of Rhodes** (third century BCE), a dactylic-hexameter poem in four books describing the gathering of Jason's companions; their voyage eastward to Colchis; their arrival there and involvement with the ruling family of Aeetes, especially his daughter, Medea; Jason's acquisition of the golden fleece; and the homeward journey of the Argonauts accompanied by the young princess. While the eventual outcome of Jason and Medea's love affair remains in the future from the perspective of Apollonius' narrator, his ancient audience already knew the full story in all its sorrowful detail from earlier literary treatments, especially Euripides' *Medea*. Apollonius' depiction of Medea's infatuation with Jason, therefore, pregnant as it is with foreshadowed doom, had a powerful influence on Vergil's depiction of Dido. New studies of Apollonius have shown, however, that his influence upon Vergil is hardly limited to the Medea/Dido parallel, but rather in its pervasiveness challenges the Homeric poems themselves.

The role of **tragedy**, both Greek and Roman, in the shaping of the *Aeneid* is also clear, although until recently it has generally received less attention from scholars than have epic influences. Indeed, the points of contact are too numerous to list here; instead, therefore, I simply note a few prominent instances worthy of further exploration. **Euripides'** *Medea* has already been alluded to; this play's reworking by **Ennius** (239–169 BCE), of which only fragments now remain, is likely to have been of equal importance. The fall of Troy so vividly depicted in Aeneas' narrative of Book 2 looks back to numerous plays on the Trojan theme, including, for example, the Euripidean and

Ennian *Andromaches*, Euripides' *Trojan Women*, and Ennius' *Alexander*; the "invasion" of Turnus by Allecto in Book 7 draws on Euripides' *Hercules Furens*; and the final combat between Turnus and Aeneas in Book 12 follows in many details the description of Hercules' engagement with Achelous, competing for Deanira, in **Sophocles'** *Trachiniae.*

The **great Roman poets of earlier generations** must have played a formative role in Vergil's early education; unfortunately, most of their work survives to us only in fragments. First and foremost was undoubtedly Ennius' *Annales*, an epic in fifteen books following the history of Rome from its foundations down to Ennius' own time. In its early articulation of the dactylic hexameter we find the origins of Vergil's beautifully balanced lines. In the early books of this poem, furthermore, Aeneas was a central character, and his struggle to achieve a Trojan foothold in Italy a central theme. The *Bellum Punicum* of **Naevius** (late third century BCE), too, was important, both in its treatment of the foundation of Rome in the early books and in its focus on the conflict between the two great peoples of the Mediterranean, the Romans and the Carthaginians. Other writers and their works, about whom we know even less, are too numerous to mention here; but whenever we are inclined to question the meaning or purpose of a particular genealogical or topographical detail in Vergil's poem, it is worth remembering how many of the texts that shaped his intellectual world are lost to us.

The interrelationship of all of Vergil's poetry with the *De rerum natura* of **Lucretius** (c. 94–55 BCE) is also evident, although exactly how this relationship should be described is a matter of some debate. Lucretius' hexameter didactic poem on the physics and metaphysics of Epicurean philosophy is a daring and powerful work, and Vergil's redeployment of Lucretian material—everything from particular words and phrases to images and even whole scenes—is undisputed. Whether Vergil's admiration of Lucretian didactic extended to his philosophy as well, however, is far less clear. On a purely technical level, a juxtaposition of Lucretian and Vergilian hexameter techniques indicates just how singular was Vergil's mastery of his poetic equipment.

Perhaps the single most important model, at least notionally, in fact, is the **Hellenistic poet** renowned for his rejection of epic—at least post-Homeric epic—and his espousal of a learned, self-conscious, and modernist poetics: I mean **Callimachus** (first half of the third century BCE), the author of numerous scholarly and literary works, most of which survive only as a list of titles but an important few of which we have at least in significant fragments. His *Aetia*, a four-book poem in elegiac couplets, was a virtuoso display of different subjects and narrative techniques, comprising a series of otherwise unrelated stories about the origins of various rituals, cults, places, and names. We also have six of his *Hymns*, modeled in some ways on the archaic *Homeric Hymns* but displaying as well the innovative style and intellectual detachment of the *Aetia*, and a large number of his *Epigrams*, again highly polished works that by their very brevity instantiate a rejection of epic values.

Because of Callimachus' evident distaste for post-Homeric epic (though not for Homer himself), scholars have long puzzled over how Vergil was able to find some compromise between the apparent polar opposites of epic and Alexandrianism, and how that compromise is articulated in the *Aeneid*. A more thoughtful appreciation of Vergil's accomplishment is made possible nonetheless—and suggests that no compromise was in fact needed—when one realizes that Callimachus' stance was not against epic *per se*, but against epic in the degraded and tedious form it often took in the centuries following the recording of the Homeric poems. In fact, Vergil's other great Hellenistic model, very much a complement to the poetry of Callimachus, is the epic *Argonautica* of Apollonius (see above)—a new epic, composed with a new sort of literary self-consciousness and in its learnedness very much suited to modern tastes.

Indeed, the depth and range of learning that was first possible in the Hellenistic world so profoundly informed Vergil's poetics that a comprehensive listing of important intellectual influences on his thought and works would be excessively long for the present purposes (if not simply impossible). In this discussion, therefore, I have chosen to focus on the most exemplary models rather than to provide a real catalogue; my readers are encouraged to make new connections on their own, using this short introduction as just that—an entry into a fascinating subject, and nothing more. But even this introduction would not be complete without the inclusion of three other names, each of whom played a direct and virtually unmediated role in the development of Vergil's poetic consciousness: Parthenius, Gallus, and Catullus. **Parthenius** of Nicaea, taken as a captive during the third Macedonian War and brought to Italy in 73 BCE, remained after being freed and became a teacher in Naples. Tradition has it that he single-handedly introduced educated elite Roman youth to the poetry of Callimachus and the other Alexandrians, and imbued his pupils with a new poetic aesthetic. While the remains of Latin poetry predating Parthenius demonstrate, scant as they are, that this is both an overstatement and oversimplification of the facts, there can be little doubt that he played a central role in the new cultural and intellectual awareness that characterized almost every aspect of life in the first half of the first century BCE. A precious indication of this is the one work of Parthenius of which we have a substantial portion, his *Erotica Pathemata* (Tales of Tormented Lovers), a textbook of sorts addressed to his pupil C. Cornelius Gallus and consisting of brief summaries of mythical love stories, for the most part obscure and for the most part concluding in tragic fashion. This document suggests *in parvo* not only how Hellenistic learning was transmitted to Roman boys but also how Hellenistic literary tastes shaped Roman ones—the stories included by Parthenius are, *mutatis mutandis*, obvious prototypes for, among other things, the story of Dido and Aeneas.

Parthenius' student **Gallus** (c. 69–26 BCE) is an equally important figure, though again we have little to go on from his own hand. The author of (at least) a collection of elegies called the *Amores*, Gallus is best known to modern readers not for the surviving ten lines of elegiac couplets attached to his name but as a figure of inspiration in Vergil's *Eclogues* 6 and 10 and as an elusive shadow behind the so-called Aristaeus epyllion with which the fourth book of the *Georgics* culminates. Whether this episode is inspired by Gallus in its subject, style, and narrative treatment, or whether Vergil composed it to replace an earlier conclusion in which Gallus himself featured, remains a matter of scholarly debate; but the episode clearly illustrates a fashion for which we also have compelling evidence from **Catullus** (c. 85–55 BCE), whose "new poetry" is likely to have made a strong impression on the adolescent Vergil. Catullus' poem 64, an epyllion on the marriage of Peleus and Thetis containing the inset narrative of Ariadne's betrayal by Theseus, has long been recognized to be a pervasive intertextual presence in Vergil's Dido and Aeneas episode; what is now becoming more apparent is that this is only the most obvious indication of Catullus' profound impact not only on Vergil's poetic sensibilities but also on his mode of expression.

Finally, I note—but can hardly do justice to here—Vergil's contemporaries, including particularly the poets **Horace** (65–8 BCE), **Propertius** (c. 54–16 BCE), and **Tibullus** (c. 55–19 BCE). Side-by-side reading of their poetry and Vergil's can only begin to suggest how these poets interacted, socially, politically, and intellectually; it offers a vivid picture nonetheless of the life-shattering turmoil which each, in his own way, survived and in which each found the inspiration to serve as spokesperson for a generation. The resulting portrait—or perhaps collage would be a better metaphor—renders the Augustan age a period for which there are few comparisons, in terms of both historical significance and creative richness.

CHARACTERS AND PLOT

Aeneas is a relatively minor Homeric character, best known for escaping from duels with both Diomedes and Achilles through divine intervention (*Iliad* Books 5 and 20, respectively); and the union of Venus and Anchises that will result in Aeneas' birth is central to the plot of the *Homeric Hymn to Aphrodite*. Aeneas is likely to have appeared in lesser or greater roles elsewhere as well in the ancient literary record, but we know of no real starring roles before the Roman poets take him up. I have already referred to his place in the poems of Ennius and Naevius; he also was a standard figure in the lists of names of ancestors with which the annalistic historians of Rome legitimized their work. The *Aeneid*, however, is effectively the first poem in which Aeneas is the central character throughout the work, and in which his characteristic *pietas* serves as a leitmotif.

The importance of this quality in Vergil's portrait of Aeneas is closely related to the prominence given to both his father **Anchises** and his son **Ascanius** in the poem. Aeneas' descent from Anchises is mentioned by Homer, and Venus' seduction of the unknowing Anchises in the *Homeric Hymn* gives Anchises a central, if somewhat passive, role in the narrative of Trojan lineage; but like his son he really only becomes a major character in the *Aeneid*. Ascanius, on the other hand, is not Homeric, and other Greek sources that attribute a young son (or sons) to Trojan Aeneas offer little more than names; rather, his prominence likely reflects the influence of local Italian traditions making Ascanius founder of Alba Longa. The emphasis on ancestral lineage that Vergil accomplishes with the close association of these three figures is thematically important to the poem, and also reflects the roles of both tradition and change in Roman cultural thought.

Much has been made since antiquity of the perceived similarities between the Vergilian Aeneas and the new *princeps*, Augustus, who brought peace to the Roman state after decades of civil strife; and indeed much contemporary evidence extraneous to the *Aeneid* indicates that this analogy was the seemingly natural outcome of a larger program of renewed emphasis on divine and heroic origins and lineage carried out through much of the first century BCE by the *gens Iulia*. Scholars are almost unanimous in their agreement, however, that an allegorical reading of the *Aeneid* (i.e., Aeneas "equals" Augustus) is not only a rash oversimplification of the facts but also ignores the complexities of Vergil's creative genius. The idea that the *Aeneid* is Augustan "propaganda" is both provocative and reductive, better used as the starting-point for a critical reading of the poem than as its conclusion.

The identificatiuon of **Creusa** as Aeneas' wife is not firmly fixed in the ancient sources before the *Aeneid* itself. Ancient representations of Aeneas' departure from Troy sometimes include a woman, but she is unnamed; and in the fragments of the Epic Cycle, she is called Eurydice. Her disappearance and death may well be Vergilian innovations, too, intended to allow both for Aeneas' subsequent relationship with **Dido** and for his eventual marriage to Lavinia. Dido makes her first appearance in late fourth-century BCE Hellenistic history, as the expansion of Carthage and other developments in the western Mediterranean give new prominence to the cultural and political reach of the Phoenicians. The encounter of Aeneas and Dido probably appeared in Naevius' *Bellum Punicum*, but at least according to Varro it was Dido's sister **Anna**, rather than Dido herself, who fell in love with the Trojan leader and committed suicide. The Vergilian version of the cultural confrontation represented by Dido's encounter with Aeneas and her subsequent demise is therefore likely to have been read as an innovation upon the traditional story, and is clearly informed by both contemporary political discourse about foreign, especially Eastern, peoples (of whom the Egyptian ruler Cleopatra is typecast as representative) and the status of women in the Roman world. Insofar as the conflict between Dido and Aeneas has been read as analogous to that between Carthage and Rome, furthermore, Dido has been interpreted as a stand-in of sorts for Hannibal. As with Aeneas, however, the temptation to allegorize is best avoided, at least in its simplest form; for it is clear that the historical models for Dido must share the limelight with her literary forerunners, like Ariadne, Medea, and Deianira.

Aside from these, there are **numerous other characters** in the *Aeneid* who play roles of some significance, both Trojans (e.g., Priam, Laocoon, Helenus, Palinurus, Achates, Nisus, Euryalus) and the ethnically diverse inhabitants of Italy (e.g., Latinus, Lavinia, Turnus, Evander, Pallas, Camilla, Iuturna, Mezentius, Lausus); the Greeks too are central to the narrative, although their roles are more often described by others than directly depicted (e.g., Odysseus [Ulysses], Achilles, Patroclus, Neoptolemus [Pyrrhus], Helen). All of these characters bear comparison with their Homeric and tragic prototypes; in these notes I shall attempt to indicate at least how to begin such comparative examination.

Arguably, however, **the gods**—or at least a few of them—are even more important than the humans in Vergil's epic narrative: Juno, Venus, Apollo, and Jupiter—as well as traditionally "minor" figures like Aeolus, Iris, and Mercury—are not only constant observers of human action in the poem but also play a central role in shaping human action. It has often been asked with some skepticism whether Vergil or his first audience, the sophisticated elite of the early principate, would have taken these gods seriously, that is, whether these gods would have been believed in and believable, both because of their obviously literary origins and because of the apparent absence of religious sentiment, at least in the modern sense, from Roman life in the first century BCE. Yet if we ignore the gods in the *Aeneid*, or see them simply as some sort of epic window-dressing, we risk writing off almost half of the poem, including moreover numerous scenes whose fundamental purpose seems to be to show the crucial part played by forces outside ourselves in human affairs: indeed, it is possible to read the *Aeneid* as evidence for the deep religiosity of the Augustan era, a religiosity that is best understood not in terms of belief or morality but in terms of cultural identity. The gods are as central to this identity as is Aeneas himself.

Vergil's Influence

The history of Vergil's reception as "the classic of all Europe," as T.S. Eliot called him, and indeed of all the West, can only be given in rough outline here; readers who wish to proceed further into this terrain are therefore advised to look at one or more of the many new treatments of Vergilian reception, and indeed of reception of Roman poetry as a whole, that have emerged in recent years. A few moments from Vergil's rich afterlife can nonetheless be noted here.

First witness to the Vergilian achievement is **Ovid**, who grew up reading Vergil's poetry and was undoubtedly deeply influenced by its language, its cadences, and its central themes. Ovid returns repeatedly in his poetry to Vergilian themes and characters, from the love letter written by the abandoned Dido to Aeneas (*Heroides* 7) to a rewriting of the *Aeneid*, from a new and sometimes subversive perspective, in the last books of the *Metamorphoses*. Ovid even exploits the Vergilian model from his place of exile, Tomis, imagining his departure from Rome in terms that are clearly modeled on Aeneas' escape from Troy (*Tristia* 1.3).

Three centuries after Ovid, the emperor **Constantine** (in a sermon dated to the early 320s CE) would read the fourth *Eclogue* as a prophecy of the birth of Jesus and thus of Christianity, and see Vergil therefore as a proto-Christian; and **Augustine** (354–430 CE) too would look to Vergil's characters as models for understanding human behavior and emotions, even as he rejected the pagan worldview of Vergil's work.

With Christian hegemony in Europe came an increasing tendency to read Vergil in Christian terms; the culmination of this trend appears in **Dante**, whose first-person narrator throughout the *Divine Comedy* (composed during the first quarter of the fourteenth century) is escorted, at least in the earliest stages of the poem's journey, by the soul of Vergil, "l'altissimo poeta." Indeed, Dante's relationship to Vergil has been seen by modern scholars as a metaphor of sorts for the way in which great works of art are kept alive, allowed—or even compelled—to transcend the boundaries of their own historical roots.

The resulting tension proved to be fertile ground for the poets of Europe throughout the ensuing centuries, particularly those engaged in the project of viewing epic through the lens of empire, and vice versa. This tradition saw its culmination, at least in some ways, in the work of **John Milton**, whose great poem *Paradise Lost* (1667) is richly Vergilian in its intertextuality even as it equates the empire-building burden of epic with the aspirations of Satan.

I leave for others, some of whom are included in the bibliographical list below, to continue this story, never-ending as it is; I mention here only two of the greatest poets of the late twentieth century, **Joseph Brodsky** and **Seamus Heaney**, each of whom has not only paid homage to Vergil but renewed Vergil in his own work. The very fact that you are reading this, before engaging in the interpretive act of translating the *Aeneid*, offers a paradigm for Vergil's vitality: with each (re-)reading the poem is renewed and transformed, as are its readers.

Timeline

	Augustan Rome - a timetable - *Barbara Weiden Boyd*		
Year(s)	Historical and Political Events	Monuments and Building Projects	Significant Texts/ Literary Events
79 BCE	Pompey's first triumph		
71	Pompey's second triumph		
70			Birth of Vergil
68	Julius Caesar's funeral oration for aunt Julia in Forum Romanum		
65			Birth of Horace

63	C. Octavius born September 23		
60	First Triumvirate formed		
59	Pompey marries Julius Caesar's daughter Julia		
55		Theater of Pompey and Temple of Venus Victrix (first use of *opus reticulatum*)	Deaths of Lucretius and Catullus
54	Julius Caesar's daughter Julia dies	Cicero purchases land for Julius Caesar's Forum (Forum Iulium)	Birth of Propertius (or 47?)
53	Battle of Carrhae – Crassus loses Roman standards to Parthians		
52	Pompey elected sole consul	Curia Hostilia and Basilica Porcia in Forum Romanum burn down	
49	Julius Caesar crosses the Rubicon		
48	Battle of Pharsalus – Julius Caesar defeats Pompey		
46	Julius Caesar's triumph in Rome	Dedication of Temple of Venus Genetrix in Forum Iulium	
44	Assassination of Julius Caesar; Antony's funeral oration for Julius Caesar in Roman forum; adoption of Octavian	Altar and column erected in Forum Romanum with inscription PARENTI PATRIAE	
43	Octavian becomes consul; formation of second Triumvirate		Birth of Ovid
42	Battle of Philippi; deification of Julius Caesar; division of empire	Building of temple of Divus Iulius in Forum Romanum decreed; Octavian vows temple to Mars Ultor	
41	Land confiscations		Vergil begins *Eclogues*
40	Antony marries Octavia		

38	Octavian marries Livia		
36	Octavian defeats Sextus Pompey at Naulochus; Lepidus removed from triumvirate		
34	Donations of Alexandria		
32	Octavian reads Antony's will; Antony divorces Octavia		
31	Battle of Actium		
30	Suicides of Antony and Cleopatra	Octavian's campsite memorial built at Actium	Horace publishes *Epodes*
29	Octavian's triple triumph	Curia Iulia in Forum Romanum finished by Octavian; temple of Divus Iulius in Forum Romanum completed	Vergil completes *Georgics*, begins *Aeneid*
28		Forum Iulium and Basilica Iulia finished by Octavian; dedication of the Temple of Apollo on the Palatine; Octavian's Mausoleum begun	
27	January 13 – *res publica restituta*; Octavian becomes Augustus		
25	Marriage of Julia and Marcellus		
23	Augustus receives tribunician powers for life; death of Marcellus; Agrippa heads to East	(approx.) Theater of Marcellus begun	Horace publishes *Odes* Books 1–3
21	Marriage of Agrippa and Julia		
20s	Lex Iulia theatralis		
20	Recovery of Roman standards from Parthia; birth of Gaius Caesar	Dedication of small Temple of Mars Ultor on Capitoline?	
19		Arch of Augustus (Parthian Arch) erected in Forum Romanum	Publication of *Aeneid*; deaths of Vergil and Tibullus

18	*Lex Iulia de maritandis ordinibus* and *Lex Iulia de adulteriis coercendis*		
17	Birth of Lucius Caesar; Augustus adopts Gaius and Lucius; *Ludi Saeculares*		Horace's *Carmen Saeculare* commissioned
16			Publication of Horace's *Odes* Book 4; death of Propertius
13	Augustus returns from Spain and Gaul	Ara Pacis Augustae vowed by Senate	
12	Death of Lepidus (or late 13?); Augustus is made Pontifex Maximus; Agrippa dies in late March		
11	Tiberius divorces Vipsania, marries Julia; Drusus marries Antonia Minor		
9	Death of Drusus	Dedication of Ara Pacis Augustae	
8			Death of Horace
2	Julia daughter of Augustus is relegated	Dedication of Forum of Augustus, including Temple of Mars Ultor; Augustus receives title PATER PATRIAE	
2 CE	Death of Lucius Caesar		
2–8 CE			Ovid works on *Fasti* and *Metamorphoses*
4 CE	Death of Gaius Caesar; adoption of Tiberius by Augustus; adoption of Germanicus son of Drusus by Tiberius		
7 CE	Julia granddaughter of Augustus is relegated; Agrippa Postumus is exiled		

8 CE			Ovid is relegated to Tomis, where he writes *Tristia* and *Epistulae ex Ponto*
9 CE	*Lex Papia Poppaea* modifies earlier social legislation		
14 CE	Death of Augustus		Augustus' *Res Gestae* read in the Senate by the Vestal Virgins

Bibliography

COLLECTIONS OF ESSAYS ON VERGIL'S LIFE AND WORK

Anderson, W. S. and L. Quartarone, eds. *Approaches to Teaching Vergil's Aeneid.* New York: Modern Language Association of America, 2002.

Harrison, S. J., ed. *Oxford Readings in Vergil's Aeneid.* Oxford and New York: Oxford University Press, 1990.

Horsfall, N. *A Companion to the Study of Virgil.* Leiden: E.J. Brill Publishers, 1995.

Martindale, C., ed. *The Cambridge Companion to Virgil.* Cambridge: Cambridge University Press, 1997.

Perkell, C., ed. *Reading Vergil's Aeneid: An Interpretive Guide.* Norman, OK: University of Oklahoma Press, 1999.

Quinn, S., ed. *Why Vergil? A Collection of Interpretations.* Wauconda, IL: Bolchazy-Carducci Publishers, Inc., 2000.

Stahl, H.-P., ed. *Vergil's Aeneid: Augustan Epic and Political Context.* London: Duckworth/The Classical Press of Wales, 1998.

THE FIRST CENTURY BCE AND THE AUGUSTAN PRINCIPATE

Galinsky, K. *Augustan Culture: An Interpretive Introduction.* Princeton: Princeton University Press, 1996.

Gurval, R. A. *Actium and Augustus: The Politics and Emotions of Civil War.* Ann Arbor: University of Michigan Press, 1995.

Raaflaub, K. A. and M. Toher, eds. *Between Republic and Empire: Interpretations of Augustus and His Principate.* Berkeley and Los Angeles: University of California Press, 1990.

Zanker, P. *The Power of Images in the Age of Augustus*. Translated by A. Shapiro. Ann Arbor: University of Michigan Press, 1988.

THE *AENEID*: LITERARY TRADITIONS

Anderson, R. J., P. J. Parsons, and R. G. M. Nisbet. "Elegiacs by Gallus from Qaṣr Ibrîm." *Journal of Roman Studies* 69 (1979) 125–55.

Clausen, W., ed. *Virgil: Eclogues*. Oxford: Clarendon Press, 1994.

Feeney, D. *The Gods in Epic*. Oxford: Clarendon Press, 1991.

Gale, M. *Virgil on the Nature of Things: The Georgics, Lucretius and the Didactic Tradition*. Cambridge: Cambridge University Press, 2000.

Gigante, M. *Philodemus in Italy: The Books from Herculaneum*. Translated by D. Obbink. Ann Arbor: University of Michigan Press, 1995.

Goldberg, S. M. *Epic in Republican Rome*. Oxford and New York: Oxford University Press, 1995.

Nelis, D. *Vergil's Aeneid and the Argonautica of Apollonius Rhodius*. Leeds: Francis Cairns Ltd., 2001.

Pease, A. S., ed. *Virgil, Aeneid IV*. Cambridge, MA: Harvard University Press, 1935.

Ross, D. O. *Backgrounds to Augustan Poetry: Gallus, Elegy and Rome*. Cambridge: Cambridge University Press, 1975.

Skutsch, O., ed. *The Annals of Quintus Ennius*. Oxford: Clarendon Press, 1985.

Thomas, R. F., ed. *Virgil: Georgics*. 2 vols. Cambridge: Cambridge University Press, 1988.

THE INFLUENCE OF VERGIL

Gransden, K. W., ed. *Virgil in English*. London and New York: Penguin Books, 1996.

Jacoff, R. and J. T. Schnapp, eds. *The Poetry of Allusion: Virgil and Ovid in Dante's Commedia*. Stanford, CA: Stanford University Press, 1991.

Martindale, C. *John Milton and the Transformation of Classical Epic*. 2d edition. London: Bristol Classical Press, 2002.

McDonough, C. M., R. E. Prior, and M. Stansbury. *Servius' Commentary on Book Four of Virgil's Aeneid: An Annotated Translation*. Wauconda, IL: Bolchazy-Carducci Publishers, Inc., 2004.

Thomas, R. F. *Virgil and the Augustan Reception*. Cambridge: Cambridge University Press, 2001.

See also the valuable chapters on Vergil's reception in the *Companions* edited by Martindale and Horsfall (listed under *Collections of Essays* above).

Signs and Abbreviations

abl. = ablative
abs. = absolute
acc. = accusative
adj. = adjective
adv. = adverb
App. = the Grammatical
    Appendix*
dat. = dative
dir. = direct
f., fem. = feminine
fut. = future
gen. = genitive
Gk. = Greek
imperat. = imperative
imperf. = imperfect
indecl. = indeclinable
indef. = indefinite
indir. = indirect
inf. = infinitive
interrog. = interrogative

Introd. = the Introduction of this
    book
lit. = literal, literally
loc. = locative
m., masc. = masculine
n., neut. = neuter
nom. = nominative
obj. = object
pass. = passive
perf. = perfect
pl. = plural
pluperf. = pluperfect
prep. = preposition
pres. = present
pron. = pronoun
quest. = question
rel. = relative
sing. = singular
stmt. = statement
voc. = vocative

(1) – This numeral after a Latin word in the vocabulary indicates that the word is a verb of the first conjugation and is to be inflected as **amō, āre, āvī, ātus**, *love, cherish.*

All Latin words in the notes and vocabularies are in bold face type. All definitions in the vocabularies are in italics. All translations in the notes are in italics.

*The Grammatical Appendix is located online at www.bolchazy.com/extras/vergilgrammaticalappendix.pdf.

THE WANDERINGS OF AENEAS

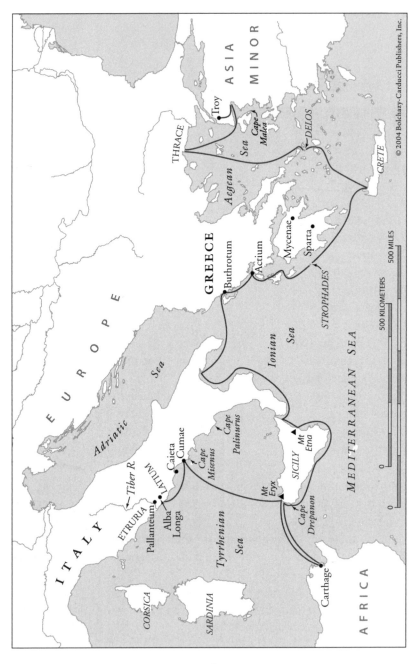

Selections from
—BOOK 1—

. . . patuit dea (1.405)

Illustration for Book 1
"Showed herself a goddess" by Thom Kapheim

Selections from Vergil's Aeneid

Book 1.1–209

Metonymy
Part = whole
arms = war

ARMA virumque canō, Troiae quī prīmus ab ōrīs
Ītaliam fātō profugus Lāvīniaque vēnit
3   lītora, multum ille et terrīs iactātus et altō

---

altum, ī *n.* the deep (sea)
canō, ere, cecinī, cantus sing (of), chant, proclaim

iactō (1) toss, buffet
Lāvīn(i)us, a, um Lavinian, of Lavinium
profugus, a, um exiled, fugitive

1–7. The theme of the poem, namely, the wanderings and wars of Aeneas, who after many struggles established the foundation for the greatness of future Rome, in accordance with the decrees of fate.

From the more extended introduction to the poem (lines 1–33) we learn: (1) the plan of the poet to describe the adventures of his hero, as is done in the *Odyssey*, and to depict wars and battles, as in the *Iliad*; (2) the importance of the gods, ruling over all mortal affairs, in the design of the poem; and (3) the story's relevance to Roman history, focusing as it does on the human trials that made possible the birth of Rome.

1. Arma virumque: the theme of the *Aeneid*; **arma** stands by METONYMY for *deeds of arms, wars*, referring to the wars in which Aeneas engaged, both in Troy and in Italy; **virum** refers to Aeneas, so well known that he is not mentioned by name until line 92. **Troiae:** with the first syllable long by position; App.

6, b. **quī prīmus ab ōrīs Troiae (ad) Ītaliam vēnit.** Aeneas was the first of the Trojans to come to Italy after his native city Troy had been captured, sacked, and destroyed by the Greeks in the Trojan War. Strictly speaking, the Trojan Antenor had preceded him, but Antenor's arrival, mentioned below at 242–49, is part of a narrative tradition different from that followed by Vergil here, and is not associated with the foundation of Rome proper.

2–3. (ad or **in) Ītaliam, (ad** or **in) lītora:** acc. of place to which; the omission of prepositions here is typical of Latin poetry, and you will see this often in the *Aeneid*; App. 315. **fātō:** abl. of means or cause; App. 331, 332; "through the will of heaven." **Lāvīn(i)a:** *of Lavinium*, an ancient city on the western coast of Italy, near the spot where Rome was later founded. Lavinium was said by many historians in antiquity to have been the first Trojan settlement in Italy and to have been named for Lavinia, the Italian princess whom Aeneas eventually married. Lavinia was the daughter of Latinus, king of the Latins. Lavinia herself first appears

A   *B*   *A*   *B*   *interlocking word order*

vī superum, saevae memorem *Iūnōnis* ob *īram,*

5   multa quoque *et bellō* passus, *dum* conderet *urbem*
īnferretque deōs Latiō; *genus* unde Latīnum
Albānīque patrēs atque altae moenia Rōmae.

Albānus, a, um Alban, of Alba Longa in
central Italy, mother city of Rome
condō, ere, didī, ditus found, establish
īnferō, ferre, tulī, lātus bring (into)
Latīnus, a, um Latin, of Latium
Latium, (i)ī *n.* district of central Italy
around Rome

memor, oris mindful, remembering,
unforgetting
ob on account of (+ *acc.*)
patior, ī, passus suffer, endure
quoque also
Rōma, ae *f.* Rome, a city and empire
saevus, a, um cruel, stern, fierce
unde whence, from which source

---

in the *Aeneid* in Book 7 (although a reference to her is made earlier by Anchises, at 6.764). Some of the oldest manuscripts of the *Aeneid* we have, dating from the 4th and 5th centuries CE, have the alternate spelling **Lāvīna**, because Vergil's earliest readers recognized that he was doing something unusual with the scansion of this line. The epithet **Lāvīn(i)a** must be scanned as two long syllables followed by one short syllable, and so the usual second **-i-** in the word must either drop out (i.e., **Lāvīna**) or be treated as a semi-consonant (i.e., **Lāvīnia**, with the second **-i-** sounding more like **-y-**, as in the English word "yoyo").

3. multum: adverbial, modifying **iactātus. ille:** Aeneas, the **virum** of line 1. **et (in) terrīs, et (in) altō:** abl. of place where; App. 319. **iactātus (est).**

4. vī: abl. of cause or means; App. 331, 332. **superum = superōrum,** gen. pl., *of the gods above.* **memorem:** an example of ENALLAGE (or TRANSFERRED EPITHET), logically describing **Iūnōnis,** but poetically applied to **īram. saevae memorem Iūnōnis ob īram:** an example of SYNCHESIS (or interlocked order), **saevae** modifying **Iūnōnis,** and **memorem** modifying **īram.** This pattern is often found in Latin poetry. **Iūnōnis ob īram:** the reasons for Juno's hatred of Aeneas and the Trojans are given by Vergil at 12–28.

5–6. conderet, īnferret: subjunctives in a purpose clause introduced by **dum,** expressing anticipated rather than completed action; App. 374.

5. urbem: Lavinium. **passus (est Aenēās). (in) bellō:** abl. of place; App. 319; referring to the enemies whom he had to conquer after landing in Italy. **multa:** obj. of the participle **passus;** App. 307, 313.

6. inferret deōs: App. 374; when travelling to found a new settlement, the migrating peoples of the ancient Greek and Roman world regularly carried with them their gods, either as images or other sacred symbols; see 68 and 378. **Latiō:** dat. of motion towards = **ad (in) Latium;** App. 306. **unde genus Latīnum (est):** Roman legends traced the origin of the Latin people, the kingdom of Alba Longa (forerunner of Rome), and the founding of Rome back to the coming of the Trojans under Aeneas to Italy.

7. (unde) Albānī patrēs (sunt): many of the noble senatorial families of Rome took much pride in tracing their families back to the early inhabitants of Alba Longa. **patrēs:** with the first syllable short; App. 17. **altae:** ENALLAGE (TRANSFERRED EPITHET). Since it more accurately describes the walls, the TRANSFERRED EPITHET suggests both the position, *situated on the (seven) high hills,* and the power and prestige of *lofty (mighty) Rome.*

> Mūsa, *mihī* causās memorā, *quō nūmine* laesō
> *quidve* dolēns *rēgīna deum* tot *volvere* cāsūs
> 10   īnsignem pietāte *virum,* tot adīre *labōrēs*
> impulerit. *Tantaene animīs* caelestibus *īrae?*

adeō, īre, iī (īvī), itus approach, encounter
causa, ae *f.* reason, cause
caelestis, e divine, heavenly
doleō, ēre, uī, itus suffer, grieve (at), be
  angry (at, with), resent
impellō, ere, pulī, pulsus strike (against),
  drive, force

īnsignis, e distinguished, marked, splendid
laedō, ere, sī, sus strike, hurt, offend,
  thwart
memorō (1) (re)call, recount, relate
Mūsa, ae *f.* Muse, patron goddess of the
  liberal arts
pietās, ātis *f.* loyalty, devotion, sense of duty
tot so many

> 8–11. Invocation of the Muse.

8. Mūsa: Jupiter and Mnemosyne ("Memory") were the parents of nine daughters, the Muses. From Homer onwards, it is the custom of epic poets to invoke one or all of the Muses for inspiration and to assign to their divine influence the gift of being able to compose poetry. **mihī:** this word in poetry may have the final **i** either long or short. The same is true of **tibi, sibi, ubi,** and **ibi. quō nūmine (Iūnōnis) laesō:** abl. abs. or abl. of cause; App. 332, 343.

9. quidve dolēns: *or vexed at what;* **quid** is the dir. obj. of **dolēns. rēgīna de(ōr)um:** Juno as Jupiter's wife was queen of the gods. **cāsūs:** dir. obj. of the inf. **volvere,** *to undergo, pass through.*

10. virum = Aenēān, subject of **volvere,** which depends upon **impulerit. pietāte:** abl. of quality (sometimes called abl. of specification), explaining in what feature Aeneas was especially outstanding (**īnsignem**); App. 330. Aeneas' **pietās,** *loyalty* or *devotion to duty,* is an important motif in the poem.

11. impulerit: perf. subjunctive in indir. quest.; App. 349, 350. **Tantaene = suntne tantae īrae caelestibus animīs? animīs:** dat. of possession; App. 299. **īrae:** poetic plural, often employed in Latin where English would ordinarily use the singular. Vergil's use of **īrae** as the concluding word of his introduction to the poem and invocation of the Muse echoes the appearance of "wrath" (**mēnis**) as the first word of Homer's *Iliad*. There is an important difference, however: Homer's theme was the wrath of his hero, Achilles; in Vergil's poem, wrath originates with the gods.

Urbs antīqua fuit (*Tyriī tenuēre* colōnī)
Karthāgō, *Italiam* contrā Tiberīna*que* longē
ōstia, dīves opum studiīs*que* asperrima *bellī,*
15   *quam Iūnō fertur terrīs* magis *omnibus ūnam*
posthabitā coluisse Samō. *hīc illius arma,*

---

asper, era, erum harsh, rough, fierce
colō, ere, uī, cultus cultivate, dwell (in),
  honor, cherish
colōnus, ī *m.* colonist, settler
contrā opposite, facing (+ *acc.*)
dī(ve)s, dī(vi)tis rich, wealthy (+ *gen.*)
Karthāgō, inis *f.* Carthage, great
  commercial city in North Africa, rival of
  Rome
longē *adv.* far (off), at a distance

magis *adv.* more, rather
ops, opis *f.* help, resources, power, wealth
ōstium, (i)ī *n.* mouth, entrance
posthabeō, ēre, uī, itus place after, esteem
  less
Samos, ī *f.* island of the Aegean, center of
  the worship of Juno
studium, (i)ī *n.* zeal, desire, pursuit
Tiberīnus, a, um of the Tiber, an Italian
  river on which Rome is situated

> 12–33. Reasons for the wrath of Juno
> against Aeneas and the Trojans.

12. Urbs antīqua fuit: it is curious that
Vergil here refers to Carthage as "ancient,"
since Carthage was in fact founded some
four hundred years later than the traditional
date of the fall of Troy, 1184 BCE. Vergil is in-
troducing the perspective of his readers into
the poem—to the Romans of the first century
BCE, as to us, Carthage was a very ancient
city indeed, and had in fact been razed to the
ground by P. Cornelius Scipio Aemilianus
(henceforth, Africanus) in 146 BCE, at the
end of the Third Punic War. **Tyriī:** *from Tyre,*
a city of Phoenicia, whence Carthage was said
to have been settled. The Phoenicians were
the great traders of their time, and Carthage,
on the northern shore of Africa and on the
Mediterranean, occupied a strategic posi-
tion for controlling the commerce of these
regions. **tenuēre:** shorter (syncopated) form
for **tenuērunt;** App. 204, 4.
    13. longē: modifying **contrā,** which gov-
erns both **Italiam** and **Tiberīna ōstia.**
    14. ōstia: see note on **īrae** (11). The gen-
eral expression **Italiam** is followed by the
more specific **Tiberīna ōstia** for the sake
of greater clearness and vividness. **opum:**

gen. of respect (also called gen. of specifica-
tion), with **dīves,** *rich in resources;* App. 294,
or gen. with special adj.; App. 287. **studiīs:**
abl. of respect, depends on **asperrima;** App.
325. This phrase would remind the Romans
of their bitter struggles with Carthage in the
Punic Wars.
    15. quam: refers to **urbs** (12) and is dir.
obj. of **coluisse. fertur:** *is said,* a common
meaning for this verb in poetry. **terrīs omni-
bus = terrīs aliīs; terrīs** is abl. with compara-
tive **magis;** App. 327. **ūnam = sōlam,** as often.
    16. posthabitā Samō: abl. abs.; App. 343.
Juno greatly loved Samos, an island off the
western coast of Asia Minor. According to
the myth, the goddess had been reared in
Samos, had married Jupiter there, and one of
her temples, among the most famous in the
world, was situated there. Vergil's point here
is probably that Juno prefers Carthage even
to her beloved Samos (although some schol-
ars still consider this abl. abs. difficult to in-
terpret). **Samō:** the final vowel is not elided,
although the following word begins with an
h. This failure to elide is called HIATUS. **illius**
(Iūnōnis): the -i of the genitive ending of the
nine pronouns and adjectives ending in -**ius**
usually long, but often short in poetry as here.
arma (fuērunt): doubtless refers to ancient
arms, chariots, and other relics preserved in
Juno's temple at Samos.

hīc currus *fuit; hoc rēgnum dea gentibus esse,*
sī quā *fāta* sinant, *iam tum tenditque* fovetque.
Prōgeniem *sed* enim Troiānō *ā sanguine dūcī*
20   *audierat Tyriās* ōlim *quae* verteret *arcēs;*
hinc populum lātē *rēgem bellōque* superbum
ventūrum excidiō Libyae; *sīc volvere* Parcās.
Id metuēns veteris*que* memor Sāturnĭa *bellī,*

---

currus, ūs *m.* chariot, car
enim for, indeed, in truth
excidium, (i)ī *n.* destruction, overthrow
foveō, ēre, fōvī, fōtus cherish, fondle
lātē *adv.* widely, far and wide
Libya, ae *f.* region of North Africa
memor, oris remembering, mindful,
   unforgetting (+ *gen.*)
metuō, ere, uī fear, dread
ōlim *adv.* (at) some time, once
Parcae, ārum *f.* the Fates

populus, ī *m.* people, nation
prōgeniēs, ēī *f.* offspring, progeny
quā *adv.* in any (some) way, where
Sāturnia, ae *f.* Juno, daughter of Saturn,
   father of the gods
sinō, ere, sīvī, situs permit, allow
superbus, a, um proud, haughty
Troiānus, a, um Trojan, of Troy
vertō, ere, ī, rsus (over)turn, change
vetus, eris old, former, ancient

16–17. hīc, hīc, hoc: repeated for emphasis; this repetition is called ANAPHORA. **hoc:** refers to **urbs** (12) but is attracted to the gender of the predicate noun **rēgnum**, *the ruling power.* **Iūno dea iam tum tenditque fovetque hanc urbem (Karthāginem) esse rēgnum omnibus gentibus, sed fāta voluērunt Rōmam esse hoc rēgnum. gentibus:** dat. of reference; App. 301.

18. quā (viā): abl. of manner; **quā** is an indef. pron. (= **aliquā**, but **ali-** is dropped after **sī**). **fāta:** the power of the fates was greater even than that of the gods.

19. Prōgeniem: the Romans. **dūcī:** *was being derived,* pres. pass. inf. used in indir. stmt.; App. 390; depends on **audi(v)erat** (20) of which Juno is the understood subject.

20. Tyriās arcēs = Karthāginem. ōlim looks to the future, i.e., to the Punic Wars. **verteret:** subjunctive of characteristic; App. 389, or rel. clause of purpose; App. 388.

21. hinc: ā **Troiānō sanguine,** or **ab hāc prōgeniē. populum:** subject of **ventūrum**

(esse) (22), an inf. in indir. stmt., depending on **audierat;** App. 390. **rēgem:** used like a participle (**rēgnantem**) here, and modified by **lātē. bēllō:** abl. of respect, depending on **superbum;** App. 325.

22. excidiō: dat. of purpose; App. 303; *for the destruction;* used with **Libyae** in the so-called double dative construction. **Libyae:** for **Āfricae,** meaning especially **Karthāginī. Parcās = fāta:** subject of **volvere.** The Parcae were represented as three sisters, Clotho (*Spinner*), who spun the thread of life for each mortal; Lachesis (*Measurer*), who measured the thread; and Atropos (*Inevitable*), who cut the thread when a human had reached his or her own allotted day. **volvere** probably describes the unrolling of the thread. **sīc (Iūnō audīverat) Parcās volvere.**

23. Id: the destined supremacy of Rome and overthrow of Carthage (19–22). **metuēns:** modifies **Sāturnia (Iūnō)** and has **Id** as obj. **Sāturnia:** *Saturn's daughter,* subject of **arcēbat** (31). **veteris bellī:** the Trojan War.

prīma quod ad Troiam prō cārīs gesserat Argīs—
25   necdum etiam causae īrārum saevīque dolōrēs
exciderant animō; manet altā mente repostum
iūdicium Paridis sprētaeque iniūria formae
et genus invīsum et raptī Ganymēdis honōrēs:
hīs accēnsa super iactātōs aequore tōtō

---

accendō, ere, ī, ēnsus inflame, enrage
Argī, ōrum *m.* Argos, a city in Greece,
 center of the worship of Juno; Greece
cārus, a, um dear, fond, beloved
causa, ae *f.* reason, cause
dolor, ōris *m.* pain, grief, anger, passion
etiam *adv.* besides, also, even
excidō, ere, ī fall from, perish
forma, ae *f.* beauty, shape, form
Ganymēdēs, is *m.* son of Laōmedon, king
 of Troy; carried off by Jupiter's eagle and
 made cupbearer to the gods
gerō, ere, gessī, gestus carry (on), wage
iactō (1) toss, buffet

iniūria, ae *f.* wrong, insult, injustice
invīsus, a, um hated, hateful, odious
iūdicium, (i)ī *n.* decision, judgment
necdum *adv.* not yet, nor yet
Paris, idis *m.* Trojan prince, son of Priam,
 took Helen from her husband Menelaus
 and thus caused the Trojan War
prō before, for, on behalf of (+ *abl.*)
rapiō, ere, uī, ptus snatch (up), plunder
repōnō, ere, posuī, pos(i)tus put (back,
 away), store up
saevus, a, um cruel, stern, fierce
spernō, ere, sprēvi, sprētus despise, reject

---

24. prīma: *(as) chief, leader, foremost,*
modifies **ea** (understood), which refers to
Juno. The goddess had taken a leading part
in assisting the Greeks against the Trojans.
The reasons for her hatred of the Trojans are
given in 27–28. **cārīs Argīs:** Argos, a noted
center of the worship of Juno, stands here for
all Greece and the Greeks.

25. īrārum: poetic plural; see note on **irae**
(11), and cf. App. 243.

26. (ex) animō: abl. of separation; App.
340. **(in) altā mente:** abl. of place where, *in
her deep mind,* i.e., *deep in her mind;* App. 319.
repos(i)tum: the longer form, with its three
successive short syllables, could not be used
in hexameter verse.

27. iūdicium Paridis: refers to the famous
Judgment of Paris. **sprētae formae:** apposi-
tional gen. with **iniūria;** App. 281; *the insult
to her slighted beauty,* shown by the adverse
decision of Paris.

28. genus invīsum: Juno hated the Trojan
people, partly because of Paris, but also be-
cause Dardanus, the founder of the Trojans,

was the son of Electra and Jupiter, and so
a constant reminder of Jupiter's betrayal.
Ganymēdis: a royal Trojan youth, brother of
Priam, was snatched up (**raptī**) by an eagle
into heaven; there he was beloved by Jupiter,
who made him his cupbearer, instead of giv-
ing the task to Juno's daughter, Hebe. Gany-
mede's story is told in more detail at 5.252–57.
Alternatively, **raptī** may be taken as nom.,
modifying **honōrēs**—the "stolen honors" of
Ganymede, i.e., stolen indirectly from Juno,
who believes they are owed to her by Jupiter.

29. hīs: abl. of means or cause; App. 331,
332, or abl. with **super;** the first option treats
hīs as dependent on **accēnsa,** and referring to
the three chief causes of Juno's hatred which
had just been mentioned in 26–28; **super** thus
functions as an adv., meaning *also, in addition*
(i.e., in addition to her fears for Carthage).
The second option would mean *angered over
these things.* The placement of a prep. after the
noun it introduces is called ANASTROPHE.
accēnsa (Iūnō). (in) aequore tōtō: abl. of
place where; App. 319.

30   Trōas, rēliquiās *Danaum atque* immītis Achillī,
      arcēbat longē Latiō, *multōsque per* annōs
      errābant āctī fātīs maria omnia circum.
      Tantae mōlis *erat* Rōmānam condere *gentem.*

Achillēs, is (ī) *m.* Greek leader before Troy
annus, ī *m.* year
arceō, ēre, uī keep off, defend, restrain
condō, ere, didī, ditus found, establish
immītis, e fierce, cruel
Latium, (i)ī *n.* district of central Italy
   around Rome

longē *adv.* far (off), afar
mōlēs, is *f.* mass, burden, difficulty
re(l)liquiae, ārum *f.* rest, remnant(s),
   leaving(s)
Rōmānus, a, um of Rome, Roman
Trōs, Trōis *m.* Trojan

---

30. Trōas: a Gk form; acc. pl. of **Trōs.**
rēliquiās: sometimes written with -ll-, to show that the first syllable is long and the word is thus able to be used in hexameter verse. **Dana(ōr)um, Achillī:** subjective genitives, *the leavings (remnants) of the Greeks and of Achilles,* i.e., those Trojans whom the Greeks and Achilles had allowed to escape.

31. arcēbat: the imperfect of continued action; App. 351, 2. **(ā) Latiō:** separation; App. 340. **longē Latiō:** note the repetition of the letter l; such a repetition is called AL-LITERATION. Alliteration, or the recurrence of the same sounds, usually consonantal, in successive syllables or words, is found in all languages, and is a characteristic feature of early Latin poetry and prose. Vergil's use of alliteration can sometimes be explained as

a conscious attempt on his part to recall the style of archaic Latin verse, especially early Latin epic (although alliteration by itself should never be over-interpreted by modern readers; the point is mainly that it makes the words memorable). It is also a special characteristic of early Germanic poetry, nearly all Old English verse being alliterative.

32. (Trōes) errābant. fātīs: abl. of means. **āctī:** participle of **agō,** modifies the understood subject **Trōes. maria omnia circum:** another example of ANASTROPHE; see above on 29.

33. Tantae mōlis: gen. of quality in the predicate; App. 285, *a.*; *of so great effort was it.* This line, summarizing the preceding lines, forms a powerful and effective close to this first section of the *Aeneid* and serves as a general introduction to the whole poem.

ᴗ◔

Anastrophe reversing of normal word order.

> *Vix ē* cōnspectū Siculae *tellūris in* altum
> 35 *vēla dabant laeti et* spūmās salis aere *ruēbant,*
> *cum Iūnō* aeternum *servāns sub pectore* vulnus
> *haec sēcum:* "*Mēne* inceptō dēsistere *victam*
> *nec posse Ītaliā Teucrōrum* āvertere *rēgem!*
> Quippe vetor *fātīs.* Pallasne exūrere *classem*
> 40 Argīvum *atque ipsōs potuit* summergere pontō

---

aes, aeris *n.* bronze
aeternus, a, um eternal, everlasting
altum, ī *n.* the deep (sea)
Argīvus, a, um Argive, Greek
āvertō, ere, ī, rsus keep off, turn aside
cōnspectus, ūs *m.* sight, view
dēsistō, ere, stitī, stitus cease (from), desist
exūrō, ere, ussī, ustus burn (up)
inceptum, ī *n.* beginning, undertaking, purpose

Pallas, adis *f.* Minerva, goddess of wisdom and the arts
pontus, ī *m.* sea
quippe truly, indeed, surely
sal, salis *n.* (or *m.*) salt (water), sea
Siculus, a, um Sicilian, of Sicily, a large island south of Italy
summergō (subm-), ere, rsī, rsus sink, drown
spūma, ae *f.* foam, froth, spray
vetō, āre, uī, itus forbid, prevent
vulnus, eris *n.* wound, blow

> 34–49. Aeneas and the Trojans set sail from Sicily for Italy, as they hope, happy at the prospect of the end of their wanderings. Juno gives a bitter soliloquy, chafing at the apparent failure of her plans to keep Aeneas and the Trojans from reaching Italy.

34. The reader is now plunged **in mediās rēs**: "into the midst of the action," and is abruptly introduced to Aeneas and his followers sailing away from the coast of Sicily. They have now been wandering for seven years since the destruction of Troy, their native city. These earlier events (the fall of Troy and their seven years of wandering) are later on narrated by Aeneas to Dido (Books 2 and 3).
35. laetī (Trōes): subject of **dabant**. **spūmās salis aere ruēbant:** note the AL-LITERATION. **salis:** METONYMY for the salt water of the sea. **aere:** the prows of the ships were sheathed with bronze; this too is a ME-TONYMY, for the prows or even the ships themselves.
36–37. Iūnō . . . haec sēcum (dīxit).

36. aeternum vulnus: the causes of this anger have been given above: her fear for Carthage, the Judgment of Paris, her love for the Greeks and hatred of the Trojans. **sub pectore:** *deep in her heart.*
37. sēcum = cum sē; App. 321, *a*; **mē:** subject of **dēsistere** and **nec posse. Mēne:** **-ne** is the interrog. particle appended to the pron. **mē.**
37–38. dēsistere . . . nec posse: infs. in an exclamatory quest.: *Am I, beaten, to desist from my undertaking and not to be able?*, etc.; App. 262. **(ab) inceptō:** abl. of separation; App. 340. **victam:** from **vincō;** it modifies **mē.**
38. (ab) Ītaliā: abl. of separation; App. 340. **Teucrōrum:** the Trojans are often referred to as **Teucrī,** a name derived from Teucer, one of the founders of the Trojan people.
39. Quippe vetor: ironical. **fātīs:** abl. of means; App. 331. **-ne = nōnne. Pallas (Athēna):** Minerva.
40. Argīvum: = **Argīvōrum;** App. 37, *d*. **ipsōs:** *(the masters) themselves,* i.e., the Argives, as contrasted with **classem. Ipse** often means *the master,* the one of most importance

ūnius ob noxam *et* furiās Aiācis Oīleī?
Ipsa Iovis rapidum iaculāta *ē* nūbibus *ignem*
disiēcit*que* ratēs ēvertit*que aequora ventīs,*
illum exspīrantem trānsfīxō *pectore flammās*
45   turbine corripuit scopulō*que* īnfīxit acūtō;
ast ego, quae dīvum incēdō *rēgina Iovisque*
et soror et coniūnx, ūnā cum gente tot annōs

---

acūtus, a, um sharp, pointed	**īnfīgō, ere, xī, xus** fasten on, impale
Aiāx, ācis *m.* Greek leader, who in the sack of Troy had taken Priam's daughter, Cassandra, by force from the sanctuary of Minerva	**noxa, ae** *f.* crime, fault, hurt, harm
	nūbēs, is *f.* cloud, mist, fog
	ob on account of (+ *acc.*)
	Oīleus, eī *m.* Greek king, father of Ajax
annus, ī *m.* year	**rapidus, a, um** swift, whirling, consuming
corripiō, ere, uī, reptus snatch (up)	**ratis, is** *f.* raft, ship
disiciō, ere, iēcī, iectus scatter, disperse	**scopulus, ī** *m.* rock, cliff, crag
ēvertō, ere, ī, rsus (over)turn	**soror, ōris** *f.* sister
exspīrō (1) breathe out, exhale	**tot** so many
furiae, ārum *f.* madness, rage	**trānsfīgō, ere, xī, xus** pierce, transfix
iaculor, ārī, ātus hurl, throw	**turbō, inis** *m.* whirl(wind, pool), storm
incēdō, ere, cessī, cessus walk (proudly), stride	

---

in a situation, as contrasted with persons or things of less importance. **pontō:** abl. of place where; App. 319, or abl. of means; App. 331.

41. ūnius Aiācis Oīleī: a whole fleet was destroyed on account of one man. For the short -i- in **ūnius** see the note on **illius** (16). **ob noxam et furiās:** Ajax, son of Oīleus, had desecrated the temple of Minerva during the sack of Troy, when before the very altar of the sanctuary he had seized Cassandra, daughter of Priam and priestess of Minerva. Enraged at such rash irreverence, Minerva later sank the ship of Ajax and destroyed him with lightning. **Aiācis Oīleī:** *of Ajax (son) of Oīleus.* The first letter of **Oīleī** is a single short syllable; the following -ī- is a long syllable; and the ending -eī is here read as one syllable by SYNIZESIS. This Ajax was less renowned than another Greek hero of the same name, Ajax, son of Telamon.

42. Ipsa: (*The goddess, Minerva*) *in person.* She was the only divinity, except Jupiter, who

could hurl Jupiter's lightning; Juno did not have this ability. **Iovis ignem:** *lightning.*

43. -que . . . -que: *both . . . and*; POLYSYN-DETON. **ventīs:** abl. of means.

44. illum (Aiācem): with emphatic first position, which contrasts it with the ships and the sea previously mentioned. **(ex) pectore:** abl. of separation; App. 340.

45. turbine: abl. of means; App. 331. **(Pallas) corripuit. scopulō:** dat. with compound verb **īnfīxit**, or abl. of place where, as **īnfīgō** may take either construction; App. 298, 319.

46. ego: with proud self-consciousness and in contrast with Minerva; **ego** is usually not expressed unless emphatic. **dīv(ōr)um:** App. 37, d.

47. tot annōs: acc. of extent (duration) of time; App. 314; ten years around Troy, and now seven more years while the Trojans wander. **ūnā cum gente = cum Teucrīs.** Note the pattern adj.+prep.+noun in this phrase, a pattern very frequent in Vergil and in Latin poetry generally.

    bella gerō. Et quisquam nūmen Iūnōnis adōrat
49   praetereā *aut supplex ārīs* impōnet *honōrem?"*

---

adōrō (1) worship, adore, honor
gerō, ere, gessī, gestus carry (on), wage
impōnō, ere, posuī, positus place on (+
   dat.)

praetereā *adv.* besides, hereafter
quisquam, quaequam, quicquam
   any(one), any(thing)
supplex, icis suppliant, humble

---

48. gerō: of past action continued into
the pres.; App. 351, 1, *b.* **Et quisquam:** Juno
thinks to herself, "Can any one hereafter re-
spect me, if I show myself such a weakling?"
Her use of the pron. **quisquam** implies that
the answer, if expressed, would be "no." This
figure is called a RHETORICAL QUESTION;

Juno does not really expect an answer.
Iūnōnis = meum: Juno is speaking, but the
use of her own name is more picturesque and
effective than the use of the possessive adj.
   49. supplex: *(as a) suppliant.* **ārīs:** dat. with
compound verb; App. 298. **honōrem:** *honor,*
i.e., an *offering* which would honor Juno.

50 *Tālia* flammātō *sēcum dea* corde volūtāns
  nimbōrum *in* patriam, *loca* fēta *furentibus* Austrīs,
  Aeoliam *venit.* hīc *vastō rēx* Aeolus antrō
  luctantēs *ventōs* tempestātēs*que* sonōrās
  imperiō premit *ac* vinclīs *et* carcere frēnat.
55 *Illī* indignantēs *magnō cum* murmure *montis*
  circum claustra fremunt; celsā sedet Aeolus *arce*
  scēptra *tenēns* mollit*que animōs et* temperat *īrās.*

Aeolia, ae *f.* one of the Liparian Islands near Sicily
Aeolus, ī *m.* god of the winds
antrum, ī *n.* cave, cavern
Auster, trī *m.* (south) wind
carcer, eris *m.* prison, inclosure
celsus, a, um lofty, high, towering
claustrum, ī *n.* bar(rier), bolt
cor, cordis *n.* heart, spirit, feelings
fētus, a, um teeming, pregnant
flammō (1) inflame, kindle
fremō, ere, uī, itus murmur, roar
frēnō (1) curb, check, restrain
indignor, ārī, ātus be angry, chafe

luctor, ārī, ātus wrestle, struggle
molliō, īre, īvī (iī), ītus soothe, tame
murmur, uris *n.* murmur, roar, rumble
nimbus, ī *m.* storm cloud, rainstorm
patria, ae *f.* homeland, country
premō, ere, pressī, pressus (re)press, control
scēptrum, ī *n.* staff, scepter, power
sedeō, ēre, sēdī, sessus sit
sonōrus, a, um roaring, howling
temperō (1) control, calm, refrain
tempestās, ātis *f.* tempest, storm
vinc(u)lum, ī *n.* bond, chain
volūtō (1) roll, revolve, ponder

50–80. Juno persuades Aeolus, god of the winds, to send forth a storm to prevent Aeneas and the Trojans from reaching Italy.

50. Tālia: used substantively, as obj. of **volūtāns**; *such things,* i.e., *such thoughts.* **(in) flammātō corde:** abl. of place where; App. 319. **sēcum = cum sē,** as in 37; App. 321, *a.*

51. patriam: with the first syllable short; App. 17. **Austrīs:** abl. with **fēta,** lit., *south winds,* but often meaning *winds* in general; App. 433. **fēta furentibus:** note the ALLITERATION.

51–52. loca . . . Aeoliam: both nouns in apposition with **patriam. Hīc:** adv., *here.* **(in) vastō antrō:** abl. of place where; App. 319.

54. vinclīs: the syncopated form of **vinculīs,** which because of its central short syllable can not be used in hexameter. **imperiō, vinc(u)līs, carcere:** abls. of means; App. 331. The two nouns **vinclīs** and **carcere** may be understood as a true pair, or may be translated as an example of HENDIADYS: "by means of the restraints of their prison"; App. 425. **frēnat:** a picture drawn from managing spirited horses, as in 63, **premere et dare laxās habēnās.**

55. magnō cum murmure montis: ALLITERATION and ONOMATOPOEIA; **murmure** is abl. of manner; App. 328.

56. (in) celsā arce: abl. of place, apparently a lofty seat within the cave or just outside on a mountain top.

57. scēptra: for the use of the poetic plural see the note on **īrae** (11). **animōs (ventōrum) et īrās (ventōrum).**

nī *faciat, maria ac terrās caelumque* profundum
quippe *ferant* rapidī *sēcum* verrant*que per aurās;*
60   sed *pater* omnipotēns spēluncīs abdidit *ātrīs*
hoc metuēns mōlem*que et montēs* īnsuper *altōs*
imposuit, *rēgemque dedit* quī foedere certō
et premere *et* laxās scīret *dare iussus* habēnās.
Ad quem tum Iūnō supplex hīs vōcibus ūsa est:
65   "Aeole (*namque tibī dīvum pater* atque hominum *rēx*
et mulcēre *dedit flūctūs et tollere ventō*),

---

abdō, ere, didī, ditus put away, hide
Aeolus, ī *m.* god of the winds
certus, a, um fixed, sure
foedus, eris *n.* agreement, condition,
   treaty
habēna, ae *f.* rein
homō, inis *m. (f.)* man, mortal, human
impōnō, ere, posuī, positus place upon
īnsuper *adv.* above, besides
laxus, a, um loose, free, lax
metuō, ere, uī fear, dread
mōlēs, is *f.* mass, burden, structure
mulceō, ēre, lsī, lsus calm, soothe

nī, nisi if not, unless
omnipotēns, entis almighty, all-powerful
premō, ere, pressī, pressus (re)press,
   control
profundus, a, um deep, high, vast
quippe indeed, surely
rapidus, a, um swift, whirling, consuming
sciō, īre, īvī (iī), ītus know (how),
   understand
spēlunca, ae *f.* cave, cavern
supplex, icis suppliant, humble
ūtor, ī, ūsus use, employ (+ *abl.*)
verrō, ere, ī, versus sweep

---

58. nī (Aeolus id) faciat = nī molliat;
faciat is pres. subjunctive in a pres. contrary-
to-fact condition (as opposed to the more
usual imperf. subjunctive); the result is a far
more vivid scene; App. 382, *c.*
   59. (ventī) rapidī: *the winds in their mad-*
ness. **sēcum = cum sē;** App. 321, *a.* **ferant,**
verrant (maria ac terrās caelumque pro-
fundum). Both pres. subjunctives continue
the condition begun in 58, **nī faciat.**
   60. pater omnipotēns: Iuppiter. (in)
spēluncīs ātrīs = antrō (52), abl. of place
where; App. 319. **abdidit (illōs ventōs).**
   61. hoc: obj. of **metuēns. mōlem et**
montēs: ALLITERATION. This is an example
of HENDIADYS (a pair of nouns translated as
a single idea).

62. rēgem (Aeolum) dedit (ventīs). foe-
dere certō: abl. of manner or of means; App.
328, 331.
   63. premere: obj. of **scīret,** *would know*
(how) to grasp tightly, so as to draw in the
reins. For the figure of horsemanship see the
note on **frēnat** (54). **scīret,** rel. clause of pur-
pose or characteristic; App. 388, 389. **dare:**
also obj. of **scīret. iussus (ā Iove):** *(when)*
ordered (by Jupiter).
   64. hīs vōcibus: abl. with **ūtor;** App. 342.
   65. Aeole: voc. **dīv(ōr)um pater atque**
hominum rēx: Iuppiter. tibī: for the length
of the final -ī, see the note on **mihi** (8).
   66. mulcēre, tollere (flūctūs): infs. used
as objs. of **dedit,** *has granted.* **ventō:** abl. of
means; App. 331.

gēns inimīca *mihī* Tyrrhēnum nāvigat *aequor*
Īlium *in Ītaliam* portāns *victōsque* penātēs:
incute *vim ventīs* submersāsque obrue *puppēs,*
70   *aut age* dīversōs *et* dissice *corpora* pontō.

Sunt *mihi* bis septem praestantī *corpore* Nymphae,
quārum quae formā pulcherrima Dēiopēa,

---

bis twice
Dēiopēa, ae *f.* a nymph
dis(s)iciō, ere, iēcī, iectus scatter, disperse
dīversus, a, um scattered, diverse
forma, ae *f.* beauty, shape, form
Īlium, (i)ī *n.* Ilium, Troy, a city of Asia Minor
incutiō, ere, cussī, cussus strike (into)
    (+ *dat.*)
inimīcus, a, um hostile, unfriendly
nāvigō (1) sail, navigate
Nympha, ae *f.* nymph, one of the minor
    divinities of nature represented as
    beautiful maidens dwelling in the forests,
    streams, meadows, mountains, etc.

obruō, ere, uī, utus overwhelm, crush
penātēs, ium *m.* household gods
pontus, ī *m.* sea
portō (1) carry, bear, bring
praestāns, antis surpassing, excellent
pulcher, chra, chrum beautiful, handsome,
    illustrious
septem seven
summergō (subm-), ere, rsī, rsus sink
Tyrrhēnus, a, um Tyrrhenian, of Etruria,
    a district of northwestern Italy

---

67. gēns inimīca mihī: i.e., *Teucrī.* **Tyrrhēnum aequor:** that part of the Mediterranean west of Italy, east of Corsica and Sardinia, and north of Sicily.

68. Īlium ... portāns victōsque penātēs: see note on **īnferret deōs** (6). They were *bearing Ilium* in their plan to found a new city, which was to continue the people and the customs of the **Īlium** (Troy) which had been destroyed. The worship of the penates, household gods at Rome, was an essential part of Roman daily life, and was seen as a link to the Romans' Trojan past. **victōs:** *defeated* by the Greeks in the Trojan War.

69. incute: imperat. **vim ventīs:** ALLITERATION; App. 411. **ventīs:** dat. with a compound; App. 298. **submersās obrue puppēs:** *overwhelm the sunken ships,* i.e., *sink and overwhelm the ships,* a good example of the figure known as PROLEPSIS, or *anticipation.*

70. age: imperat. **dīversōs (Teucrōs):** i.e., drive the Trojans in different directions and scatter their corpses over the sea; another example of PROLEPSIS. **dissice:** usually written with one **-s-**; the doubled consonant here gives Juno's words an extra hissing sound, perhaps not coincidentally. **pontō:** abl. of place where; App. 319.

71. mihi: dat. of possession; App. 299. **bis septem:** *twice seven;* more poetic than to say simply *fourteen.* **praestantī corpore:** abl. of quality; App. 330.

72. formā: abl. of respect; App. 325; dependent on **pulcherrima. Dēiopēa:** nom. by attraction into the case of the rel. pron., **quae;** the accusative would be expected, as obj. of **iungam;** App. 242, *a.* **quārum:** use the English demonstrative in translation, and read accordingly: **Dēiopēam, quae (est) eārum (nymphārum) pulcherrima formā, iungam (tibi) stabilī cōnūbiō et (eam) dicābō (tuam) propriam.**

cōnūbiō iungam stabilī propriam*que* dicābō,
omnēs ut tēcum meritīs prō tālibus annōs
75   exigat *et* pulchrā *faciat tē* prōle *parentem.*"
    Aeolus *haec* contrā: "*Tuus,* Ō *rēgīna, quid* optēs
    explōrāre *labor; mihi* iussa capessere *fās est.*
    Tū mihi quodcumque *hoc rēgnī, tū* scēptra *Iovemque*
    conciliās, *tū dās* epulīs accumbere *dīvum*
80   nimbōrum*que facis* tempestātum*que* potentem."

---

accumbō, ere, cubuī, cubitus recline (at) (+ *dat.*)	**iussum, ī** *n.* command, order
Aeolus, ī *m.* god of the winds	**meritum, ī** *n.* reward, merit
annus, ī *m.* year	**nimbus, ī** *m.* storm cloud, rainstorm
capessō, ere, īvī, ītus (under)take, perform	**optō** (1) desire, choose, hope (for)
conciliō (1) win over, unite	**potēns, entis** powerful, ruling (+ *gen.*)
contra opposite, against, in reply (+ *acc.*)	**prō** before, for (+ *abl.*)
cōnūbium, (i)ī *n.* marriage, wedlock	**prōlēs, is** *f.* offspring, progeny
dicō (1) consecrate, dedicate	**proprius, a, um** one's own, permanent
epulae, ārum *f.* banquet, feast	**pulcher, chra, chrum** beautiful, handsome, illustrious
exigō, ere, ēgī, āctus complete, pass	**quīcumque, quaecumque, quodcumque** whoever, whatever
explōrō (1) examine, search out	**scēptrum, ī** *n.* staff, scepter, power
fās *n. indecl.* right, divine law, duty	**stabilis, e** firm, lasting, stable
iungō, ere, iūnxī, iūnctus join, yoke, unite	**tempestās, ātis** *f.* tempest, storm; time

---

73. cōnūbiō: *in wedlock,* abl. of place where or means; App. 319, 331. **cōnūbiō** is either trisyllabic by SYNIZESIS, and pronounced as though written **cōnūbyō** (i.e., consonantal -i-), or quadrisyllabic, with the variable syllable -nub- scanned as short. **iungam (tibi) dicābō (eam) propriam:** *I shall dedicate her (Deiopea) to you (as) your very own.* Juno was goddess of marriage. **propriam:** with the first syllable short; App. 17.

74. tēcum = cum tē; App. 321, *a.*

75. prōle: abl. of quality; App. 330, or means; App. 331. **pulchrā prōle parentem:** ALLITERATION. **exigat, faciat:** subjunctives of result or purpose; App. 364, 388. **parentem = patrem.**

76. haec (dīxit). optēs: indir. quest.; App. 349. **Tuus (est) labor:** *yours (is) the task.* Aeolus thus absolves himself from responsibility, if his obedience to Juno gets him into trouble.

77. mihi: dat. of reference; App. 301. **iussa (tua).**

78. quodcumque hoc (est) rēgnī: *whatever this is (in the way) of a kingdom,* an expression of modesty. **rēgnī:** partitive gen. with **quodcumque;** App. 286. **Tū:** always emphatic, and an example of ANAPHORA, the repetition of a single word at the beginning of successive clauses or phrases.

79. conciliās: this one verb should be translated twice, first with its obj. **quodcumque hoc rēgnī** ("win for") and then with its objs. **scēptra Iovemque** ("win over"). **epulīs:** dat. with compound; App. 298. The ancient Romans regularly reclined at meals. **dīv(ōr)um:** App. 37, *d.* **accumbere:** inf. used as obj. of **dās,** *you grant (me) the privilege of reclining.* As one of the lesser gods, Aeolus was dependent upon the favor of the more powerful divinities.

80. facis (mē) potentem nimbōrum tempestātumque.

Haec ubi dicta, cavum conversā cuspide *montem*
impulit *in* latus; *ac ventī* velut *agmine factō,*
quā *data* porta, *ruunt et terrās* turbine perflant.
Incubuēre *marī tōtumque ā sēdibus īmīs*
85   ūnā Eurus*que* Notus*que* ruunt crēber*que* procellīs
Āfricus, *et vastōs volvunt ad lītora flūctūs.*
Īnsequitur *clāmorque virum* strīdorque *rudentum;*
ēripiunt subitō nūbēs *caelumque diemque*

Āfricus, ī *m.* (southwest) wind
cavus, a, um hollow, vaulted
convertō, ere, ī, rsus turn (around), reverse
crēber, bra, brum frequent, crowded
cuspis, idis *f.* point, spear
Eurus, ī *m.* (east) wind
impellō, ere, pulī, pulsus drive, strike
   (against)
incumbō, ere, cubuī, cubitus lie upon,
   brood over (+ *dat.*)
īnsequor, ī, secūtus follow, pursue
latus, eris *n.* side, flank

Notus, ī *m.* (south) wind
nūbēs, is *f.* cloud, fog, mist
perflō (1) blow (over, through)
porta, ae *f.* gate, door, opening
procella, ae *f.* blast, gust
quā *adv.* where, in any way
rudēns, entis *m.* rope, cable
strīdor, ōris *m.* creaking, grating, whirring
subitō *adv.* suddenly
turbō, inis *m.* whirl(wind, pool), storm
ūnā *adv.* together, at the same time
velut(ī) (even) as, just as

81–123. A storm wrecks some of the
Trojan ships and scatters the rest. The
entire scene is indebted to the descrip-
tion of a storm at sea given by Homer in
Odyssey 5.

**81. ubi haec dicta (sunt ab Aeolō).
cavum conversā cuspide:** observe the
ALLITERATION.

82. impulit: Aeolus thus opens the barri-
ers and lets out the winds. **agmine factō:** abl.
abs.; App. 343; a SIMILE (**velut**) drawn from
the imagery of military life.

83. Observe the ALLITERATION: every
word but one in this line contains a **t. data
(est). turbine:** abl. of manner; App. 328; or
means.

84. Incubuēre = incubuērunt, from
incumbō. The perfect, after a series of presents,
denotes rapid or instantaneous action; *they have
fallen upon the sea.* **marī:** dat. with compound;
App. 298. **tōtum (mare):** obj. of **ruunt** (85).

85. ruunt: *overturn.* **Eurus, Notus, Āfricus:**
all the winds blow at once, and in their strug-
gles produce a mighty storm. **procellīs:** abl. of
respect or means with **crēber**; App. 325, 331.
-que, -que, -que: POLYSYNDETON; App. 439.

86. vastōs volvunt: ALLITERATION, em-
ployed very effectively here to evoke the noise
of the storm.

87. vir(ōr)um: Aeneas and the other Tro-
jans. **-que, -que:** POLYSYNDETON.

88. diem = lūcem diēī; alternatively, **cae-
lumque diemque** may be construed as an in-
stance of HENDIADYS, = **caelum diēī. -que,
-que:** POLYSYNDETON.

Teucrōrum ex oculīs; pontō nox incubat *ātra;*
90   intonuēre polī *et* crēbrīs micat *ignibus* aethēr
       praesentem*que virīs* intentant *omnia mortem.*
       Extemplō *Aenēae* solvuntur frīgore membra;
       ingemit *et* duplicēs *tendēns ad sīdera* palmās
       tālia vōce refert: "Ō ter*que* quater*que* beātī,
95   *quīs ante ōra patrum Troiae sub moenibus altīs*
       contigit oppetere! *Ō Danaum* fortissime *gentis*
       Tȳdīdē! *Mēne* Īliacis occumbere *campīs*

---

aethēr, eris *m.* upper air, sky, ether
beātus, a, um happy, blessed
contingō, ere, tigī, tāctus touch, befall
crēber, bra, brum frequent, crowded
duplex, icis double, both
extemplō *adv.* immediately, straightaway
fortis, e strong, brave, valiant
frīgus, oris *n.* cold, chill
Īliacus, a, um of Ilium, Trojan
incubō, āre, uī (āvī), itus (ātus) lie upon, brood over (+ *dat.*)
ingemō, ere, uī groan
intentō (1) threaten, aim
intonō, āre, uī thunder, roar
membrum, ī *n.* limb, member, part
micō, āre, uī quiver, flash

occumbō, ere, cubuī, cubitus fall (in death)
oppetō, ere, īvī (iī), ītus encounter, meet (death)
palma, ae *f.* palm, hand
polus, ī *m.* pole, sky, heaven
pontus, ī *m.* sea
praesēns, entis present, instant
quater four times
solvō, ere, ī, solūtus relax, loose(n)
ter thrice, three times
Tȳdīdēs, ae *m.* son of Tydeus, Diomedes, who fought against Aeneas in single combat before Troy and would have killed him had Venus not spirited her son away

---

89. pontō: dat. with compound; App. 298.
90. Intonuēre = **intonuērunt;** App. 204, 4. **ignibus (Iovis):** *lightning;* abl. of means or manner; App. 328, 331.
91. virīs = **Teucrīs;** dat. of reference; App. 301. **omnia:** used substantively, *all things,* as subject of **intentant.** The terror that comes over the Trojans is all-encompassing.
92. frīgore: *chilly fear;* the ancient heroes were not ashamed to display their emotions, and often gave way to terror or grief, weeping copiously on occasion.
93. duplicēs palmās: In prayer the ancient Greeks and Romans extended their hands with the palms upward, ready to accept the gods' blessing.
94. tālia (dicta). beātī (vōs): voc.
95. quīs ante ōra patrum (vestrum) sub moenibus Troiae contigit oppetere (mortem). quīs = **quibus;** App. 109, *c;* observe

the quantity of the -i-; dat. with **contigit;** App. 298. **ante ōra:** where their kinsmen and friends might witness their glorious deeds and death and would bury their bodies, thus giving rest to their souls; for the souls of the unburied must wander restlessly after death.
96. oppetere (mortem): subject of **contigit. Dana(ōr)um:** App. 37, *d.*
97. Mē: subject of **potuisse. Mēne potuisse:** *could I not,* etc. inf. in an exclamatory quest.; App. 262. The construction, opening as it does with **Mēne,** recalls Juno's rhetorical quest. at 37. **Tȳdīdē:** Gk. voc.: the final **-e** is long. Aeneas engaged in a disastrous duel in the *Iliad* with Diomedes and barely escaped with his life, being rescued by his mother, the goddess Venus. **(in) campīs:** abl. of place where; App. 319. **occumbere (mortī):** complementary inf. with **potuisse,** as is also **effundere** in 98.

nōn potuisse tuāque animam hanc effundere dextrā,   - Soliloquy
   saevus ubi Aeacidae tēlō iacet Hector, ubi ingēns   - prayer
100 Sarpēdōn, ubi tot Simoīs correpta sub undīs
   scūta virum galeāsque et fortia corpora volvit!"
   Tālia iactantī strīdēns Aquilōne procella
   vēlum adversa ferit, flūctūsque ad sīdera tollit.
   Franguntur rēmī, tum prōra āvertit et undīs
105 dat latus, īnsequitur cumulō praeruptus aquae mōns.
   Hī summō in flūctū pendent; hīs unda dehīscēns

---

adversus, a, um opposite
Aeacidēs, ae *m.* descendant of Aeacus, Achilles, Greek chieftain
aqua, ae *f.* water
Aquilō, ōnis *m.* (north) wind
āvertō, ere, ī, rsus turn away, avert
corripiō, ere, uī, reptus snatch (up)
cumulus, ī *m.* heap, mass
dehīscō, ere, hīvī gape, split, open
effundō, ere, fūdī, fūsus pour out
feriō, īre strike, beat
fortis, e strong, brave, valiant
frangō, ere, frēgī, frāctus break, shatter
galea, ae *f.* helmet
Hector, oris *m.* leader of the Trojans

īnsequor, ī, secūtus follow, pursue
iaceō, ēre, uī, itus lie (low, outspread)
iactō (1) toss, buffet; utter
latus, eris *n.* side, flank
pendeō, ēre, pependī hang
praeruptus, a, um steep, towering
procella, ae *f.* blast, gale
prōra, ae *f.* prow
saevus, a, um fierce, cruel, stern
Sarpēdōn, onis *m.* king of Lydia, ally of the Trojans
scūtum, ī *n.* shield
Simoīs, entis *m.* river near Troy
strīd(e)ō, ēre, dī creak, rustle, roar
tot so many

---

98. hanc = meam. (tuā) dextrā (manū): abl. of means; App. 331.

99. tēlō: construe as if with **ictus** *(slain by the spear)* as abl. of means, or with **iacet** *(lies dead because of the spear)* as abl. of cause; App. 331, 332. Observe the emphasis obtained by ANAPHORA of **ubi**; App. 413.

100. Sarpēdōn (iacet): an ally of the Trojans, and son of Jupiter. **Simoīs . . . volvit.**

101. vir(ōr)um. correpta sub undīs: goes with **scūta** and **galeās** as well as with **corpora** and refers to the corpses and armor of slain warriors swept along by (under) the water.

102. (Aenēae) iactantī: dat. of reference; App. 301. **Tālia (dicta):** obj. of **iactantī**. **Aquilōne:** abl. of means; App. 331.

103. ferit: from **feriō**; not to be confused with the verb **ferō. adversa (procella). ad sīdera:** such exaggerated language is called HYPERBOLE.

104. rēmī: the ancient ship used both oars and sails. **prōra (sē) āvertit et undīs dat latus (nāvis).**

105. cumulō: abl. of manner; App. 328. **mōns:** more HYPERBOLE; note the smashing effect of the monosyllable at the end of the line.

106. Hī (virī). hīs (virīs): dat. of reference; App. 301. **hī . . . hīs:** *these . . . for those; some . . . for others,* referring to the crews of different ships; ANAPHORA.

Altars - where
you're
sacrificed.

terram inter flūctūs aperit, *furit* aestūs harēnīs.
Trēs Notus abreptās *in saxa* latentia torquet
(*saxa vocant* Italī *mediīs quae in flūctibus* Ārās,
110   dorsum *immāne marī summō*), trēs Eurus *ab* altō
in brevia *et* syrtēs urget, miserābile *vīsū,*
inlīditque vadīs *atque* aggere cingit harēnae.
Ūnam, quae Lyciōs fīdumque vehēbat Orontēn,
ipsius ante oculōs ingēns ā vertice pontus

---

abripiō, ere, uī, reptus carry off, snatch away
aestus, ūs *m.* boiling (surge), tide
agger, eris *m.* mound, bank
altum, ī *n.* the deep (sea)
aperiō, īre, uī, ertus open, disclose
Ārae, ārum *f.* the Altars, a ledge of rocks between Sicily and Africa
brevis, e short, shallow
cingō, ere, cīnxī, cīnctus gird(le), encircle
dorsum, ī *n.* back, ridge, reef
Eurus, ī *m.* (east) wind
fīdus, a, um faithful, trustworthy
harēna, ae *f.* sand, beach
inlīdō, ere, sī, sus dash against (into) (+ *dat.*)

Italus, a, um Italian
lateō, ēre, uī lie hid, hide, lurk
Lycius, a, um Lycian, of Lycia, a country of Asia Minor
miserābilis, e pitiable, wretched
Notus, ī *m.* (south) wind
Orontēs, is (ī) *m.* comrade of Aeneas
pontus, ī *m.* sea
syrtis, is *f.* sand bar, reef
torqueō, ēre, rsī, rtus turn, twist, whirl
trēs, tria three
urgeō, ēre, ursī drive, force, press
vadum, ī *n.* shallow, shoal, depth(s)
vehō, ere, vēxī, vectus carry, convey
vertex, icis *m.* peak, summit, head, top; whirlpool

---

107. terram: *the bottom* (of the sea); the HYPERBOLE is continued. **harēnīs:** *with the sands,* abl. of means; App. 331.

108–9. Trēs (nāvēs) abreptās: obj. of torquet. **saxa . . . saxa:** ANAPHORA. **mediīs in flūctibus:** *in the middle (of the) waves;* App. 246. **quae saxa Italī vocant Ārās:** **quae** is a rel. adj. agreeing with **saxa**; **saxa** is obj. of **vocant**, and **Ārās** is predicate acc. **Ārās:** *the Altars,* the Roman name for a ledge of rocks off the African coast, just outside the harbor of ancient Carthage.

110. (in) marī summō: *at the surface of the sea;* abl. of place where; App. 319, 246. **dorsum:** apposition with **saxa. trēs (nāvēs):** obj. of **urget**.

111. miserābile vīsū: *piteous to behold;* **miserābile** is a neut. adj. modifying the idea expressed in the preceding sentence, while **vīsū** is the supine of **videō** and an abl. of respect; App. 325.

112. vadīs = in vada, understand either as dat. of direction, sometimes used instead of the acc. of place to which; App. 306, or as dat. with a compound verb; App. 298.

113. Ūnam (nāvem). Orontēn: acc., a Gk. form.

114. ipsius (Aeneāe): *of the master,* a common use of **ipse.** Cf. **ipsa** (42) and **ipsōs** (40). Note the shortening of **-i-** in the **-ius** gen. ending of this adj., and see the note on **illius** (16). **ā vertice:** *from high above.*

115   *in puppim ferit: excutitur prōnusque magister*
     volvitur in caput, ast illam ter flūctus ibīdem
     torquet agēns circum et rapidus vorat aequore vertex.
     Appārent rārī nantēs in gurgite vastō,
     arma virum tabulaeque et Trōia gaza per undās.
120   *Iam validam Īlioneī nāvem, iam fortis Achātae,*
     et quā vectus Abās, et quā grandaevus Alētēs,
     vīcit hiems; laxīs laterum compāgibus omnēs
     accipiunt inimīcum imbrem rīmīsque fatīscunt.

Abās, antis *m.* Trojan leader
Achātēs, ae *m.* faithful comrade of Aeneas
Alētēs, ae *m.* Trojan leader
appāreō, ēre, uī, itus appear
compāgēs, is *f.* joint, seam, fastening
excutiō, ere, cussī, cussus cast out, shake off
fatīscō, ere split, open, gape
feriō, īre strike, beat
fortis, e brave, strong, valiant
gaza, ae *f.* treasure, wealth
grandaevus, a, um aged, old
gurges, itis *m.* abyss, gulf, whirlpool
hiems, emis *f.* winter, storm
ibīdem *adv.* in the same place
Īlioneus, eī *m.* Trojan leader
imber, bris *m.* rain, flood, water

inimīcus, a, um hostile, unfriendly
latus, eris *n.* side, flank
laxus, a, um loose, open, lax
magister, trī *m.* master, pilot
nō (1) swim, float
prōnus, a, um leaning forward, headlong
rapidus, a, um swift, whirling, consuming
rārus, a, um scattered, far apart
rīma, ae *f.* crack, fissure
tabula, ae *f.* plank, board
ter three times, thrice
torqueō, ēre, rsī, rtus turn, twist, whirl
Trōius, a, um Trojan, of Troy
validus, a, um strong, mighty
vehō, ere, vēxī, vectus carry, convey
vertex, icis *m.* top, summit; whirlpool
vorō (1) swallow (up)

---

115. ferit: from **feriō. in:** *upon.* **excutitur** (ē nāvī).

116. in caput: *headlong.* **illam (nāvem):** contrasted with the helmsman (**magister**).

117. (in) aequore: abl. of place where; App. 319.

118. nantēs: pres. participle of **nō**, modifying **rārī (virī)**, **arma**, **tabulae**, and **gaza**, but agreeing with the nearest word, **rārī** (**virī**), *men here and there*; App. 238.

119. vir(ōr)um. arma: such as wooden shields and leather helmets made of light and buoyant material. **gaza:** the first syllable is long by position; App. 15.

120. Īlioneī: gen., with the final **eī** pronounced as one syllable by SYNIZESIS. (nāvem) fortis Achātae. Iam . . . iam: ANAPHORA.

121. et (nāvem) quā vectus (est) Abās, et (nāvem) quā (vectus est) Alētēs. et quā . . . et quā: ANAPHORA.

122. laxīs compāgibus: abl. of means or instrument, or abl. abs. **omnēs (nāvēs)**.

123. rīmīs: abl. of means or manner; App. 328, 331. Cf. 83, 105. **imbrem = aquam maris.**

Intereā *magnō* miscērī murmure pontum
125   ēmissam*que* hiemem sēnsit Neptūnus *et īmīs*
stāgna refūsa vadīs, graviter commōtus, *et altō*
prōspiciēns *summā* placidum *caput* extulit *undā.*
Disiectam *Aenēae tōtō videt aequore classem,*
flūctibus oppressōs Trōas *caelīque* ruīnā;
130   *Nec* latuēre dolī frātrem *Iūnōnis et īrae.*
Eurum *ad sē* Zephyrum*que vocat,* dehinc *tālia fātur:*
"Tantane vōs generis tenuit fīdūcia vestrī?
Iam caelum terramque meō sine *nūmine, ventī,*

---

altum, ī *n.* the deep (sea)
commoveō, ēre, mōvī, mōtus move,
  disturb
dehinc *adv.* then, thereupon
disiciō, ere, iēcī, iectus scatter, disperse
dolus, ī *m.* deceit, wiles, trick, fraud
efferō, ferre, extulī, ēlātus raise, lift (up)
ēmittō, ere, mīsī, missus send forth
Eurus, ī *m.* (east)wind
fīdūcia, ae *f.* confidence, trust
frāter, tris *m.* brother
graviter *adv.* heavily, violently, greatly
hiems, hiemis *f.* winter, storm
intereā *adv.* meanwhile, meantime
lateō, ēre, uī lie hid, escape the notice (of)
misceō, ēre, uī, mixtus mix, confuse, stir
murmur, uris *n.* murmur, roar, rumble

Neptūnus, ī *m.* Neptune, god of the sea
opprimō, ere, pressī, pressus overwhelm,
  crush
placidus, a, um calm, quiet, peaceful
pontus, ī *m.* sea
prōspiciō, ere, spexī, spectus look out
  (on), see
refundō, ere, fūdī, fūsus pour back
ruīna, ae *f.* downfall, ruin
sentiō, īre, sēnsī, sēnsus feel, perceive
sine without (+ *abl.*)
stāgnum, ī *n.* still waters, depth
Trōs, Trōis *m.* Trojan
vadum, ī *n.* shallow, shoal, depth(s)
vester, tra, trum your(s), your own
Zephyrus, ī *m.* (west) wind

124–56. Neptune, god of the sea, inter-
venes; he rebukes the winds and calms
the sea.

124. magnō miscērī murmure: ALLITER-
ATION (**m**) and ONOMATOPOEIA. **murmure:**
abl. of attendant circumstance or manner;
App. 329, 328.
  125. ēmissam (esse).
  126. refūsa (esse). vadīs: either abl. of sepa-
ration; App. 340, or dat. of direction; App. 306.
The ambiguity of construction may be meant
to reflect the confused movement of the water.
(**in**) **altō:** *over the sea*; abl. of place where; App.
319. **commōtus (animō):** although disturbed
in spirit as a god he maintains an outward calm
(**placidum caput** of 127).

  127. (ex) undā: abl. of separation; App.
340; *from the crest of the wave;* App. 246.
  128. (in) tōtō aequore: abl. of place
where; App. 319.
  129. Trōas: acc. pl., a Gk. form. (**et vi-
det**) **Trōas oppressōs (esse). caelī ruīnā:**
HYPERBOLE.
  130. latuēre = **latuērunt;** App. 204, 4.
frātrem: Neptune, as Juno's brother, knew her
tricky nature (**dolī**) and her ugly temper (**īrae**).
  131. dehinc: one syllable by SYNIZESIS.
tālia (dicta).
  132. generis fīdūcia vestrī: this verse is
sarcastic; the winds were of divine origin,
being descended from Aurora, goddess of
the dawn, and from Astraeus, a Titan rival of
the gods.
  133. caelum terramque: HYPERBOLE.

miscēre *et tantās audētis tollere* mōlēs?
135 *Quōs ego–sed mōtōs* praestat compōnere *flūctūs.*
Post *mihi nōn similī poenā* commissa luētis.
Mātūrāte *fugam rēgīque haec dīcite* vestrō:
nōn illī imperium pelagī saevum*que* tridentem,
sed mihi sorte *datum. Tenet ille immānia saxa,*
140 vestrās, Eure, *domōs; illā sē* iactet *in aulā*
Aeolus *et* clausō *ventōrum* carcere rēgnet."
Sīc ait, et dictō citius tumida aequora plācat
collēctās*que* fugat nūbēs sōlem*que* redūcit.

Aeolus, ī *m.* god of the winds
audeō, ēre, ausus sum dare, venture
aula, ae *f.* court, hall
carcer, eris *m.* prison, inclosure
citō *adv.* quickly, soon
claudō, ere, sī, sus (en)close, hem in
colligō, ere, lēgī, lēctus collect, gather
commissum, ī *n.* fault, crime
compōnō, ere, posuī, pos(i)tus compose, construct, calm, quiet
Eurus, ī *m.* (east)wind
fugō (1) put to flight, rout
iactō (1) toss, buffet, vaunt
luō, ere, luī atone for
mātūrō (1) hasten, speed; ripen
misceō, ēre, uī, mixtus mix, confuse, stir

mōlēs, is *f.* mass, burden, heap
nūbēs, is *f.* cloud, mist, fog
plācō (1) calm, quiet
post *adv.* afterward; *prep. + acc.* after, behind
praestō, āre, stitī, stitus surpass, be better
redūcō, ere, dūxī, ductus lead back, bring back
rēgnō (1) rule, reign
saevus, a, um fierce, cruel, stern
similis, e like, similar
sōl, sōlis *m.* sun, day
sors, rtis *f.* lot, fate, destiny
tridēns, entis *m.* trident, symbol of Neptune as god of the sea
tumidus, a, um swelling, swollen
vester, tra, trum your(s), your own

---

134. miscēre, tollere: depend on **audētis**, as complementary infs.; App. 259.

135. Quōs = Vōs. Quōs ego—: a good and famous example of APOSIOPESIS; i.e., instead of completing his sentence, the speaker breaks off abruptly and leaves to the imagination, as being beyond the power of adequate expression in words, just what sort of dire punishment he may inflict upon the guilty winds; **Quōs** is thus the obj. and **ego** the subject of the unexpressed verb.

136. nōn similī poenā: abl. of means; App. 331; *by no similar punishment,* i.e., by a much greater one; this figure of speech is called LITOTES.

137. rēgī vestrō = Aeolō.

138. illī: dat. of indir. obj. in emphatic position contrasted with **mihi** in the same position in the following line. **tridentem:** subject of **datum (esse)**, an inf. in indir. stmt., dependent on **dīcite**, in 137.

139. sorte: when Saturn was overthrown, the three gods, Jupiter, Neptune, and Pluto, divided his dominion among them by lot, Jupiter receiving the dominion of heaven, Neptune of the sea, and Pluto of the realm of the dead in the lower world.

140. vestrās: referring to all the winds, although Neptune is directly addressing Eurus only.

140–41. illā, clausō: emphatic by position. **iactet, rēgnet:** volitive or jussive subjunctives; App. 254. **(in) clausō carcere:** abl. of place where; App. 319.

142. ait: 3rd person sing. of **aiō. dictō:** abl. with comparative; App. 327.

Cȳmothoē *simul et* Trītōn adnixus acūtō
145   dētrūdunt *nāvēs* scopulō; levat *ipse* tridentī
et *vastās* aperit syrtēs *et* temperat *aequor*
atque rotīs *summās* levibus perlābitur *undās*.
Ac velutī *magnō in* populō *cum* saepe coōrta *est*
sēditiō saevit*que* animīs ignōbile vulgus
150   *iamque* facēs *et saxa* volant, furor *arma* ministrat;
tum, pietāte gravem *ac* meritīs *sī forte virum quem*
cōnspexēre, silent arrēctīs*que* auribus astant;

---

acūtus, a, um sharp, pointed, keen
adnītor, ī, sus (nixus) strive, lean against
aperiō, īre, uī, ertus open, disclose
arrigō, ere, rēxī, rēctus raise, prick up
a(d)stō, āre, stitī stand (near, by)
auris, is *f.* ear
cōnspiciō, ere, spexī, spectus see,
    behold
coōrior, īrī, ortus (a)rise
Cȳmothoē, ēs *f.* a sea nymph
dētrūdō, ere, sī, sus push off, dislodge
fax, facis *f.* firebrand, torch
furor, ōris *m.* madness, frenzy, rage
gravis, e heavy, weighty; venerable
ignōbilis, e inglorious, common
levis, e light, swift
levō (1) lift, raise
meritum, ī *n.* reward, service, merit

ministrō (1) tend, serve, supply
perlābor, ī, lāpsus glide over
pietās, ātis *f.* loyalty, devotion, duty
populus, ī *m.* people, nation, crowd
rota, ae *f.* wheel; chariot
saepe *adv.* often
saeviō, īre, īvī (iī), ītus rage, be fierce
scopulus, ī *m.* rock, cliff, crag
sēditiō, ōnis *f.* riot, strife
sileō, ēre, uī be silent, be still
syrtis, is *f.* sand bar, reef
temperō (1) calm, control
tridēns, entis *m.* trident, symbol of
    Neptune
Trītōn, onis *m.* Triton, a minor sea-god
velut(ī) as, just as
volō (1) fly, speed
vulgus, ī *n. (m.)* crowd, throng, herd

---

144. Cȳmothoē: nom.; a Gk. form.

145. ipse: *the master* (Neptune). See note on **ipsōs** (40). **(dē) scopulō:** abl. of separation; App. 340. **levat:** with the trident as a lever. **tridentī:** abl. of an *i-* stem.

147. rotīs levibus: abl. of manner; App. 328, or of means.

148. velutī saepe cum: *just as often (happens) when;* this phrase introduces one of Vergil's most famous SIMILES, the first to appear in the *Aeneid.*

149. animīs: abl. of place where or manner; App. 319, 328.

150. facēs: very dangerous in a city with so many wooden buildings as there were in ancient Rome. **furor arma ministrat:** *Madness provides weapons,* i.e., in the people's fury any object serves as a weapon.

151. quem: *some,* the indef. pron. **pietāte, meritīs:** abl. of cause or respect with **gravem;** App. 325, 332.

152. arrēctīs auribus: abl. abs. or abl. of manner; App. 343, 328. **arrēctīs auribus astant:** ALLITERATION. **cōnspexēre** = **cōnspexērunt;** App. 204, 4. **silent, astant:** plurals, because of the collective idea in **vulgus** and **populō;** App. 236, *a.*

ille rēgit *dictīs animōs et pectora* mulcet:
sīc cūnctus pelagī cecidit fragor, *aequora* postquam
155   prōspiciēns *genitor caelōque* invectus apertō
flectit *equōs* currū*que* volāns *dat* lōra secundō.

---

apertus, a, um open, clear
cadō, ere, cedidī, cāsus fall, subside
currus, ūs *m.* chariot, car
flectō, ere, exī, exus bend, turn, guide
fragor, ōris *m.* crash, uproar
invehō, ere, ēxī, ectus carry in, convey
lōrum, ī *n.* rein, thong

mulceō, ēre, lsī, lsus soothe, calm
postquam after (that), when
prōspiciō, ere, spexī, spectus look out on
secundus, a, um following, favorable,
    obedient
rego, ere, rēxī, rēctus rule, control
volō (1) fly, speed

154–5. sic: correlative with **velutī** in 148. **postquam genitor . . . flectit et . . . dat. aequora:** obj. of **prōspiciēns**.
155. (in) caelō apertō: abl. of place where; App. 319. **genitor:** Neptune. **invectus (currū):** *riding in his car.*

156. flectit . . . dat: historical pres.; App. 351,1, *a.* **currū:** dat. of indir. obj.; App. 295.

Neptune on his sea-chariot, mosaic from Ostia.

Dēfessī Aeneadae *quae* proxima *lītora cursū*
contendunt *petere, et* Libyae vertuntur *ad ōrās.*
Est in sēcessū *longō locus: īnsula portum*
160   efficit obiectū laterum, *quibus omnis ab* altō
frangitur *inque* sinūs scindit *sēsē unda* reductōs.
Hinc atque hinc vastae rūpēs *geminīque* minantur
in caelum scopulī, *quōrum sub* vertice lātē
aequora tūta silent; *tum silvīs* scaena coruscīs
165   dēsuper, horrentī*que ātrum* nemus imminet *umbrā.*

Aeneadae, (ār)um *m.* descendants
  (followers) of Aeneas
altum, ī *n.* the deep (sea); heaven
contendō, ere, ī, ntus strive; hasten
coruscus, a, um waving, quivering,
  flashing
dēfessus, a, um weary, tired, worn
dēsuper *adv.* from above
efficiō, ere, fēcī, fectus make, form
frangō, ere, frēgī, frāctus break, shatter
horreō, ēre, uī bristle, shudder, tremble
immineō, ēre hang over, threaten
īnsula, ae *f.* island
lātē *adv.* widely, far and wide
latus, eris *n.* side, flank
Libya, ae *f.* region of North Africa

minor, ārī, ātus threaten, tower
nemus, oris *n.* grove, forest
obiectus, ūs *m.* projection, overhang
proximus, a, um nearest
redūcō, ere, dūxī, ductus bring back, lead
  back
rūpēs, is *f.* crag, cliff
scaena, ae *f.* background, stage
scindō, ere, scidī, scissus split, divide
scopulus, ī *m.* rock, cliff
sēcessus, ūs *m.* inlet, recess
sileō, ēre, uī be silent, be still
sinus, ūs *m.* fold, gulf, bay
tūtus, a, um safe, protected, secure
vertex, icis *m.* summit, top
vertō, ere, ī, rsus (over)turn, (ex)change

157–209. Aeneas, with seven out of twenty ships, lands on the coast of North Africa near Carthage. He kills seven fine stags, which he divides among his comrades, whom he tries to console and encourage.

157–8. Aeneadae lītora, quae (sunt) proxima, cursū petere contendunt. The word **cursū** has two implications, both of which are probably relevant here: the men are moving with speed, i.e., "running"; and they travel on their "course."

159. The opening words **est . . . locus** mark this passage as an ECPHRASIS, the detailed and vivid description of a place or work of art.

159–60. īnsula efficit (hunc locum) portum. portum: predicate acc. **in sēcessū longō:** the inlet extends deep into the land.

160. quibus: abl. of means; App. 331; the antecedent is **laterum.**

160–61. omnis unda (veniēns) ab altō frangitur et sē in sinūs reductōs scindit. sēsē = sē. Observe the ALLITERATION.

162. Hinc atque hinc: *on (from) this side and that,* i.e., on both sides. **rūpēs (sunt).**

164. scaena: the place resembles a stage with its scenery. **silvīs coruscīs:** abl. of quality; App. 330.

165. horrentī umbrā: abl. of cause if taken with **ātrum,** or of manner if taken with **imminet;** App. 332, 328. It is curious that Vergil uses here a verb the literal meaning of which, "threatens" (cf. **minantur,** 162), is at odds with the apparent peacefulness of the scene. This is meant to be a safe harbor for Aeneas and his men; yet twice its features are characterized in a less than entirely benign

Fronte *sub* adversā scopulīs pendentibus antrum;
intus aquae dulcēs vīvōque sedīlia saxō,
Nymphārum domus. *hīc fessās nōn vincula nāvēs*
ūlla tenent, uncō *nōn* alligat ancora morsū.
170   *Hūc* septem Aenēās collēctīs nāvibus omnī
ex numerō subit, *ac magnō tellūris amōre*
ēgressī optātā potiuntur Trōes harēnā
et sale tābentēs artūs *in lītore pōnunt.*

---

adversus, a, um opposite, facing
alligō (1) bind, hold (to)
ancora, ae *f.* anchor
antrum, ī *n.* cave, cavern
aqua, ae *f.* water
artus, ūs *m.* joint, limb
colligō, ere, lēgī, lēctus collect, gather
dulcis, e sweet, dear, fresh
ēgredior, ī, gressus go out, disembark
frōns, ontis *f.* front, face, brow
harēna, ae *f.* sand, beach
intus *adv.* within
morsus, ūs *m.* bite, bit
numerus, ī *m.* number, multitude

Nympha, ae *f.* nymph, a minor divinity of
nature, represented as a beautiful maiden
optō (1) choose, desire, hope (for)
pendeō, ēre, pependi hang
potior, īrī, ītus gain (+ *abl.*)
sal, salis *n.* (*m.*) salt (water), sea
scopulus, ī *m.* rock, cliff
sedīle, is *n.* seat, bench
septem seven
tābeō, ēre drip, soak, melt, waste
Trōs, Trōis *m.* Trojan
uncus, a, um curved, bent, hooked
vinc(u)lum, ī *n.* chain, bent, hooked
vīvus, a, um living, natural, alive

---

manner. **horrentī:** abl. of an *i-* stem; this word is probably used here to suggest the shade of bristling evergreens, such as cedars, firs, or pines.

166. fronte sub adversā: i.e., the cave is at the innermost end of the bay, facing the island. **scopulīs pendentibus:** abl. of quality or material; App. 330, 324.

167. vīvō saxō: denotes natural, not artificial, seats.

168. domus: in apposition with **antrum,** the cave just described; nymphs were supposed to frequent remote spots with beautiful natural scenery. **Hīc:** adv., *here;* observe that the -i- is long in the adv. but short in the pron.

fessās nāvēs: PERSONIFICATION; or possibly a TRANSFERRED EPITHET, since it is actually the Trojans who are tired; App. 446.

169. ancora: anachronistic; hooked anchors were not used in the Bronze Age. **alligat (nāvēs). uncō morsū:** abl. of means; App. 331.

170. collēctīs nāvibus: abl. abs.; App. 343. **omnī ex numerō:** we see from 393 that Aeneas had set out with twenty ships. For this pattern of words, see the note on 47.

171. magnō amōre: abl. of manner; App. 328.

172. Trōes: nom. pl., a Gk. form.
173. sale: abl. of means with **tābentēs.**

Ac prīmum silicī scintillam excūdit Achātēs
175   suscēpit*que ignem* foliīs *atque* ārida *circum*
nūtrīmenta *dedit* rapuit*que in* fōmite *flammam.*
Tum Cererem corruptam *undīs* Cereālia*que arma*
expediunt *fessī* rērum, frūgēs*que* receptās
et torrēre *parant* flammīs *et* frangere *saxō.*
180   *Aenēās* scopulum intereā cōnscendit, *et omnem*
prōspectum lātē *pelagō petit,* Anthea *sī quem*
iactātum *ventō videat* Phrygiās*que* birēmēs
aut Capyn *aut* celsīs *in puppibus arma* Caīcī.

Achātēs, ae *m.* faithful comrade of Aeneas
Antheus, eī, *acc.* **ea,** *m.* comrade of Aeneas
āridus, a, um dry
birēmis, is *f.* bireme, galley (with two banks
    of oars)
Caīcus, ī *m.* comrade of Aeneas
Capys, yos, *acc.* **yn** *m.* comrade of Aeneas
celsus, a, um high, lofty, towering
Cereālis, e of Ceres, goddess of grain
Cerēs, eris *f.* goddess of grain
cōnscendō, ere, ī, ēnsus climb, mount
corrumpō, ere, rūpī, ruptus spoil, ruin
excūdō, ere, dī, sus strike out
expediō, īre, īvī (iī), ītus bring out, prepare
folium, (i)ī *n.* leaf
fōmes, itis *m.* tinder, fuel, shaving

frangō, ere, frēgī, frāctus break, crush
frūx, frūgis *f.* fruit, grain
iactō (1) toss, buffet
intereā *adv.* meanwhile, meantime
lātē *adv.* widely, far and wide
nūtrīmentum, ī *n.* food, fuel, nourishment
Phrygius, a, um Phrygian, Trojan
prōspectus, ūs *m.* view
rapiō, ere, uī, ptus snatch (up), whirl
recipiō, ere, cēpī, ceptus take back, recover
scintilla, ae *f.* spark
scopulus, ī *m.* rock, cliff, crag
silix, icis *m.* (*f.*) flint
suscipiō, ere, cēpī, ceptus catch (up),
    receive
torreō, ēre, uī, tostus parch, roast

---

174. silicī: dat. of separation; App. 305.

175. foliīs: abl. of means; App. 331.
circum: adv. modifying **dedit:** *he places
fuel around;* or else understand **circum**
(**ignem**).

177. Cererem: *the goddess of grain.* The
use of her name here to signify the gift she
gives to humans, grain, is an example of
METONYMY. **Cereālia arma:** *the utensils of
Ceres,* i.e., utensils or tools for grinding and
for cooking grain.

178. expediunt (**ex nāvibus**). **rērum:** gen.
with the adj. **fessī;** App. 287, *weary of their
misfortunes.* **receptās** (**ex marī**).

179. torrēre: to make it easier to grind.
frangere: to make coarse meal. **flammīs ...
saxō:** abl. of means; App. 331.

181. pelagō: dat. of direction = **in pela-
gus;** App. 306, or else = **in pelagō,** abl. of
place where; App. 319. **quem:** indef. *any,*
modifying **Anthea,** acc., a Gk. form, *if he can
see any Antheus;* in English we should say *if he
can see anything of Antheus.*

182. videat: subjunctive in an indir.
quest.; App. 349.

183. Capyn: acc., a Gk. form. **puppibus:**
poetic plural. **arma:** especially shields fastened
on the ship and conspicuous at a great distance.

Nāvem in cōnspectū nūllam, trēs lītore cervōs
185 prōspicit errantēs; hōs tōta armenta sequuntur
ā tergō et longum per vallēs pascitur agmen.
Cōnstitit hīc arcumque manū celerēsque sagittās
corripuit fīdus quae tēla gerēbat Achātēs,
ductorēsque ipsōs prīmum capita alta ferentēs
190 cornibus arboreīs sternit, tum vulgus et omnem
miscet agēns tēlīs nemora inter frondea turbam;
nec prius absistit quam septem ingentia victor
corpora fundat humī et numerum cum nāvibus aequet;

---

absistō, ere, stitī cease, stop
Achātēs, ae m. faithful comrade of Aeneas
aequō (1) (make) equal
arboreus, a, um branching, tree-like
arcus, ūs m. bow
armentum, ī n. herd, drove
celer, eris, ere swift
cervus, ī m. stag, deer
cōnsistō, ere, stitī, stitus stop, settle
cōnspectus, ūs m. sight, view
cornū, ūs n. horn
corripiō, ere, uī, reptus snatch (up)
ductor, ōris m. leader
fīdus, a, um faithful, trusty
frondeus, a, um leafy
gerō, ere, gessī, gestus carry (on)
humus, ī f. ground, soil, earth

misceō, ēre, uī, mixtus confuse, mix, mingle
nemus, oris n. grove, forest
numerus, ī m. number, multitude
pascor, ī, pāstus feed, graze
prius adv. first, sooner
prōspiciō, ere, spexī, spectus look out on, see
quam how, than, as
sagitta, ae f. arrow
septem seven
sternō, ere, strāvī, strātus lay low, spread, strew
tergum, ī n. back, hide, rear
trēs, tria three
turba, ae f. mob, crowd
vallis, is f. valley
vulgus, ī n. (m.) crowd, throng, herd

---

184. Nāvem (prōspicit). (in) lītore: abl. of place where; App. 319. **Nāvem nūllam, trēs cervōs:** CHIASMUS and ASYNDETON.

185. hōs (cervōs): the three stags are at the head of the feeding herd.

186. vallēs: pl., but probably referring to a single valley; see the note on **īrae** (11), and cf. App. 243.

187. Cōnstitit (Aenēās). hīc: adv., here; distinguish from the pron., which has a short -i-.

188. tēla: attracted into the rel. clause, it refers back to **arcum** and **sagittās**, objs. of **corripuit.**

189–91. ductōrēs: the three stags (184). **tum vulgus (sternit) et omnem turbam miscet, agēns (eōs = cervōs) tēlīs inter frondea nemora.**

190. cornibus arboreīs: abl. of quality; App. 330. **tum vulgus (sternit). vulgus:** acc., the herd, as opposed to the leaders, **ductōrēs.**

191. nemora: poetic plural. **turbam:** the **vulgus** has now become a panic-stricken and tumultuous **turba,** a mob.

192. victor: (as) victor; apposition with **Aenēās,** the understood subject.

193. humī: loc.; App. 37, c. **numerum (cervōrum). cum nāvibus = cum numerō nāvium. aequet:** temporal or anticipatory subjunctive with **priusquam;** App. 376, a.

hinc portum petit et sociōs partitur in omnēs.
195   Vina bonus *quae* deinde cadīs onerārat *Acestēs*
      lītore Trīnacriō *dederatque* abeuntibus hērōs
      dīvidit, *et dictīs* maerentia *pectora* mulcet:
      "Ō sociī (*neque* enim ignārī *sumus ante* malōrum),
      Ō passī graviōra, *dabit deus hīs* quoque *finem*.
200   Vōs et Scyllaeam rabiem penitus*que* sonantēs
      accestis scopulōs, *vōs et* Cyclōpia *saxa*
      expertī: revocāte *animōs* maestum*que* timōrem

---

abeō, īre, iī (īvī), itus depart
accēdō, ere, cessī, cessus approach
bonus, a, um good, kind(ly), useful
cadus, ī *m.* jar, urn
Cyclōpius, a, um Cyclopean, of the
   Cyclopes, huge one-eyed giants of Sicily
deinde *adv.* then, thereupon, next
dīvidō, ere, vīsī, vīsus divide, distribute
enim *adv.* for, indeed, surely
experior, īrī, pertus try, experience
gravis, e heavy, grievous, serious
hērōs, ōis *m.* hero, mighty warrior
ignārus, a, um ignorant, inexperienced
maereō, ēre mourn, grieve (for)
malum, ī *n.* evil, misfortune, trouble
maestus, a, um sad, mournful, gloomy
mulceō, ēre, lsī, lsus soothe, calm
onerō (1) load, burden

partior, īrī, ītus distribute, divide
patior, ī, passus suffer, endure
penitus *adv.* within, deep(ly), wholly
quoque also
rabiēs, ēī *f.* rage, madness, fury
revocō (1) recall, restore
scopulus, ī *m.* rock, cliff, crag
Scyllaeus, a, um of Scylla, a ravenous
   sea-monster, part woman and part sea
   creature, girdled with fierce dogs and
   destructive to mariners who attempted
   to sail past her cave situated on a narrow
   strait opposite the great whirlpool
   Charybdis
sonō, āre, uī, itus (re)sound, roar
timor, ōris *m.* fear, dread, anxiety
Trīnacrius, a, um Trinacrian, Sicilian
vīnum, ī *n.* wine

---

194. et partītur (cervōs) in (*among*)
omnēs sociōs (suōs).
   195–97. Deinde vīna, quae bonus Acestēs
onerā(ve)rat (in) cadīs (in) Trīnacriō lītore
et quae (ille) hērōs dederat (illīs = Teucrīs)
abeuntibus, dīvidit (Aenēās). deinde: two
syllables by SYNIZESIS. **onerā(ve)rat:** App.
204. **cadīs:** dat. of direction; App. 306; or else
= **in cadīs,** abl. of place where; App. 319. **Vīna**
... dīvidit (Aenēās).
   196. hērōs (Acestēs): nom. sing., a Gk.
form. Acestes had entertained Aeneas and
his comrades during the preceding winter
and had funished them with supplies for the
rest of their journey. **abeuntibus (Teucrīs):**
indir. obj. of **dederat.**

197. pectora (suōrum sociōrum).
   199. Ō (vōs) passī graviōra (mala). hīs
(**malīs**): indir. obj. of **dabit;** App. 295.
   201. acces(sis)tis: syncopated perf.; App.
204. **vōs et:** correlative with **vōs et** in 200;
ANAPHORA; App. 413. **Cyclōpia:** *of the Cy-*
clopes, huge one-eyed giants, one of whom,
Polyphemus, had killed and eaten several of
the comrades of Odysseus while they were
shut up in his cave. Odysseus and his men fi-
nally succeeded in blinding Polyphemus and
escaping. For the story, see 3.613–38, and
Book 9 of Homer's *Odyssey.*
   202. expertī (estis).

mittite; forsan *et haec* ōlim meminisse iuvābit.
Per variōs *cāsūs, per* tot discrīmina *rērum*
205 *tendimus in* Latium, *sēdēs ubi fāta* quiētās
ostendunt; illīc fās *rēgna* resurgere *Troiae.*
Dūrāte, *et vōsmet rēbus servāte secundis.*"
Tālia vōce refert cūrīsque ingentibus aeger
spem vultū simulat, premit *altum* corde dolōrem.

aeger, gra, grum sick, weary	**ōlim** *adv.* once, at some time
cor, cordis *n.* heart, spirit, feelings	**ostendō, ere, ī, ntus** show, promise
discrīmen, inis *n.* crisis, danger	**quiētus, a, um** calm, peaceful
dolor, ōris *m.* grief, pain, suffering	**premō, ere, pressī, pressus** (re)press,
dūrō (1) harden, endure	control
fās *n. indecl.* divine will, right, duty	**resurgō, ere, surrēxī, surrēctus** rise again
fors(it)an *adv.* perhaps, perchance, possibly	**secundus, a, um** following, favorable
illīc *adv.* there	**simulō** (1) imitate, pretend, feign
iuvō, āre, iūvī, iūtus help, please	**spēs, eī** *f.* hope, expectation
Latium, (i)ī *n.* district of central Italy	**tot** so many
around Rome	**varius, a, um** varied, different
meminī, isse remember, recall	**vultus, ūs** *m.* countenance, face

203. mittite: *dismiss.* **et** = **etiam,** *even.* **haec:** obj. of **meminisse. forsan et haec,** etc.: *perhaps at some time we shall be glad to remember even these things.* A famous verse, often quoted. **iuvābit (nōs):** *it will please (us),* with **meminisse** as subject.

205. tendimus (cursum) in Latium: it is curious that here Aeneas mentions Latium, since previously he has not known the name of their destination.

206. fās (est), etc.: *it is divine will that the realms of Troy rise there again.* **rēgna:** poetic plural; App. 243.

207. vōsmet: an emphatic form of **vōs.**

208. Tālia (dicta). vōce: contrasted with **corde** (209). **refert (Aenēās). cūrīs ingentibus:** abl. of cause with **aeger;** App. 332. **aeger:** concessive, i.e., *(although) sick at heart.*

209. (in) vultū: abl. of place where or (less likely) means, sharply contrasted with **corde. corde:** abl. of place where or (less likely) means. **spem:** contrasted with **dolōrem. altum corde:** *deep in his heart.* **spem . . . simulat, premit . . . dolōrem:** this figure is known as CHIASMUS. The contrast is here emphasized by placing the two pairs of words in inverse (reverse) order; that is, **spem** begins the first clause and is contrasted with **dolōrem,** which ends the second, while **simulat** ends the first clause and is thus contrasted with **premit,** which begins the second; App. 420; see the note on 184. Note also the ASYNDETON (lack of connective) between the two clauses, making the CHIASMUS all the more emphatic.

Book 1.418–440

Corripuēre *viam* intereā, quā sēmita mōnstrat.
Iamque ascendēbant collem, *quī plūrimus urbī*
420   imminet adversās*que* aspectat dēsuper *arcēs.*
Mīrātur mōlem *Aenēās,* māgalia *quondam,*
mīrātur portās strepitum*que* et strāta *viārum.*   *Sīsʃ·ʃʰᵘS*
Īnstant *ardentēs Tyriī: pars dūcere* mūrōs
mōlīri*que* arcem et manibus subvolvere *saxa,*
425   *pars* optāre *locum tēctō et* conclūdere sulcō;
iūra magistrātūs*que* legunt sānctum*que* senātum.
Hīc portūs aliī effodiunt; *hīc alta* theātrīs
fundāmenta locant *aliī, immānēs*que columnās

---

adversus, a, um opposite, facing
ascendō, ere, ī, ēnsus ascend, mount
a(d)spectō (1) look at, see, face
collis, is *m.* hill
columna, ae *f.* column, pillar
conclūdō, ere, sī, sus (en)close
corripiō, ere, uī, reptus snatch (up)
dēsuper *adv.* from above
effodiō, ere, fōdī, fossus dig out, excavate
fundāmentum, ī *n.* foundation
immineō, ēre hang over, menace (+ *dat.*)
īnstō, āre, stitī urge on, press on (+ *dat.*)
intereā *adv.* meanwhile, meantime
iūs, iūris *n.* law, justice, decree
legō, ere, lēgī, lēctus choose, gather
locō (1) place, locate, establish
māgālia, ium *n.* huts, hovels

magistrātus, ūs *m.* magistrate, officer
miror, ārī, ātus wonder (at), admire
mōlēs, is *f.* mass, burden, structure
mōlior, īrī, ītus work, effect, make
mōnstrō (1) show, point out
mūrus, ī *m.* (city) wall, rampart
optō (1) choose, desire, hope (for)
porta, ae *f.* gate, door, opening
quā *adv.* where(by), in any way
sānctus, a, um sacred, holy, revered
sēmita, ae *f.* path
senātus, ūs *m.* senate, council of elders
strātum, ī *n.* pavement; bed
strepitus, ūs *m.* noise, uproar
subvolvō, ere, ī, volūtus roll up
sulcus, ī *m.* furrow, trench, ditch
theātrum, ī *n.* theater

418–40. Aeneas and Achates, rendered invisible by Venus, proceed to Carthage and admire the rising city.

418. (Aenēās Achātēsque) corripuērunt viam: *they hurried along their way.* **sēmita (sē) mōnstrat.**

419. plūrimus: *with imposing size.* **urbī:** dat. with compound; App. 298.

421. mōlem (urbis). quondam: before the building of the city. **Mīrātur … mīrātur:** ANAPHORA, here—as often—combined with ASYNDETON.

423. dūcere: *extend;* this and the following infs. either depend on **Īnstant;** App. 259, or are to be construed as historical infs.; App. 257.

423–25. pars, pars: in partitive apposition with **Tyriī.**

425. tēctō: *for a house:* dat. of purpose; App. 303. **conclūdere (locum tēctī) sulcō:** for the foundation.

426. magistrātūs: acc. pl.

427–28. aliī … aliī: *some … others.*

rūpibus excīdunt, scaenīs decora *alta futūrīs.*

430   Quālis apēs aestāte *novā per* flōrea rūra   Simile
     exercet *sub* sōle *labor, cum gentis* adultōs
     ēdūcunt fētūs, *aut cum* līquentia mella
     stīpant *et* dulcī distendunt nectare cellās,
     aut onera *accipiunt venientum, aut agmine factō*

435   ignāvum fūcōs pecus *ā* praesēpibus arcent;
     fervet opus redolent*que* thymō fraglantia mella.
     "Ō fortūnātī, quōrum iam moenia surgunt!"
     Aenēās ait et fastīgia suspicit *urbis.*

---

adultus, a, um grown, adult
aestās, ātis *f.* summer
apis, is *f.* bee
arceō, ēre, uī keep off, defend
cella, ae *f.* cell, storeroom
decus, oris *n.* ornament, beauty, dignity
distendō, ere, ī, ntus distend, stretch
dulcis, e sweet, dear, fresh
ēdūcō, ere, dūxī, ductus lead forth
excīdō, ere, ī, sus cut out, destroy
exerceō, ēre, uī, itus be busy, train
fastīgium, (i)ī *n.* summit, top, height
ferv(e)ō, ēre, ferbuī glow, boil
fētus, ūs *m.* offspring, brood, swarm
flōreus, a, um flowery
fortūnātus, a, um fortunate, blessed
fraglāns, antis fragrant, sweet-smelling
fūcus, ī *n.* drone

ignāvus, a, um lazy, idle
līquēns, entis liquid, flowing
mel, mellis *n.* honey
nectar, aris *n.* nectar
onus, eris *n.* burden, load
opus, eris *n.* work, deed, toil
pecus, oris *n.* flock, herd, swarm
praesēpe, is *n.* stall, hive
quālis, e such (as), of what sort, as
redoleō, ēre, uī be fragrant, smell (of)
rūpēs, is *f.* rock, cliff, crag
rūs, rūris *n.* country, rural area
scaena, ae *f.* stage, background
sōl, sōlis *m.* sun; day
stīpō (1) stuff, crowd, stow
suspiciō, ere, spexī, spectus look up (at)
thymum, ī *n.* thyme, a flowering plant

---

429. (ex) rūpibus: the typical open-air theater of classical Greece (less frequently, Rome) was commonly excavated from a hillside. **scaenīs:** dat. **decora:** apposition with **columnās.**

430–31. (tālis est labor illīs) quālis (labor) exercet apēs: the SIMILE is famous. **aestāte novā:** abl. of time; App. 322.

434. venient(i)um (apium).

435. fūcōs: *the drones;* apposition with **ignāvum pecus.**

436. fraglantia: this unusual form, which appears as **flagrantia** in some of the earliest manuscripts of Vergil's works, is cognate with the English *fragrant;* but in Latin words, one of two similar consonantal sounds (here, **l** and **r**) sometimes changes so as to become more pronounceable (the process is called "dissimilation" by linguists).

437. Ō fortūnātī: substantively, *O fortunate ones!* **iam moenia surgunt:** Aeneas is impatiently looking forward to the time when the walls of his own city will rise.

438. ait: 3rd person sing. of **aiō.**

Īnfert *sē* saeptus nebulā (mīrābile *dictū*)
440   *per mediōs,* miscet*que virīs neque cernitur ūllī.*

īnferō, ferre, tulī, lātus bear (in, into)
mīrābilis, e wonderful, marvelous
misceō, ēre, uī, mixtus mix, mingle

nebula, ae *f.* cloud, mist, fog
saepiō, īre, psī, ptus hedge in, inclose

---

439. dictū: supine, abl. of respect with **mīrābile;** App. 271, 325.

440. per mediōs (virōs): *through the midst (of) the men;* App. 246. **(sē) miscet virīs: virīs** is dat. with **miscet;** App. 297. **ūllī:** dat. of agent; App. 302.

Book 1.494–578

Haec dum Dardaniō *Aenēae* mīranda v̲i̲d̲e̲n̲t̲u̲r̲,
495   *dum* s̲t̲u̲p̲e̲t̲ obtūtū*que* h̲a̲e̲r̲e̲t̲ dēfīxus *in ūnō,*
     rēgīna ad templum, formā pulcherrima *Dīdō,*
     incessit *magnā* iuvenum stīpante catervā.
     Quālis *in* Eurōtae rīpīs *aut per* iuga Cynthī
     e̲x̲e̲r̲c̲e̲t̲ Dīāna chorōs, *quam* mīlle *secūtae*
500   *hinc atque hinc* g̲l̲o̲m̲e̲r̲a̲n̲t̲u̲r̲ Oreādes; *illa* pharetram
     f̲e̲r̲t̲ *umerō* gradiēns*que deās* superēminet *omnēs*
     (Lātōnae tacitum p̲e̲r̲t̲e̲m̲p̲t̲a̲n̲t̲ gaudia *pectus*):
     tālis e̲r̲a̲t̲ *Dīdō, tālem sē laeta* f̲e̲r̲ē̲b̲a̲t̲
     per mediōs īnstāns operī *rēgnīsque futūrīs.*

---

caterva, ae *f.* band, troop, crowd
chorus, ī *m.* chorus, dance, band
Cynthus, ī *m.* mountain in Delos, birthplace of Apollo and Diana
Dardanius, a, um Dardanian, Trojan
Dīāna, ae *f.* goddess of the hunt and of the mountains
dēfīgō, ere, fīxī, fīxus fix, fasten
Eurōtās, ae *m.* river of Sparta, center of the worship of Diana
exerceō, ēre, uī, itus busy, train
forma, ae *f.* form, beauty, shape
gaudium, (i)ī *n.* joy, rejoicing
glomerō (1) gather, roll together
gradior, ī, gressus step, go, proceed
haereō, ēre, haesī, haesus hang, cling (to)
incēdo, ere, cessī, cessus march, go (majestically)
īnstō, āre, stitī press on, urge (+ *dat.*)
iugum, ī *n.* yoke, (mountain) ridge

iuvenis, is *m.* *(f.)* youth, young (man or woman)
Lātōna, ae *f.* mother of Apollo and Diana
mīlle; *pl.* **mīlia, ium** *n.* thousand
mīrandus, a, um wonderful, marvelous
obtūtus, ūs *m.* gaze, view
opus, eris *n.* work, deed, toil
Oreās, adis *f.* Oread, a mountain nymph
pertemptō (1) try; master, possess
pharetra, ae *f.* quiver
pulcher, chra, chrum beautiful, handsome, illustrious
quālis, e such (as), of what sort
rīpa, ae *f.* bank, shore
stīpō (1) stuff, crowd, throng, stow
stupeō, ēre, uī stand agape, be dazed
superēmineō, ēre tower above
tacitus, a, um silent, speechless, still
templum, ī *n.* temple, shrine, sanctuary

> 494–519. Dido visits the temple and welcomes the newly arrived Trojans.

494. Dardaniō: *Trojan;* reminding us why the scenes depicted on the temple had so much meaning for Aeneas.

496. formā: abl. of respect with **pulcherrima**; App. 325.

497. stīpante catervā: abl. abs.; App. 343.

498. Quālis: correlative with **tālis** (503). This SIMILE was inspired by Homer, who described the Phaeacian princess Nausicaa in similar terms when she was first seen by Odysseus (*Odyssey* Book 6).

499. Dīāna: with long -i-; elsewhere with short -i-.

500. illa: Dīāna. **hinc atque hinc:** *on this side and on that; on both sides.*

501. (in) umerō. deās (Oreādas).

502. tacitum pectus: indicating joy too deep for words.

504. per mediōs (virōs).

505   *Tum* foribus *dīvae, mediā* testūdine templī,
      saepta *armīs* soliō*que* altē subnixa resēdit.
      Iūra *dabat* lēgēs*que* virīs, operum*que labōrem*
      partibus aequābat iūstīs *aut* sorte *trahēbat,*
      cum subitō *Aenēās* concursū accēdere *magnō*
510   Anthea Sergestum*que videt* fortem*que* Cloanthum
      Teucrōrumque aliōs, āter quōs aequore turbō
      dispulerat penitus*que aliās* āvēxerat *ōrās.*
      Obstipuit *simul ipse, simul* percussus Achātēs
      laetitiā*que* metū*que;* avidī coniungere *dextrās*
515   *ardēbant, sed rēs animōs* incognita turbat.

---

accēdō, ere, cessī, cessus approach
Achātēs, ae *m.* faithful comrade of Aeneas
aequō (1) equal(ize)
altē *adv.* on high, loftily
Antheus, eī, *acc.* **ea,** *m.* Trojan leader
āvehō, ere, vēxī, vectus bear away
avidus, a, um eager, greedy
Cloanthus, ī *m.* Trojan leader
concursus, ūs *m.* throng, crowd
coniungō, ere, iūnxī, iūnctus join
dispellō, ere, pulī, pulsus drive apart,
    disperse, scatter
foris, is *f.* door, gate, entrance
fortis, e strong, brave, valiant
incognitus, a, um unknown
iūs, iūris *n.* law, justice, right
iūstus, a, um just, fair, right(eous)
laetitia, ae *f.* joy, gladness, delight

lēx, lēgis *f.* law, regulation, decree
metus, ūs *m.* fear, anxiety, dread
obstipēscō, ere, stipuī stand agape
opus, eris *n.* work, deed, toil
penitus *adv.* deep within, deeply, wholly
percutiō, ere, cussī, cussus strike, astound
resīdō, ere, sēdī sit down
saepiō, īre, psī, ptus hedge in, enclose
Sergestus, ī *m.* Trojan leader
solium, (i)ī *n.* throne, seat
sors, rtis *f.* lot, fate, destiny
subitō *adv.* suddenly
subnixus, a, um resting on (+ *abl.*)
templum, ī *n.* temple, shrine, sanctuary
testūdō, inis *f.* tortoise, vault, dome
turbō (1) confuse, disturb, perplex
turbō, inis *m.* whirl(wind, pool), storm

---

505. dīvae: *of the shrine* (lit. *of the goddess*).

505–6. (in) **foribus,** (in) **testūdine,** (in) **soliō.**

507. virīs (Tyriīs): her subjects. The use of temples for the transaction of public business was very common in ancient Rome; hence Vergil assigns a similar custom to the Carthaginians.

508. sorte trahēbat: *assigned the work by lot.*

509–12. cum Aenēās subitō videt accēdere Anthea (acc.) **Sergestumque fortemque Cloanthum aliōsque Teucrōrum, quōs āter turbō dispulerat** (in) **aequore. concursū magnō:** abl. of manner; App. 328. (ad) **aliās ōrās.**

513. ipse: Aeneas; see the note on 114. **simul ... simul** = et ... et. **percussus** (est).

515. rēs incognita: the uncertainty of the situation keeps them silent.

Dissimulant *et* nūbe cavā speculantur amictī
quae fortūna virīs, classem quō lītore linquant,
quid *veniant;* cūnctīs nam lēctī nāvibus ībant
519 ōrantēs veniam *et* templum *clāmōre petēbant.*

---

amiciō, īre, uī (ixī), ictus enfold, wrap
cavus, a, um hollow
dissimulō (1) hide, disguise
legō, ere, lēgī, lēctus choose, gather
linquō, ere, līquī, lictus leave, desert

nūbēs, is *f.* cloud, mist, fog
ōrō (1) pray (for), entreat, beseech
speculor, ārī, ātus spy out, watch
templum, ī *n.* temple, shrine, sanctuary
venia, ae *f.* favor, grace, pardon

---

516. Dissimulant (animōs).
517. quae (sit) fortūna: indir. quest.; App.
349. **virīs:** dat. of possession. **(in) quō lītore.**
517–18. linquant, veniant: subjunctives
in indir. quest.; App. 349.

518. quid = **cūr,** *why?* **(virī) lēctī. (ex)**
cūnctīs nāvibus.
519. clāmōre: abl. of manner; App. 328.

520   Postquam intrōgressī *et* cōram *data* cōpia *fandī,*
       maximus Īlioneus placidō *sīc pectore* coepit:
       "*Ō rēgīna, novam cui* condere *Iuppiter urbem*
       iūstitiā*que* dedit *gentēs* frēnāre superbās,
       Trōes *tē miserī, ventīs maria omnia* vectī,
525   ōrāmus: prohibē īnfandos *ā nāvibus ignēs,*

---

coepī, isse, ptus begin, commence
condō, ere, didī, ditus found, establish;
   hide, bury
cōpia, ae *f.* abundance, plenty, forces
cōram *adv.* before the face, face to face,
   openly
frēnō (1) curb, check, restrain
Īlioneus, eī *m.* Trojan leader
īnfandus, a, um unspeakable, accursed
intrōgredior, ī, gressus step in, enter

iūstitia, ae *f.* justice, equity, righteousness,
   uprightness
ōrō (1) beseech, pray (for), entreat
placidus, a, um peaceful, calm, quiet
postquam after (that), when
prohibeō, ēre, uī, itus prohibit, hold back,
   keep away
superbus, a, um proud, haughty
Trōs, Trōis *m.* Trojan
vehō, ere, vēxī, vectus carry, convey

520–60. Ilioneus, leader of a group of Aeneas' followers who do not know whether their leader has survived the storm at sea, addresses the Carthaginian queen Dido, asking for her assistance and protection. In his speech, he summarizes the purpose of the Trojans' journey, and gives the queen a brief but glowing introduction to the character of Aeneas. Aeneas and Achates, protected by the cloud poured around them by Venus, observe the exchange but are themselves unobserved.

520. intrōgressī (sunt): a metrically convenient variation on **ingressī. data (est).**

521. maximus Īlioneus: greatest because he is probably the oldest of the Trojan exiles in Aeneas' entourage, and so the most suited to lead. The ending of his name, **-eus**, is a diphthong (i.e., a single syllable). **placidō . . . pectore:** abl. of description or manner; Ilioneus speaks in peaceful tones in hopes of being welcomed by Dido.

522–23. cui . . . Iuppiter . . . dedit: the HYPERBATON of Ilioneus' opening words suggests the lofty aspiration of his speech. **condere . . . frēnāre:** infinitival dir. objs. of **dedit.**

523. iūstitiā: abl. of means or manner; to be understood with **frēnāre.** The way the noun is set off here at the beginning of the line places added emphasis on it. **gentēs . . . superbās:** the surrounding peoples of north Africa, with whom Dido had to negotiate to acquire the land settled by her people.

524. Trōes . . . miserī: by characterizing them as helpless, Ilioneus throws himself and his men on Dido's mercy. **(per) maria omnia.**

525–26. Ilioneus uses a TRICOLON marked by ALLITERATION to express his request for assistance; the emphasis thus created draws attention to the most important word in these two lines, **piō.**

parce *piō generī et* propius *rēs* aspice *nostrās.*
Nōn nōs aut ferrō Libycōs populāre penātes
vēnimus, aut raptās *ad lītora* vertere praedās;
non ea vīs animō nec tanta superbia *victīs.*
530   *Est locus,* Hesperiam Graī cognōmine *dīcunt,*
terra antīqua, potēns *armīs atque* ūbere glaebae;
Oenōtrī coluēre *virī; nunc fāma* minōrēs
Ītaliam dīxisse ducis *dē nōmine gentem.*

---

aspiciō, ere, spexī, spectus look at, look
  upon, behold, look
cognōmen, inis *n.* (sur)name, cognomen,
  nickname
colo, ere, ui, cultus cultivate, dwell (in),
  cherish, honor
dux, ducis *m.* (*f.*) leader, conductor, guide
glaeba, ae *f.* a lump of earth, clod
Graius, a, um Greek
Hesperia, ae *f.* Hesperia, Italy; lit., the
  western place
Libycus, a, um Libyan, of Libya, a country
  of North Africa
minores, um *m.* lit. smaller or younger ones;
  descendants (comparative of *parvus*)

Oenōtrus, a, um Oenotrian
parcō, ere, pepercī, parsus spare (+ *dat.*)
penātēs, ium *m.* household gods
populō (1) devastate, plunder, ravage
potēns, entis powerful, ruling (+ *gen.*)
praeda, ae *f.* booty, spoils, prey
propior, propius nearer, closer
rapiō, ere, uī, ptus snatch (away), seize,
  ravish; whirl
superbia, ae *f.* loftiness, haughtiness, pride,
  arrogance
ūber, eris *n.* udder, breast; (symbol of)
  fertility
vertō, ere, ī, rsus (over)turn, (ex)change

527–28. Ilioneus assures Dido that they are
not pirates or thieves. **populāre** and **vertere**
are complementary infs. with **vēnimus** (perf.),
standing in for the usual construction of ex-
pressions of purpose with **ut** + subjunctive, i.e.,
ut populārēmus / ut verterēmus. vertere:
i.e., to divert the stolen property from its right-
ful location and take it towards the ships. The
simple form of the verb is substituted here for
a compound, probably **advertere.**

    529. non . . . animō nec . . . victīs (est): the
two nouns, both dat. of reference or posses-
sion, may be construed separately or as a an
instance of HENDIADYS, i.e., **animō victōrum.**

530. cognōmine: abl. of specification.

    531. potēns armīs atque ūbere glaebae:
the two nouns, abl. of specification or respect,
define Hesperia as a land suited for both war
(**armīs**) and peace (**ūbere glaebae**).

    532. Oenōtrī: inhabitants of southern
Italy. **coluēre = coluērunt. fāma (est):** fol-
lowed by indir. stmt.

    **533. Ītaliam . . . ducis dē nōmine gen-
tem:** the adj. **Ītal(i)us**, according to Ilione-
us, is said to be derived from the name of the
leader of the Oenotrians, i.e., Italus.

> *Hic cursus fuit,*
535 *cum* subitō adsurgēns *flūctū* nimbōsus Orīōn
> *in* vada caeca *tulit* penitus*que* procācibus Austrīs
> *perque undās* superante salō *perque* invia *saxa*
> *dispulit*; *hūc* paucī vestrīs adnāvimus ōrīs.

---

adnō (1) swim, to, swim up to
adsurgō, ere, surrēxī, surrēctus rise up,
  rise, stand up
Auster, trī *m.* the south wind
caecus, a, um blind, dark, hidden
dispellō, ere, pulī, pulsus drive apart,
  disperse, scatter
invius, a, um pathless, trackless
nimbōsus, a, um stormy, rainy
Orīōn, ōnis *m.* the storm-bringing
  constellation, named for a famous
  hunter transported to heaven

paucus, a, um little, few, light, scanty
penitus *adv.* deep within, deeply,
  wholly
procāx, procācis bold, insolent,
  wanton
salum, ī *n.* swell (of the sea); sea
subitō *adv.* suddenly
superō (1) surmount, surpass,
  overcome, survive
vadum, ī *n.* shallow, shoal, depth(s)
vester, tra, trum your(s), your own

---

534. This is the first of about fifty "half-lines" in the *Aeneid*. Some scholars consider them to be proof that Vergil did not quite finish the *Aeneid* before he died, although it is sometimes possible to hypothesize that the slight breaks these lines introduce into the rhythm of the poem are meant to underscore the meaning of the text. Here, for example, it is possible to imagine Ilioneus pausing momentarily, perhaps overwhelmed by his memories, before plunging into a description of the destructive storm.
   535. flūctū: abl. of place where. **nimbōsus Orīōn:** the constellation known as Orion was

thought to represent a mythical hunter transformed by Jupiter into a constellation, visible in the northern hemisphere during the fall and winter. His epithet associates him with the storms common at this time of year.
   536–38. tulit . . . dispulit (understand **nōs** or **nāvēs**). **procācibus Austrīs:** abl. abs.
   537. perque . . . perque: POLYSYNDETON emphasizes the incessant battering they received in the storm. **superante salō:** abl. abs.
   538. paucī: nom. pl. subject of **adnāvimus**. **vestrīs . . . ōrīs:** dat. of motion towards rather than the more usual **ad** (+ acc.).

Quod genus hoc hominum? *Quaeve hunc* tam barbara mōrem
540   permittit patria? Hospitiō prohibēmur harēnae;
bella cient prīmāque vetant cōnsistere terrā.
Sī genus hūmānum *et* mortālia temnitis *arma,*
at spērāte *deōs* memorēs fandī *atque* nefandī.
Rēx erat Aenēās nōbīs, quō iūstior alter,
545   *nec* pietāte *fuit, nec bellō maior et armīs.*

Stop here

---

alter, era, erum one (of two), other
   (of two), second
barbarus, a, um foreign, strange,
   barbarous, uncivilized
cieō, ēre, cīvī, citus (a)rouse, stir (up)
cōnsistō, ere, stitī, stitus stand (fast),
   rest, stop, settle
fandus, a um to be uttered, right, just
harēna, ae *f.* sand
homō, inis *m. (f.)* man, mortal, human
hospitium, (i)ī *n.* hospitality, welcome
hūmānus, a, um of man, human
iūstus, a, um just, fair, right(eous)
memor, oris remembering, mindful,
   unforgetting (+ *gen.*)

mortālis, e human, mortal
mōs, mōris *m.* custom, ritual, manner
nefandus, a, um unspeakable,
   unutterable
patria, ae *f.* homeland, country
permittō, ere, mīsī, missus entrust,
   allow
pietās, ātis *f.* loyalty, devotion, (sense of)
   duty
prohibeō, ēre, uī, itus prohibit, hold back,
   keep away
spērō (1) hope (for, to), expect, suppose
tam *adv.* so (much), such
temnō, ere scorn, disdain, despise
vetō, āre, uī, itus forbid, prevent

---

539. Quod (est)? **hoc:** a long syllable, re-flecting the earlier form of the demonstrative, **hocce. hominum:** partitive gen. **hunc . . . mōrem:** Ilioneus will explain what he means by this phrase in the next two verses.

540–41. Ilioneus refers here to events not described by Vergil: it seems that someone (he presumes the Carthaginians are respon-sible) is actively attempting to prevent him and the other survivors of the storm from landing on the shore and taking shelter there; they are threatening war if the Trojans do not move on. **Hospitiō:** abl. of separation with **prohibēmur. prīmā . . . terrā:** abl. of place where. Land is described as **prīma** here to re-flect the perspective of those at sea: the shore

is the first thing sailors see, and the first thing they touch upon landing.

542–43. A pres. general condition; the adversative particle **at** suggests that **sī** should be translated *even if.* **genus hūmānum et mortālia . . . arma:** CHIASMUS. **deōs memorēs (futūrōs esse):** indir. stmt. after **spērāte. fandī atque nefandī:** originally gerunds, but here they have lost most of their verbal quality and can be simply translated as *right and wrong.*

544. nōbīs: dat. of possession. **quō:** abl. of comparison with **iūstior** and **maior** (545).

545. pietāte: abl. of respect or specifica-tion with **iūstior. bellō . . . armīs:** abl. of respect or specification with **maior.**

Quem sī fāta virum servant, sī vēscitur aurā
aetheriā *neque* adhūc crūdēlibus occubat *umbrīs,*
nōn metus, officiō *nec tē* certāsse priōrem
paeniteat. *Sunt et* Siculīs regiōnibus *urbēs*
550   *armaque* Troiānōque *ā sanguine* clārus *Acestēs.*
Quassātam *ventīs* liceat subdūcere *classem*
et silvīs aptāre trabēs *et* stringere *rēmōs,*
sī datur Ītaliam sociīs et rēge receptō
tendere, ut Ītaliam laetī Latiumque *petāmus;*

---

adhūc *adv.* to this point, till now

aetherius, a, um of the upper air, high in the air, airy, ethereal

aptō (1) equip, make ready, furnish

certō (1) strive, fight, vie, contend

clārus, a, um clear, bright, illustrious

crūdēlis, e cruel, bloody, bitter

Latium, (i)ī *n.* Latium, district of central Italy

licet, ēre, uit, itum it is permitted

metus, ūs *m.* fear, anxiety, dread

occubō, āre lie prostrate, lie dead

officium, ī *n.* service, kindness, favor, courtesy

paeniteō, ēre, uī repent, be sorry

prior, ius sooner, former, first, prior

quassō (1) shake, shatter, toss

recipiō, ere, cēpī, ceptus receive, accept, take back, recover

regiō, ōnis *f.* district, region, quarter

Siculus, a, um Sicilian, of Sicily, a large island south of Italy

stringō, ere, strinxī, strictus graze

subdūcō, ere, dūxī, ductus take away, remove, beach, bring out of water

trabs (trabēs), trabis *f.* beam, timber, tree

Troiānus, a, um Trojan, of Troy

vēscor, ī use as food, feed upon, eat (+ *abl.*)

546–47. Quem = hunc. sī vēscitur aurā aetheriā: a picturesque equivalent of **sī vīvit. vēscitur:** takes abl; App. 342.

548–49. nōn metus (est nōbīs et tibī). officiō: abl. of specification. **nec tē certā(vi)sse priōrem (esse). paeniteat:** jussive subjunctive.

549–50. Sunt et: as his confidence grows in Dido's presence, Ilioneus begins to think of additional information he might offer her to convince her to help them. **urbēs armaque . . . Acestēs:** Ilioneus assures Dido that he and his followers have some resources after all: Sicily offers the Trojans centers of civilization (**urbēs**), the ability to protect themselves (**arma**), and a distinguished leader (**Acestēs**) to take Aeneas' place if need be.

551–52. ventīs: abl. of means. **subdūcere . . . aptāre . . . stringere:** complementary inf. with **liceat** (jussive subjunctive). **silvīs:** abl. of place where. **stringere:** Ilioneus uses this verb to describe the process of stripping tree branches of foliage in order to turn them into oars.

553–54. Ītaliam: acc. of place towards which; the prep. is sometimes omitted (as here) in poetry. **sociīs et rēge receptō:** abl. abs.; the participle is sing. in agreement with the noun closer to it, but should be understood with both. **Ītaliam laetī Latiumque:** the combination of **l-, -a-,** and **t-** sounds in these words is an example of ASSONANCE enhanced by ALLITERATION; here, it draws attention to **laetī** (and hints at a pun on **laetī** and **Latium**).

555   sīn absūmpta salūs, *et tē, pater* optime *Teucrum,*
      pontus *habet*Libyae *nec* spēs *iam* restat Iūlī,
      at freta Sīcaniae saltem *sēdēsque parātās,*
      unde *hūc* advectī, *rēgemque petāmus Acestēn."*
      Tālibus Īlioneus; *cūnctī simul ōre* fremēbant
560   Dardanidae.

---

absūmō, ere, sūmpsī, sūmptus take away, diminish, use up, consume
ādvehō, ere, vēxī, vectus carry, convey (away)
Dardanidēs, ae *m.* Dardanian, Trojan
fremō, ere, uī, itus murmur, lament, groan, roar, rage
fretum, ī *n.* strait, sound, channel, narrow sea
Īlioneus, eī *m.* Trojan leader
Iūlus, ī *m.* Ascanius, son of Aeneas

Libya, ae *f.* country of North Africa
optimus, a, um best, finest (superl. of **bonus**)
pontus, ī *m.* sea, waves
restō, āre, stitī remain, be left
saltem *adv.* at least, at any rate
salūs, ūtis *f.* safety, salvation, health
Sīcania, ae *f.* Sicily, a large island south of Italy
sīn if however, if on the contrary, but if
spēs, speī *f.* hope, expectation
unde from where, from which source

---

555. absūmpta (est) salūs. tē, pater optime Teucrum: APOSTROPHE, used ironically here. Ilioneus thinks Aeneas may well be dead, when in fact he is present but unseen.

556. spēs . . . Iūlī: i.e., hope for his survival; **Iūlī** is objective gen.

557. at . . . saltem: *still, at least.*

558. advectī (sumus). petāmus: hortatory subjunctive.

560. On the half-lines in the *Aeneid,* see note on 534.

Tum breviter *Dīdō* vultum dēmissa profātur:
"Solvite corde metum, *Teucrī*, sēclūdite *cūrās.*
Rēs dūra *et rēgnī* novitās *mē tālia* cōgunt
mōlīrī *et* lātē *fīnēs* custōde tuērī.
565   *Quis genus* Aeneadum, *quis Troiae* nesciat *urbem,*
virtūtēs*que* virōs*que aut tantī* incendia *bellī?*
Nōn obtūnsa adeō gestāmus *pectora* Poenī,
nec tam āversus *equōs Tyriā* Sōl iungit *ab urbe.*

---

adeō *adv.* to such an extent, so (much)
Aeneadae, (ār)um *m.* descendants
   (followers) of Aeneas
āvertō, ere, ī, rsus turn away, avert
breviter *adv.* shortly, briefly, concisely
cōgō, ere, coēgī, coāctus bring together,
   force, muster, compel
cor, cordis *n.* heart, spirit, feelings
custōs, ōdis *m.* (*f.*) guard(ian), keeper
dēmittō, ere, mīsī, missus send down, let
   down, drop, lower, derive
dūrus, a, um hard(y), harsh, rough, stern
gestō (1) bear, wear, carry
incendium, ī *n.* a burning, fire, conflagration
iungō, ere, iūnxī, iūnctus join, unite
lātē *adv.* widely, far and wide
metus, ūs *m.* fear, anxiety, dread
mōlior, īrī, ītus undertake, (strive
   to) accomplish, do

nesciō, īre, īvī, (iī) not know, know not, be
   ignorant
novitās, ātis *f.* newness, novelty
obtundō, ere, tudī, tūsus (tūnsus) blunt,
   weaken, exhaust, make dull
Poenus, a, um Phoenician, Carthaginian
profor, ārī, ātus speak (out), say
sēclūdō, ere, sī, sus shut off, seclude, part
sōl, sōlis *m.* sun; day; personified as **Sōl,**
   Sōlis *m.* sun-god
solvō, ere, ī, solūtus loose(n), release, break
   down, free, pay
tueor, ērī, itus (tūtus) watch, look at,
   protect, eye
tam *adv.* so (much), such
virtūs, ūtis *f.* manliness, excellence in
   battle, valor
vultus, ūs *m.* countenance, face

561–78. Dido responds to Ilioneus, offering
the Trojans her hospitality. She indicates
her willingness to let them settle in Car-
thage with her people if they wish, but also
says that, should they prefer, she will assist
them to continue their voyage. Finally, she
promises to send out a search party to ascer-
tain the whereabouts of Aeneas.

561. vultum: to be construed either as
dir. obj. of the participle **dēmissa** (*having
been cast down*), treated here as a Gk. middle
participle capable of having a dir. obj. (*hav-
ing cast down her face*) or as an acc. of respect,
often called the Greek accusative (*having been
cast down with respect to her face*); App. 309, *a.*

562. corde: abl. of separation.

564. custōde: abl. of means; the sing. is
used as a collective in place of the pl.

565. nesciat: potential or deliberative
subjunctive.

567. Poenī: nom. pl.; Dido speaks on be-
half of her people.

568. *Nor does the Sun yoke his horses so far
from the Tyrian city.* Dido uses this expres-
sion to convey the idea that her people and
the Trojans are not so different from each
other—they live in the same part of the
world, and share the same sunlight. Ilioneus
can thus be confident that his requests will
be met with civilized hospitality, similar to
what the Trojans themselves would offer to
newcomers.

Dido: fair, hospitable, a little naive.

Seu *vōs* Hesperiam *magnam* Sāturnia*que arva*
570 sīve Erycis *fīnēs* rēgem*que* optātis *Acestēn,*
auxiliō tūtōs dīmittam opibus*que* iuvābō.
Vultis et hīs mēcum pariter cōnsīdere *rēgnīs?*
Urbem quam statuō, vestra *est;* subdūcite *nāvēs;*
Trōs Tyriusque *mihī nūllō* discrīmine *agētur.*
575 *Atque* utinam *rēx ipse* Notō compulsus *eōdem*
adforet Aenēās! Equidem *per lītora* certōs
dīmittam *et* Libyae lūstrāre extrēma *iubēbō,*
sī quibus ēiectus *silvīs aut urbibus errat.*"

---

auxilium, (i)ī *n.* aid, help, assistance
certus, a, um fixed, sure, certain, reliable
compellō, ere, pulī, pulsus drive, compel, force
cōnsīdō, ere, sēdī, sessus sit (down), settle
discrīmen, inis *n.* crisis, danger
dīmittō, ere, mīsī, mīssus send out, scatter, dismiss
ēiciō, ēicere, ēiēcī, ēiectus cast out, eject
equidem *adv.* indeed, truly, surely
Eryx, ycis *m.* Eryx, a mountain in western Sicily named after a son of Venus (and half-brother of Aeneas) who settled there
extrēmus, a, um extreme, farthest, last
Hesperia, ae *f.* Hesperia, Italy; lit., the western place
iuvō, āre, iūvī, iūtus help, please

Libya, ae *f.* country of North Africa
lūstrō (1) purify, survey, traverse
Notus, ī *m.* (south) wind
ops, opis *f.* help, resources, power, wealth
optō (1) choose, desire, hope (for)
pariter *adv.* equally, side by side
Sāturnius, a, um (born) of Saturn, father of Jupiter and Juno
sīve, seu whether, or, either if, or if
statuō, ere, uī, ūtus set (up), found
subdūcō, ere, dūxī, ductus take away, remove, beach, bring out of water
Trōs, Trōis *m.* Trojan
tūtus, a, um protected, safe, secure
utinam *adv.* oh that!, I wish that!
vester, tra, trum your(s), your own

569–70. Dido displays her familiarity with the geography of the western Mediterranean—she not only refers to the places and people mentioned by Ilioneus (**Hesperiam magnam; rēgem . . . Acestēn**) but adds a few details that will be important later in the *Aeneid*: when the Trojans return to Sicily in Book 5, they will be in the territory once ruled by Eryx, a son of Venus (and so half-brother of Aeneas); and in Book 8, Evander will explain to Aeneas that Italy is called Saturnian because Saturn came to hide there when he was driven into exile by Jupiter.
571. auxiliō . . . opibusque: abl. of means.

572. hīs . . . rēgnīs: abl. of place where.
573. Urbem: acc. in agreement with **quam** rather than the more logical nom.; this construction is sometimes known by the name relative attraction.
574. mihī: dat. of agent.
576. adforet = adfutūrus esset; the infinitival form **fore** (= **esse**) and the compounds derived from it provide a convenient metrical alternative for the longer forms. **certōs:** *men I can be sure of.*
578. sī (ali)quibus . . . silvīs aut urbibus: abl. of place where.

Selections from
—BOOK 2—

Invadunt urbem somno vinoque sepultam (2.265)

Illustration for Book 2
"Into the darkened city" by Thom Kapheim

Book 2.40–56

40   *Prīmus* ibi *ante omnēs magnā* comitante catervā
      Lāocoōn *ardēns summā* dēcurrit *ab arce,*
      et procul 'Ō miserī, quae tanta īnsānia, cīvēs?
      Crēditis āvectōs hostēs? *Aut ūlla* putātis
      dōna carēre dolīs *Danaum? Sīc* nōtus Ulixēs?
45   *Aut hōc* inclūsī lignō occultantur Achīvī,
      aut haec in nostrōs fabricāta *est* māchina mūrōs,
      īnspectūra domōs ventūraque dēsuper *urbī,*
      aut aliquis latet error; *equō nē* crēdite, *Teucrī.*
      Quidquid *id est,* timeō *Danaōs et dōna ferentēs.'*

Achīvus, a, um Achaean, Greek
aliquis (quī), qua, quid (quod) some(one), any(one)
āvehō, ere, vēxī, vectus carry, convey (away)
careō, ēre, uī, itus be free from, lack (+ *abl.*)
caterva, ae *f.* crowd, band, troop
cīvis, is *m.* (*f.*) citizen, compatriot
comitō (1) accompany, attend, escort, follow
crēdō, ere, didī, ditus believe, trust (+ *dat.*)
dēcurrō, ere, (cu)currī, cursus run down
dēsuper *adv.* from above
dolus, ī *m.* deceit, wiles, trick, fraud
error, ōris *m.* error, deceit, trick
fabricō (1) fashion, make
hostis, is *m.* (*f.*) enemy, foe, stranger
ibi *adv.* there, then
inclūdō, ere, sī, sus (en)close, confine

īnsānia, ae *f.* madness, frenzy, folly
īnspiciō, ere, spexī, spectus look into
Lāocoōn, ontis *m.* Trojan priest of Neptune
lateō, ēre, uī lie hidden, hide, lurk
lignum, ī *n.* wood, timber
māchina, ae *f.* machine, engine, device
mūrus, ī *m.* (city) wall, rampart
nōtus, a, um (well) known, familiar
occultō (1) hide, conceal, secrete
putō (1) suppose, think, consider
quisquis, quidquid whoever, whatever
timeō, ēre, uī fear, dread, be anxious
Ulixēs, is (eī, ī) *m.* Odysseus, the wily Greek leader who is the central character in Homer's *Odyssey* (his name in Latin is **Ulixes**, or Ulysses)

40–56. Laocoon, priest of Neptune, tries to avert disaster by taking the lead and striking the side of the horse with his spear.

40. comitante catervā: abl. abs.; App. 343.
42. et procul (clāmat). īnsānia (est ista).
43. āvectōs (esse).
44. dolīs: abl. of separation with **carēre;** App. 340. **dōna Dana(ōr)um. nōtus (est vōbīs) Ulixēs:** Odysseus (Latin, **Ulixēs** or Ulysses), Greek instigator of cunning, craft, and treachery. Here, his name is symbolic of the Greeks as a whole.

45. (in) hōc lignō = in hōc equō, quī est dē lignō factus: METONYMY.
46. māchina (bellī).
47. īnspectūra, ventūra: the fut. participles denote purpose; App. 274. **urbī:** dat. of direction = **in urbem;** App. 306.
48. nē crēdite: nē with the imperat. is a poetic use, = **nōlite crēdere;** App. 256, *a.* **equō:** dat. with **crēdō;** App. 297.
49. timeō Danaōs et dōna ferentēs: a proverbial line. The Greeks are so treacherous that they are not to be trusted even when making gifts (sacrificing, as in this case) to their gods.

50   *Sīc fātus* validīs *ingentem vīribus* hastam
in latus *inque* ferī curvam compāgibus alvum
contorsit. *Stetit illa* tremēns, uterō*que* recussō
īnsonuēre cavae gemitum*que dedēre* cavernae.
Et, sī fāta deum, sī mēns nōn laeva fuisset,
55   impulerat *ferrō* Argolicās foedāre latebrās,
Troiaque nunc stāret, Priamīque arx alta manērēs.

---

alvus, ī *f.* belly, body
Argolicus, a, um Argive, Greek
caverna, ae *f.* hollow, cavity, cave
cavus, a, um hollow, vaulted
compāgēs, is *f.* joint, seam, fastening
contorqueō, ēre, rsī, rtus hurl, twirl
curvus, a, um *f.* curved, crooked
ferus, ī *m.* beast, monster, horse
foedō (1) befoul, defile; mar, mangle
gemitus, ūs *m.* groan, roar, moan
hasta, ae *f.* spear, lance, dart

impellō, ere, pulī, pulsus impel, drive
īnsonō, āre, uī (re)sound, roar, echo
laevus, a, um left, foolish, unlucky
latebra, ae *f.* hiding place, cavern, lair
latus, eris *n.* side, flank
recutiō, ere, cussī, cussus strike (back), shake
tremō, ere, uī tremble, quiver, shake
uterus, ī *m.* belly, womb
validus, a, um strong, mighty

---

50. validīs ingentem vīribus hastam: interlocked order, SYNCHYSIS; App. 442. **vīribus:** abl. of manner; App. 328; from **vīs**, not **vir**, as may be seen from the quantity of the -i- as well as from its third-declension ending.

51. ferī = equī. compāgibus: with **curvam**, abl. of manner or means; App. 328, 331.

52. illa = hasta. uterō recussō: abl. abs. with causal force; App. 343, *a*.

53. īnsonuēre, dedēre = īnsonuērunt, dedērunt: App. 204, 4. **gemitum:** the hollow sound is described ominously, and almost as if the wooden horse were alive.

54–56. fuisset, stāret, manērēs: contrary-to-fact condition, with indicative (**impulerat**) instead of the standard subjunctive (**impulisset**) in the apodosis; App. 382, *d*. **sī fāta deum, sī mēns nōn laeva fuisset:** the combination of ANAPHORA and ASYNDETON links the two subjects closely, and suggests that the verb and predicate adj. are to be understood with each. **laeva:** here, not just passively *unlucky*, but downright *hostile*.

55. (Lāocoōn nōs) impulerat.

56. manērēs: observe the change to the 2nd person sing.; personification and APOSTROPHE add to the pathos.

Laocoon and his sons, Vatican
Photograph by Raymond V. Schoder, S.J.

Book 2.201–249

Lāocoōn, *ductus* Neptūnō sorte sacerdōs,
sollemnēs taurum *ingentem* mactābat *ad ārās.*
Ecce autem *geminī ā* Tenedō tranquilla *per* alta
(horrēscō *referēns*) immēnsīs orbibus anguēs
205   incumbunt *pelagō* pariter*que ad lītora tendunt;*
pectora quōrum *inter flūctūs* arrēcta iubae*que*
sanguineae superant *undās, pars* cētera pontum
pōne legit sinuat*que* immēnsa volūmine terga.

---

altum, ī *n.* the deep (sea); heaven
anguis, is *m.* *(f.)* snake, serpent
arrigō, ere, rēxī, rēctus raise, rear
autem *adv.* moreover, but, however
cēterus, a, um rest, remaining, other
ecce see! look! behold!
horrēscō, ere, horruī shudder, tremble
immēnsus, a, um immense, immeasurable
incumbō, ere, cubuī, cubitus lean upon,
    hang over, lower (over) (+ *dat.*)
iuba, ae *f.* mane, crest
Lāocoōn, ontis *m.* Trojan priest of Neptune
legō, ere, lēgī, lēctus choose; skim
mactō (1) sacrifice, slaughter; honor
Neptūnus, ī *m.* Neptune, god of the sea

orbis, is *m.* circle, fold, coil; earth
pariter *adv.* equally, side by side
pōne *adv.* behind, after
pontus, ī *m.* sea, waves
sacerdōs, dōtis *m.* *(f.)* priest(ess)
sanguineus, a, um bloody, blood-red
sinuō (1) fold, curve, twist, wind
sollemnis, e annual, customary, solemn
sors, rtis *f.* lot, fate, destiny, oracle
superō (1) surmount, overcome, survive
taurus, ī *m.* bull, bullock, ox
Tenedos, ī *f.* small island near Troy
tergum, ī *n.* back, body, rear
tranquillus, a, um tranquil, calm
volūmen, inis *n.* fold, coil, roll

201–227. As a punishment for Laocoon, who had struck the wooden horse with his spear, two serpents come from Tenedos and destroy him and his two little sons.

201. Neptūnō: dat. of reference; App. 301. **ductus sorte:** *drawn (chosen) by lot.*

203–4. autem ecce geminī anguēs immēnsīs orbibus—**horrēscō (haec dicta) referēns**—**(venientēs) ā Tenedō:** symboliz-ing the later coming of the Greek ships from

Tenedos, bringing destruction with them. **horrēscō referēns:** Aeneas was indeed an eyewitness, and his use of the pres. tense through much of this passage makes the rec-ollection vivid for his listeners. **immēnsīs orbibus:** abl. of quality or manner; App. 330, 328.

205. pelagō: dat. with compound **incum-bunt;** App. 298.

206. pectora arrēcta: the snakes seem almost to stand on the water.

208. volūmine: abl. of manner or respect; App. 328, 325.

Fit sonitus spūmante salō; *iamque arva tenēbant*
210   *ardentēsque oculōs* suffectī *sanguine et ignī*
       sībila lambēbant linguīs vibrantibus *ōra*.
       Diffugimus vīsū exsanguēs. *Illī agmine* certō
       Lāocoōnta *petunt; et prīmum* parva duōrum
       corpora nātōrum serpēns amplexus uterque
215   implicat *et miserōs* morsū dēpascitur artūs;
       post *ipsum* auxiliō *subeuntem ac tēla ferentem*
       corripiunt spīrīs*que ligant ingentibus; et iam*
       bis *medium* amplexī, bis collō squāmea *circum*

---

amplector, ī, plexus embrace, enfold
artus, ūs *m.* joint, limb, body
auxilium, (i)ī *n.* help, aid, assistance
bis twice
certus, a, um sure, fixed, certain, reliable
collum, ī *n.* neck
corripiō, ere, uī, reptus seize, snatch up
dēpascor, ī, pāstus feed on, devour
diffugiō, ere, fūgī flee apart, scatter
duo, ae, o two
exsanguis, e bloodless, lifeless, pale
fīō, fierī, factus become, arise
implicō, āre, āvī (uī), ātus (itus) entwine
Lāocoōn, ontis *m.* Trojan priest of Neptune
lambō, ere lick, lap
ligō (1) bind, tie, fasten

lingua, ae *f.* tongue, language
morsus, ūs *m.* bite, biting, jaws, fangs
parvus, a, um small, little
post *adv.* afterward; *prep. + acc.* after, behind
salum, ī *n.* sea, swell (of the sea)
serpēns, entis *m.* (*f.*) serpent, snake
sībilus, a, um hissing, whirring
sonitus, ūs *m.* sound, roar, noise, crash
spīra, ae *f.* fold, coil, spire
spūmō (1) foam, froth, spray
squāmeus, a, um scaly
sufficiō, ere, fēcī, fectus supply, suffuse
uterque, utraque, utrumque each, both
vibrō (1) quiver, vibrate, dart
vīsus, ūs *m.* sight, view, vision, aspect

---

209. spūmante salō: abl. abs.; App. 343.

210. oculōs: obj. of the participle **suffectī**, treated here as a Gk. middle participle capable of having a dir. obj.; alternatively, **oculōs** is a so-called Gk. acc., i.e., acc. of respect (*suffused with respect to their eyes*); App. 309, *a*.

212. Diffugimus: Aeneas inserts himself and his companions again into the scene. **vīsū:** either abl. of cause with **exsanguēs**, or abl. of separation with **diffugimus**; App. 332.

213. Lāocoōnta: acc., a Gk. form; App. 68.

213–14. parva duōrum / corpora nātōrum: the interlocked word order is a verbal approximation of the sight described.

216. ipsum (Lāocoōnta). auxiliō: dat. of purpose; App. 303.

218. circum: with **datī** = **circumdatī**, *placed around*; the separation into two separate words of the parts of a compound is called TMESIS ("cutting"). **medium (illum =** **Lāocoōnta). collō:** dat. with the compound **circumdatī**; App. 298.

terga *datī* superant *capite et* cervīcibus *altīs.*
220   *Ille simul manibus tendit* dīvellere nōdos
     perfūsus saniē vittās *ātrōque* venēnō,
     clāmōrēs simul horrendōs *ad sīdera tollit:*
     quālis mūgītus, *fugit cum* saucius *āram*
     taurus *et* incertam excussit cervīce secūrim.
225   *At geminī* lāpsū dēlūbra *ad summa* dracōnēs
     effugiunt saevae*que petunt* Trītōnidis *arcem,*
     sub pedibusque deae clipeī*que sub* orbe teguntur.

---

cervīx, īcis *f.* neck
clipeus, ī *m.* shield, buckler
dēlūbrum, ī *n.* shrine, temple
dīvellō, ere, ī (or **vulsī**), **vulsus** tear apart
dracō, ōnis *m.* dragon, serpent
effugiō, ere, fūgī flee, escape
excutiō, ere, cussī, cussus shake off
horrendus, a, um horrible, horrifying
incertus, a, um uncertain
lāpsus, ūs *m.* gliding, rolling, sinking
mūgītus, ūs *m.* bellow(ing), roar
nōdus, ī *m.* knot; fold, coil
orbis, is *m.* circle, fold, coil; earth
perfundō, ere, fūdī, fūsus soak, drench

quālis, e (such) as, of what sort
saevus, a, um fierce, cruel, stern
saniēs, ēī *f.* blood, gore
saucius, a, um wounded, stricken
secūris, is *f.* ax
superō (1) surmount, overcome, survive
tegō, ere, tēxī, tēctus cover, hide
tergum, ī *n.* back, body, rear
taurus, ī *m.* bull, bullock, ox
Trītōnis, idis *f.* Minerva, goddess of
     wisdom and the arts
venēnum, ī *n.* poison, venom, drug
vitta, ae *f.* fillet, garland, band

---

219. terga: obj. of the participle **circumdatī** (*having placed*), treated here as a Gk. middle participle capable of having a dir. obj.; alternatively, **terga** is a so-called Gk. acc., i.e., acc. of respect (*having been placed around with respect to their bodies*); App. 309, *a.* **superant (illum =** **Lāocoönta). capite:** for **capitibus,** which could not be used in dactylic verse because of its three successive short syllables; abl. of means or degree of difference; App. 331, 335.

220. Ille: Lāocoön. manibus: abl. of means.

221. saniē ātrōque venēnō: abl. of means. **vittās:** acc. obj. of the participle **perfūsus,** treated here as a Gk. middle participle capable of having a dir. obj.; alternatively, **vittās** is a so-called Gk. acc., i.e., acc. of respect (*soaked with respect to his headbands*); App. 309, *a,* 311.

223. (tālis est mūgītus Lāocoöntis) quālis (est) mūgītus (taurī): a SIMILE; App. 441.

224. (ā) cervīce.

225. lāpsū: *with a gliding (movement):* abl. of manner; App. 328. Note how with this word Aeneas passes over in silence the death of Laocoon. **dēlūbra summa = dēlūbra arcis Troiae,** where the temple of Minerva stood (226).

227. deae = here, the statue of the goddess. **teguntur: = sē tegunt,** as if a Gk. verb in the middle voice; App. 309. The serpents return to the goddess who, at least indirectly (i.e., by her staunch patronage of the Greeks in general and Odysseus in particular), is responsible for their appearance.

Tum vērō tremefacta *novus per pectora cūnctīs*
īnsinuat pavor, *et* scelus expendisse merentem
230 Lāocoōnta *ferunt, sacrum quī* cūspide rōbur
laeserit *et* tergō scelerātam intorserit hastam.
Dūcendum ad sēdēs simulācrum ōranda*que dīvae*
nūmina conclāmant.
Dīvidimus mūrōs *et moenia* pandimus *urbis.*
235 Accingunt *omnēs* operī *pedibusque* rotārum
subiciunt lāpsūs, *et* stuppea vincula collō

---

accingō, ere, cīnxī, cīnctus gird (on),
  equip
collum, ī *n.* neck
conclāmō (1) cry, shout, exclaim
cuspis, pidis *f.* point, spear, lance
dīvidō, ere, vīsī, vīsus divide, separate
expendō, ere, ī, pēnsus expiate, pay (for)
hasta, ae *f.* spear, dart, lance
īnsinuō (1) wind, creep, coil
intorqueō, ēre, rsī, rtus hurl (against) (+ *dat.*)
laedō, ere, ī, sus strike, hurt, offend
Lāocoōn, ontis *m.* Trojan priest of Neptune
lāpsus, ūs *m.* gliding, rolling, sinking
mereō, ēre, uī, itus deserve, merit, earn
mūrus, ī *m.* wall, rampart
opus, eris *n.* work, task, deed, labor

ōrō (1) entreat, pray (for), beseech
pandō, ere, ī, passus spread, open, loosen
pavor, ōris *m.* terror, shuddering, alarm
rōbur, oris *n.* oak; strength
rota, ae *f.* wheel
scelerātus, a, um criminal, wicked
scelus, eris *n.* crime, impiety, sin
simulācrum, ī *n.* image, statue, likeness
stuppeus, a, um (of) flax or hemp (used in
  the production of rope)
subiciō, ere, iēcī, iectus place under (+ *dat.*)
tergum, ī *n.* back, body, rear
tremefaciō, ere, fēcī, factus make tremble,
  appall, alarm
vērō *adv.* truly, indeed, but
vinc(u)lum, ī *n.* chain, bond, cable

228–49. The Trojans make a breach in
the walls of the city, drag the horse inside,
and celebrate in thanksgiving to the gods
for the preservation of their city.

228. cūnctīs (nōbis): dat. of reference;
App. 301.
229–30. īnsinuat (sē). expendisse: indir.
stmt. with **ferunt,** *say;* App. 263.
231. laeserit, intorserit: causal rel. clause,
or characteristic clause with causal force;
App. 389. **tergō:** dat. with compound **in-**
torserit; App. 298.

232. Dūcendum (esse), ōranda (esse):
infs. in indir. stmt. with **conclāmant. ad**
sēdēs (deōrum) = ad dēlūbra summa (225)
= arcem. dīvae (Minervae).
233. This is one of the half-lines in the *Ae-*
neid. Most scholars think the presence of these
lines indicates that Vergil had not yet complet-
ed the *Aeneid* when he died. Cf. note on 1.534.
235. omnēs (sē) accingunt operī. operī:
dat. of purpose; App. 303. **rotārum lāpsūs:**
rollings (glidings) of wheels = rolling wheels;
App. 425. **pedibus (equī):** dat. with com-
pound **subiciunt.**
236. (ā) collō: abl. of separation; App. 340;
or dat. with compound **intendunt;** App. 298.

intendunt: scandit fātālis māchina mūrōs
fēta *armīs*. *Puerī circum* innūptae*que* puellae
sacra canunt fūnem*que manū* contingere gaudent;
240 *illa* subit *mediaeque* mināns inlābitur *urbī*.
Ō *patria, Ō dīvum domus* Īlium *et incluta bellō*
moenia Dardanidum! quater *ipsō in līmine* portae
substitit *atque* uterō sonitum quater *arma* dedēre;
īnstāmus tamen immemorēs caecī*que* furōre
245 *et* mōnstrum *īnfēlīx* sacrātā sistimus *arce*.
Tunc etiam *fātīs* aperit Cassandra *futūrīs*
ōra deī iussū *nōn* umquam crēdita *Teucrīs*.

---

aperiō, īre, uī, rtus open, disclose
caecus, a, um blind, hidden, dark
canō, ere, cecinī, cantus sing (of), chant
Cassandra, ae *f.* Trojan prophetess,
    punished by Apollo and so never believed
contingō, ere, tigī, tāctus touch, befall
crēdō, ere, didī, ditus believe, trust (+ *dat.*)
Dardanidēs, ae *m.* Dardanian, Trojan
etiam *adv.* also, even, besides, yet, still
fātālis, e fatal, deadly, fated, fateful
fētus, a, um teeming, pregnant, filled
fūnis, is *m.* rope, cable
furor, ōris *m.* madness, frenzy, fury
gaudeō, ēre, gāvisus sum rejoice, exult
Īlium, (i)ī *n.* Ilium, Troy
immemor, oris unmindful, heedless
inclutus, a, um famous, renowned
inlābor, ī, lāpsus glide in(to) (+ *dat.*)
īnstō, āre, stitī press on, pursue

intendō, ere, ī, ntus stretch, extend
innūptus, a, um unmarried, virgin
iussus, ūs *m.* command, order, behest
māchina, ae *f.* machine, engine, device
minor, ārī, ātus tower (over); threaten (+ *dat.*)
mōnstrum, ī *n.* omen, portent, monster
mūrus, ī *m.* (city) wall, rampart
patria, ae *f.* homeland, country
porta, ae *f.* gate, entrance, exit, portal
puella, ae *f.* girl
quater four times
sacrō (1) dedicate, consecrate, hallow
scandō, ere, ī, scānsus mount, climb
sistō, ere, stetī, status stand, stop, stay
sonitus, ūs *m.* sound, roar, crash, noise
subsistō, ere, stitī stop, halt, resist
tamen *adv.* nevertheless, however, but
umquam *adv.* ever, at any time
uterus, ī *m.* belly, womb

---

238. armīs: abl. with **fēta**; App. 337. **circum (equum)**.

239. sacra (carmina): *sacred songs.*

240. illa (māchina) = equus. mediae urbī: dat. with compound **inlābitur**; App. 298.

241. dīv(ōr)um domus: in apposition with **Īlium**. Note the APOSTROPHE and personification, often used together in epic at moments of great pathos.

242. Dardanid(ār)um: App. 34, *b.* **in līmine:** to stop or stumble on the threshold was considered by the Romans a bad omen and sure to bring misfortune.

243. (ab) uterō: abl. of source or separation; App. 323, 340. **dedēre = dedērunt;** App. 204, 4.

245. (in) sacrātā arce: since it contained the temple and statues of the gods; abl. of place where; App. 319, *b.*

246. fātīs futūrīs: abl. of means or dat. of purpose; App. 331, 303.

247. deī: Apollo. **nōn crēdita:** Cassandra had been beloved of Apollo, who had granted her the gift of prophecy. Because she reneged on her promise to be his in return for this gift, Apollo turned the gift into a curse, placing

Nōs dēlūbra *deum miserī, quibus* ultimus *esset*
ille diēs, fēstā vēlāmus fronde *per urbem.*

---

dēlūbrum, ī *n.* shrine, temple
fēstus, a, um festal, festive
frōns, frondis *f.* branch, foliage

ultimus, a, um last, final, farthest
vēlō (1) veil, cover, deck, clothe

---

upon her the necessity of forever prophesying and of never being believed. Even today a person who predicts a future event rightly yet is not believed at the time is called a *Cassandra.* **Teucrīs:** dat. of agent; App. 302.

248. quibus esset: rel. clause of characteristic with accessory notion of cause; App. 388, 389.

248–49. Nōs: emphatic; App. 247. **Nōs miserī, quibus ille diēs esset ultimus, vēlāmus dēlūbra de(ōr)um.**

Book 2.268–297

Tempus (*erat*) *quō prīma* quiēs mortālibus aegrīs
(*incipit*) *et dōnō dīvum* grātissima (*serpit*).

270   *In somnīs, ecce, ante oculōs* maestissimus Hector
vīsus adesse mihī largōs*que* (*effundere*) flētūs,
raptātus bīgīs *ut quondam, āterque* cruentō
(*pulvere*) *perque pedēs* trāiectus lōra tumentēs.
Ei *mihi,* quālis (*erat,*) quantum mūtātus *ab illō*

275   Hectore *quī* (*redit*) *exuviās* indūtus Achillī

Achillēs, ī (**is, eī**) *m.* Greek leader who is
  the central character in Homer's *Iliad*
aeger, gra, grum sick, weary, wretched
bīgae, ārum *f.* two-horse chariot
cruentus, a, um bloody, cruel
ecce look! behold!
effundō, ere, fūdī, fūsus pour out
ei alas! ah!
exuviae, ārum *f.* spoils, booty
flētus, ūs *m.* weeping, tears, lament
grātus, a, um welcome, pleasing, grateful
Hector, oris *m.* Trojan leader
incipiō, ere, cēpī, ceptus begin, undertake
induō, ere, uī, ūtus don, clothe, put on
largus, a, um abundant, copious

lōrum, ī *n.* thong, leather strap, rein
maestus, a, um sad, mournful, gloomy
mortālis, is *m.* mortal, man, human
mūtō (1) (ex)change, transform, alter
pulvis, pulveris *m.* dust
quālis, e (such) as, of what sort
quantus, a, um how great, how much, how
  many, as
quiēs, ētis *f.* quiet, rest, sleep, peace
raptō (1) snatch, drag, carry off
redeō, īre, iī (īvī), itus return
serpō, ere, psī creep (on), crawl
trāiciō, ere, iēcī, iectus throw across,
  pierce
tumeō, ēre, uī swell, be swollen

268–97. The ghost of Hector appears to
Aeneas in a dream and urges him to flee
from the doomed city and to rescue the
paternal gods from destruction.

268. quō: abl. of time when; App. 322.
With this scene, Aeneas directs the focus of
the story onto himself; at the same time, the
action of the story is suspended, and the ten-
sion is allowed to build.

269. dīv(ōr)um. serpit: the description of
sleep, apparently so good to mortals, ends on an
ominous note, reminding us of the snakes which
came across the sea to kill Laocoon and his sons.

270. (meōs) oculōs.

271. vīsus (est) adesse: *seemed to appear.* In
Latin poetry (as in Greek), dreams are conven-
tionally introduced this way: persons "seem"
or "appear to" manifest themselves and speak.

272. raptātus bīgīs (Achillis): for the
story, cf. 1.483–84.

273. pedēs trāiectus lōra: *his feet pierced
with thongs;* **pedēs** is obj. of the prep. **per** and
lōra is obj. of the participle **trāiectus** used as a
Gk. middle participle, i.e., Gk. acc.; App. 309, *a.*

274. mihi: dat. of reference or interest
with the interjection **ei**; App. 301.

275. exuviās: acc. obj. of **indūtus**, used as a
Gk. middle participle, i.e., Gk. acc.; App. 309, *a.*
Hector had slain and despoiled Patroclus, who
was wearing the armor of his friend Achilles.

vel Danaum Phrygiōs iaculātus *puppibus ignēs;*
squālentem barbam *et* concrētōs *sanguine* crīnēs
vulnera*que illa* gerēns, *quae circum plūrima* mūrōs
accēpit*patriōs*. Ultrō flēns *ipse videbar*
280   compellāre *virum et* maestās exprōmere *vōcēs:*
'Ō *lūx* Dardaniae, spēs Ō fidissima *Teucrum,*
quae tantae tenuēre morae? *Quibus* Hector *ab ōrīs*
exspectāte *venīs? Ut tē* post *multa tuōrum*
fūnera, post variōs hominum*que urbisque labōrēs*
285   dēfessī aspicimus! *Quae* causa indigna serēnōs
foedāvit vultūs? *Aut* cūr *haec* vulnera *cernō?'*
Ille nihil, *nec mē quaerentem* vāna morātur,
sed graviter gemitūs *īmō dē pectore dūcēns,*

---

a(d)spiciō, ere, spexī, spectus see, look (at)
barba, ae *f.* beard, whiskers
causa, ae *f.* cause, reason, occasion
compellō (1) address, accost, speak to
concrētus, a, um grown together, hardened,
    matted
crīnis, is *m.* hair, locks, tresses
cūr why? for what reason?
Dardania, ae *f.* city of Dardanus, Troy
dēfessus, a, um weary, tired, worn
exprōmō, ere, mpsī, mptus express, bring
    forth
exspectō (1) await (eagerly), expect
fīdus, a, um faithful, trustworthy, safe
fleō, ēre, ēvī, ētus weep, lament
foedō (1) defile, befoul, mar, mangle
fūnus, eris *n.* funeral, death, disaster
gemitus, ūs *m.* groan, lament, roar
gerō, ere, gessī, gestus bear, carry (on)
graviter *adv.* heavily, violently

Hector, oris *m.* Trojan leader
homō, inis *m. (f.)* man, mortal, human
iaculor, ārī, ātus hurl, throw, fling
indignus, a, um undeserved, unworthy
maestus, a, um sad, mournful, gloomy
mora, ae *f.* delay, hesitation, hindrance
moror, ārī, ātus delay, tarry, heed
mūrus, ī *m.* (city) wall, rampart
nihil, nīl nothing, not at all
Phrygius, a, um Phrygian, Trojan
post *adv.* afterward; *prep. + acc.* after,
    behind
serēnus, a, um serene, calm, fair, clear
spēs, speī *f.* hope, expectation
squāleō, ēre, uī be rough, be filthy
ultrō *adv.* voluntarily, further
vānus, a, um vain, idle, useless, false
varius, a, um various, manifold, diverse
vulnus, eris *n.* wound, deadly blow
vultus, ūs *m.* countenance, face, aspect

---

276. Dana(ōr)um puppibus: dat. of direction or reference; App. 306, 301. Vergil refers to the battle around the Greek ships described in *Iliad* 15, when the Trojans under Hector almost captured the Greek camp and set fire to several of the ships.

   278. quae . . . plūrima: acc. circum . . . mūrōs.

   281. Teucr(ōr)um.

   282. tenuēre = (tē) tenuērunt.

282–83. Hector exspectāte: voc. **(tū) venīs.**

   283. Ut: *how (gladly)*—although the implication that Aeneas feels pleasure at the sight of Hector in his gruesome post-mortem condition is ironic, to say the least.

   285–86. serēnōs vultūs (tuōs), haec vulnera (tua).

   287. Ille (dīcit) nihil.

'*Heu fuge, nāte deā, tēque his' ait 'ēripe flammīs.*

290   Hostis *habet* mūrōs; *ruit* altō ā culmine *Troia.*
       Sat patriae *Priamōque datum: sī* Pergama *dextrā*
       dēfendī *possent,* etiam *hāc* dēfēnsa *fuissent.*
       Sacra suōsque tibī commendat *Troia* penātēs;
       hōs cape fātōrum comitēs, hīs moenia quaere
295   *magna,* pererrātō statuēs *quae* dēnique pontō.'
       Sīc ait et manibus vittās Vestam*que* potentem
       aeternum*que* adytīs *effert* penetrālibus *ignem.*

S ḃ p

---

adytum, ī *n.* inner shrine, sanctuary
aeternus, a, um eternal, undying
commendō (1) entrust, commit
culmen, inis *n.* top, summit, peak, roof
dēfendō, ere, ī, fēnsus defend, protect
dēnique *adv.* finally, at last
efferō, ferre, extulī, ēlatus carry forth, lift
etiam *adv.* also, even, besides, yet, still
hostis, is *m. (f.)* enemy, foe, stranger
mūrus, ī *m.* (city) wall, rampart
patria, ae *f.* homeland, country

penātēs, ium *m.* household gods
penetrālis, e inmost, interior
pererrō (1) wander through, traverse
Pergama, ōrum *n.* (citadel of) Troy
potēns, entis powerful, mighty
pontus, ī *m.* sea, waves
sat(is) *adv.* enough, sufficient(ly)
statuō, ere, uī, ūtus set up, establish
Vesta, ae *f.* goddess of the hearth
vitta, ae *f.* fillet, garland, band

---

289. nāte: voc. **deā:** abl. of separation. **nāte deā:** *goddess-born;* lit., *born from a goddess.*

291–92. Sat ... datum (est ā tē). sī (quā) dextrā dēfendī possent, hāc (dextrā meā) dēfēnsa fuissent. The combination of imperf. and pluperf. subjunctives here creates what is called a mixed condition; each clause should be translated in accordance with the English approximation appropriate in each case, i.e., "were to" with the imperf. subjunctive, "would have" with the pluperf. subjunctive.

293. (sua) sacra: objects used in the performance of rituals, statues, etc. **comitēs:** *(as) comrades,* in apposition with **hōs.**

294. moenia = urbem, as often. **hīs (penātibus):** dat. of reference; App. 301.

295. pererrātō pontō: abl. abs.; App. 343. **quae (moenia magna) dēnique statuēs.**

297. aeternum ignem: the sacred fire of Vesta was never allowed to go out, and from it was always kindled the fire which was given to each colony sent out from Rome. The Romans believed that the eternal burning of Vesta's flame ensured the permanence of Rome.

Book 2.559–620

At mē tum prīmum saevus circumstetit horror.
560 Obstipuī; subiit cārī genitōris imāgō,
    ut rēgem aequaevum crūdēlī vulnere vīdī
    vītam exhālantem, subiit dēserta Creūsa
    et dīrepta domus et parvī cāsus Iūlī.
    Respiciō et quae sit mē circum cōpia lūstrō.
565 Dēseruēre omnēs dēfessī, et corpora saltū
    ad terram misēre aut ignibus aegra dedēre.

---

aeger, gra, grum sick, weary, wretched
aequaevus, a, um of equal age
cārus, a, um dear, beloved, fond
circumstō, āre, stetī surround, stand around
cōpia, ae *f.* abundance, plenty, forces
Creūsa, ae *f.* wife of Aeneas, lost at the sack of Troy
crūdēlis, e cruel, bloody, bitter
dēfessus, a, um weary, tired, worn
dēserō, ere, uī, rtus desert, forsake
dīripiō, ere, uī, reptus plunder, ravage
exhālō (1) breathe out, exhale

horror, ōris *m.* horror, terror, shudder(ing)
imāgō, inis *f.* likeness, image, ghost, soul, form
Iūlus, ī *m.* Ascanius, son of Aeneas
lūstrō (1) purify, survey, traverse
obstipēscō, ere, stipuī be dazed, stand agape
parvus, a, um small, little
saevus, a, um fierce, harsh, stern
respiciō, ere, spexī, spectus look (back) at, regard
saltus, ūs *m.* forest, glade, pasture; leap, bound, dancing
vulnus, eris *n.* wound, deadly blow

559–87. Stunned by Priam's death, Aeneas thinks of those closest to him and of all he has lost, and looks for his followers, only to find them gone. He sees only one person alive: the Greek Helen, whose abandonment of her home and husband Menelaus and departure for Troy in the company of Paris provided the reason for the war. In an internal monologue, Aeneas reflects bitterly on her responsibility and the destruction she has caused, and considers killing her.

560. subiit: understand **meam mentem** as implied dir. obj., or take intransitively (*arose*).

561. aequaevum: Anchises was of about the same age as Priam.

563. dīrepta: i.e., in Aeneas' imagination. **domus:** nom. sing. with the final syllable long before the caesura; App. 394, *a*. The unusual metrical effect emphasizes Aeneas' sense of loss.

564. respiciō: Aeneas on the roof of the palace had been so transfixed in looking down on the murder of Priam that he had forgotten everything else. He now looks around but sees nothing to comfort him. **quae cōpia (virōrum) sit:** indir. quest.; App. 349. **mē circum = circum mē,** a common type of ANASTROPHE.

565. saltū: abl. of means or manner.

565–66. dēseruēre, misēre, dedēre = **dēseruērunt, misērunt, dedērunt. corpora ... aegra:** dir. obj. of both **misēre** and **dedēre.**

[*Iamque adeō super ūnus eram, cum līmina* Vestae
servantem et tacitam sēcrētā *in sēde* latentem
Tyndarida aspiciō; dant clāram incendia *lūcem*
570   *errantī* passimque oculōs per cūncta ferentī.
Illa sibi infēstōs ēversa ob Pergama *Teucrōs*
et Danaum poenam et dēsertī *coniugis īrās*
praemetuēns, *Troiae et* patriae commūnis Erīnys,
abdiderat *sēsē atque ārīs* invīsa sedēbat.

---

abdō, ere, didī, ditus hide, put away, bury
adeō *adv.* to such an extent, so (much)
a(d)spiciō, ere, spexī, spectus see, behold, look (at)
clārus, a, um clear, bright, illustrious
commūnis, e (in) common, joint, mutual
dēserō, ere, uī, rtus desert, forsake
Erīnys, yos *f.* Fury, Curse (personified)
ēvertō, ere, ī, rsus overturn, destroy
incendium, (i)ī *n.* blaze, conflagration
īnfēstus, a, um hostile, threatening
invīsus, a, um hateful, hated, odious

lateō, ēre, uī lie hidden, hide, lurk, escape the notice (of)
ob on account of (+ *acc.*)
passim *adv.* everywhere, all about
patria, ae *f.* homeland, country
Pergama, ōrum *n.* (citadel of) Troy
praemetuō, ere fear beforehand
sēcrētus, a, um remote, hidden, secret
sedeō, ēre, sēdī, sessus sit, settle
tacitus, a, um silent, still, quiet
Tyndaris, idis *f.* daughter of Tyndarus, Helen
Vesta, ae *f.* goddess of the hearth

567–88. Editors use brackets here to indicate that they do not believe that this passage was written by Vergil; they think that it was inserted into a copy of the manuscript not long after the poem began to circulate in the Roman world. Some stylistic oddities in the passage have long made scholars question the authenticity of the scene, known as "The Helen Episode." Many scholars believe that it was written by someone eager to emulate Vergil at some time after the original publication of the *Aeneid*; these scholars believe that this episode was then integrated into the poem by the scholar Servius in the fourth century CE. The inherent interest of the passage, focusing as it does on the universally despised Helen, will have guaranteed its survival thereafter. Authentic or not, The Helen Episode offers valuable insight into the character of Aeneas and the *Aeneid*'s ethical code.

567. Iamque adeō: adeō emphasizes the word it follows, and helps to mark a transition to a new sight. **Super . . . eram:** *I survived*; an effective example of TMESIS, placing emphasis on the word **ūnus.**

567–69. cum . . . aspiciō: cum is temporal with the indicative; App. 377; the present

tense contributes to the vividness of Aeneas' recollection of the moment when he first caught sight of Helen. **Tyndarida:** Gk. acc. of a feminine patronymic.

570. (mihi) errantī passimque . . . ferentī.

571. sibi: dat. with **infēstōs . . . Teucrōs. ēversa ob Pergama:** this word order pattern, adj. + prep. + noun, is common in poetry and elegant prose.

572. Dana(ōr)um: subjective gen. with **poenam**; App. 284. **dēsertī coniugis:** Menelaus, king of Mycenae.

573. praemetuēns: modifies **Illa** (571). The prefix **prae-** added to the verb **metuō** emphasizes the anticipation of the retribution that Helen fears because of her guilty conscience. **Troiae et patriae commūnis Erīnys:** the entire phrase, characterizing Helen as a source of divine retribution for both the Trojans and the Greeks, is in apposition with **Illa** (571).

574. ārīs: abl. of place where. **invīsa:** most likely derived from verb **invideō** (*hate, despise*), although the emphasis throughout this passage on sight (561, **vīdī**; 564, **respiciō, lūstrō**; 569, **aspiciō**; 570, **oculōs . . . ferentī**) may suggest a wordplay with the perf. pass. participle of **invīsō** (*look upon*); cf. also 601.

575   ~~Exarsere~~ *ignēs animō;* ~~subit~~ *ira* cadentem
      ~~ulcīscī~~ patriam *et* scelerātās ~~sūmere~~ *poenās.*
No →   ~~Scilicet~~ *haec* Spartam incolumis *patriāsque* Mycēnās
      aspiciet, partōque *ibit rēgina* triumphō?
      Coniugiumque domumque patris nātōsque vidēbit
580   Īliadum turbā *et* Phrygiīs comitāta ministrīs?

---

a(d)spiciō, ere, spexī, spectus see, behold,
  look (at)
cadō, ere, cecidī, cāsus fall, fail, sink, die
comitōr, ārī, ātus accompany, attend,
  escort, follow
coniugium, (i)ī n. wedlock; husband, wife
exardēscō, ere, arsī, arsus blaze (up)
Īlias, adis f. Trojan woman
incolumis, e safe, sound, unharmed
minister, trī m. attendant, servant
Mycēnae, ārum f. city of central Greece,
  home of Agamemnon, leader of the Greek
  expedition against Troy

pariō, ere, peperī, partus (re)produce,
  gain, acquire, give birth to
patria, ae f. homeland, country
Phrygius, a, um Phrygian, Trojan
scelerātus, a, um criminal, wicked
scīlicet adv. of course, to be sure, doubtless
Sparta, ae f. region of Greece, home of
  Helen and Menelaus
sūmō, ere, mpsī, mptus take, assume; (+
  poenam) exact (a penalty)
triumphus, ī m. triumph, victory
turba, ae f. mob, crowd
ulcīscor, ī, ultus avenge, punish

575–76. exarsēre = exarsērunt. ignēs: the nature of these fires is explained by **īra** later in the line. **subit (mihi) īra . . . ulcīscī . . . et . . . sūmere**: the subject, **īra**, introduces Aeneas' desire, the nature of which is specified with the complementary infs.; App. 259, 264. **scelerātās . . . poenās**: Aeneas realizes now that killing a woman would have been a criminal act on his part, but when he saw Helen he considered doing so.

577–87. Aeneas recalls the internal debate that went through his head when he saw Helen in the ruins of Troy.

577. **Scīlicet**: introduces a series of sarcastic RHETORICAL QUESTIONS; the sarcasm is directed at Aeneas himself, as he considers the possibility that Helen may well return home unscathed although she has provoked untold suffering and destruction.

578. **partō triumphō**: abl. abs.

579. **Coniugium**: Aeneas uses an abstract noun instead of the specific **coniugem** (i.e., Menelaus).

580. **turbā, ministrīs**: abl. of accompaniment with **comitāta**. Aeneas imagines that Helen will bring captive Trojans back to Sparta as slaves.

Occiderit *ferrō* Priamus? *Troia arserit ignī?*
Dardanium totiēns sūdārit *sanguine lītus?*
Nōn ita. *Namque* etsī *nūllum* memorābile *nōmen*
fēmineā *in poenā est, habet haec* victōria laudem;
585 exstīnxisse nefās tamen *et* sūmpsisse merentēs
laudābor *poenās, animumque* explesse *iuvābit*
ultrīcis †*fāmam et* cinerēs *satiāsse meōrum.*"

---

cinis, eris *m.* ashes (of the dead), embers
Dardanius, a, um Dardanian, Trojan
etsī although, even if
expleō, ēre, ēvī, ētus fill (out), fulfil
exsting(u)ō, ere, īnxī, īnctus extinguish,
  blot out, destroy, ruin
fēmineus, a, um feminine, of women
ita *adv.* thus, so
iuvō, āre, iūvī, iūtus help, please
laudō (1) praise
laus, laudis *f.* glory, praise, merit
memorābilis, e memorable, glorious

mereō, ēre, uī, itus deserve, earn, merit
nefās *n. indecl.* impiety, unspeakable thing,
  crime
occidō, ere, ī, cāsus fall, perish, end, die
satiō (1) satisfy, sate, satiate, glut
sūdō (1) sweat, perspire
sūmō, ere, mpsī, mptus take, assume;
  (+ **poenam**) exact (a penalty)
tamen *adv.* nevertheless, however
totiēns so often, so many times
ultrīx, īcis avenging, vengeful
victōria, ae *f.* victory, conquest, triumph

581–82. Occiderit, arserit, sūdā(ve)rit:
future perf. indicative verbs reflect Aeneas'
anticipation of what will happen to Helen
after the war: will she get home safely after
these events (will) have happened? **totiēns:**
a reminder that the war extended over a ten-
year period, with numerous encounters on
the battlefield. **sūdārit sanguine lītus:** the
image is strangely violent: it is not normal for
the shore to sweat, and even stranger that its
sweat take the form of blood. **sanguine:** abl.
of specification.

583. Nōn ita (erit *or* sit). Aeneas responds
with determination to his own RHETORICAL
QUESTIONS.

584. fēmineā in poenā = in poenā fēminae,
in the punishment of a woman; the adjectival form
(**fēmineus**) in place of the substantive (**fēmina**)
in the gen. is frequent in poetry.

**585–86. extīnxisse . . . et sūmpsisse . . .
laudābor:** an unusual indir. stmt. equivalent
to a causal clause, i.e., **mē laudābunt quod
nefās extīnxī . . . et poenās sūmpsī. nefās:**
Aeneas avoids naming Helen directly, simul-
taneously defining her and her role in the war
as "unspeakable."

**586–87. explē(vi)sse . . . et . . . satiā(vi)
sse:** the infs. are the subjects of the impersonal
al verb (**mē**) **iuvābit. ultrīcis †fāmam:** The
symbol †, called an *obelos* (from the Gk. word
lance), is used by editors of classical texts to
mark a phrase or word that appears to have
been corrupted in the process of copying and
so presents a problem for comprehension of
the text. Here, the original words of the be-
ginning of the line cannot be reconstructed;
Aeneas was probably saying something here
about exacting revenge on Helen.

Tālia iactābam et furiātā mente ferēbar,]
cum mihi sē, nōn ante oculīs tam clāra, videndam
590   obtulit et pūrā per noctem in lūce refulsit
alma parēns, cōnfessa deam quālisque vidērī
caelicolīs et quanta solet, dextrāque prehēnsum
continuit roseōque haec īnsuper addidit ōre:
"Nāte, quis indomitās tantus dolor excitat īrās?
595   Quid furis? Aut quōnam nostrī tibi cūra recessit?

---

addō, ere, didī, ditus add
almus, a, um nurturing, kind(ly)
caelicola, ae m. (f.) divinity, deity
clārus, a, um clear, bright, illustrious
cōnfiteor, ērī, fessus confess, reveal
contineō, ēre, uī, tentus hold together,
   restrain, check
dolor, ōris m. grief, pain, passion, anger
excitō (1) arouse, stir up, excite
furiō (1) madden, frenzy, infuriate
iactō (1) toss, buffet, boast, utter
indomitus, a, um uncontrolled,
   ungoverned

īnsuper adv. above, besides
offerō, offerre, obtulī, oblātus present
pre(he)ndō, ere, ī, ēnsus seize, grasp
pūrus, a, um pure, bright, clean, clear
quālis, e (such) as, of what sort
quantus, a, um how great, how much, how
   many, as much (as)
quōnam adv. whither, (to) where on earth
recēdō, ere, cessī, cessus depart, withdraw
refulgeō, ēre, lsī, lsus gleam, shine, glitter
roseus, a, um rosy, pink
soleō, ēre, itus sum be accustomed
tam adv. so (much), such

588–620. Venus appears to her son and
restrains him, explaining that nothing can
save Troy now, since its fate has been deter-
mined; at least she can help him in his flight.

588. ferēbar (per viās).
589–91. The HYPERBATON of these lines,
underscored by the postponement of the sub-
ject (alma parēns) to the end of the clause,
mimics Aeneas' experience: the shining pres-
ence approaching him only gradually assumes
the identifiable shape of his mother Venus. The
scene both echoes and is in contrast to Venus'
earlier epiphany in disguise at 1.314–417.

589. ante: adverbial, = antea. oculīs: dat.
of reference with clāra; App. 301. videndam:
agrees with sē.
591–92. cōnfessa (sē esse) deam. quālis,
quanta: gods are typically perceived by mor-
tals as being different both in nature (quālis)
and in size (quanta). (mē) prehēnsum: dir.
obj. of continuit (593); Venus prevents her
son from attacking Helen.
594. quis (modifying dolor) is used here
instead of the usual form of the interrog.
adj., quī.
595. nostrī: objective gen. with cūra. tibi:
dat. of reference or advantage.

> Nōn prius aspiciēs *ubi fessum* aetāte *parentem*
> līqueris *Anchīsēn,* superet *coniūnxne* Creūsa
> Ascaniusque *puer*? *Quōs omnēs* undique Graiae
> circum errant aciēs *et, nī mea cūra resistat,*
> 600 *iam flammae tulerint* inimīcus *et* hauserit ēnsis.
> Nōn *tibi* Tyndaridis faciēs invīsa Lacaenae
> culpātusve Paris, *dīvum* inclēmentia, *dīvum*

---

aciēs, ēī *f.* edge; eye(sight); battle line, army
a(d)spiciō, ere, spexī, spectus see, look (at)
aetās, ātis *f.* age, time
Ascanius, (i)ī *m.* son of Aeneas
circum *adv.* around, about
Creūsa, ae *f.* wife of Aeneas, lost during the sack of Troy
culpō (1) blame, censure, reprove
ēnsis, is *m.* sword, knife
faciēs, ēī *f.* appearance, face, aspect
Graius, a, um Greek
hauriō, īre, hausī, haustus drain, drink (in)
inclēmentia, ae *f.* cruelty, harshness
inimīcus, a, um hostile, enemy, unfriendly

invīsus, a, um hateful, hated, odious
Lacaenus, a, um Spartan, Lacedaemonian
linquō, ere, līquī, lictus leave, desert
nī, nisi if not, unless, except
Paris, idis *m.* Trojan prince, son of Priam, took Helen from her husband Menelaus and thus caused the Trojan War
prius *adv.* former(ly), sooner, first
resistō, ere, stitī stop, resist (+ *dat.*)
superō (1) surmount, surpass, overcome, survive
Tyndaris, idis *f.* daughter of Tyndarus, Helen
undique *adv.* everywhere, from all sides

596–98. ubi . . . līqueris, superet coniūnxne: indir. quests. dependent on **aspiciēs. superet:** sing. in agreement with the closest subject, **Creūsa**; **Ascaniusque puer** is the second subject.
  598–99. quōs omnēs . . . circum = circum eōs omnēs.
  599–600. nī . . . resistat, . . . tulerint . . . et hauserit: a mixed contrary-to-fact condition, with pres. and perf. subjunctives providing a more vivid alternative to the usual imperf. (**resisteret**) and pluperf. (**tulissent, hausisset**).

601–3. Nōn . . . Tyndaridis faciēs invīsa . . . culpātusve Paris . . . hās ēvertit opēs: neither Helen nor Paris is truly responsible for the fall of Troy; Venus uses ASYNDETON and EPANALEPSIS (**dīvum, dīvum**) to direct Aeneas' attention to the real cause, **dīv(ōr)um inclēmentia. tibi:** dat. of reference. **culpātus:** modifies **Paris**, but should be understood also with **Tyndaridis faciēs**.

hās ēvertit opēs sternitque ā culmine Troiam.
Aspice (namque omnem, quae nunc obducta tuentī
605   mortālēs hebetat vīsūs *tibi et* ūmida *circum*
cālīgat, nūbem *ēripiam; tū nē qua parentis*
iussa timē neu praeceptīs pārēre recūsā):
hīc, ubi disiectās mōlēs āvulsa*que saxīs*
saxa vidēs, mixtōque undantem pulvere fūmum,

---

a(d)spiciō, ere, spexī, spectus see, behold, look (at)

āvellō, ere, (vuls)ī, vulsus tear (off, from)

cālīgō, āre, āvī be dark, darken

culmen, inis *n.* roof, peak, summit, top

dis(s)iciō, ere, iēcī, iectus scatter, disperse

ēvertō, ere, ī, rsus overturn, destroy

fūmus, ī *m.* smoke, vapor, fog, fume

hebetō (1) blunt, dull, dim, weaken

iussum, ī *n.* order, command, behest

misceō, ēre, uī, mixtus confuse, mix, mingle, stir (up)

mōlēs, is *f.* mass, burden, heap, structure; difficulty

mortālis, e mortal, human, earthly

neu, nēve and (that) not, and lest

nūbēs, is *f.* cloud, fog, mist

obdūcō, ere, dūxī, ductus draw over

ops, opis *f.* help, resources, power, wealth

pāreō, ēre, uī, itus obey, yield (+ *dat.*)

praeceptum, ī *n.* advice, instruction

pulvis, eris *m.* dust

recūsō (1) refuse, decline, object

sternō, ere, strāvī, stratus lay low, spread, strew

timeō, ēre, uī fear, dread, be anxious

tueor, ērī, itus (tūtus) watch, look at, protect, eye

ūmidus, a, um moist, damp, dewy

undō (1) swell, roll, wave

vīsus, ūs *m.* sight, view, vision, aspect

604–6. omnem … nūbem: the separation of the noun from its adjective suggests the function of the cloud it describes, surrounding everything and obscuring Aeneas' view. **quae:** the grammatical antecedent is **nūbem**, although it does not here appear before the relative pronoun. **obducta, ūmida:** both modify **quae. tuentī … tibi:** dat. of reference or indir. obj.; a second example of enclosing word order occurs within the first.

606–7. nē … timē, neu … recūsā: negating the imperative with **nē** is a poetic alternative to the construction more commonly found in prose, **nōlī(te)** + inf. **praeceptīs:** dat. with **pārēre.**

608. saxīs: abl. of separation with **āvulsa.**

609. mixtō … pulvere: abl. abs.

610 Neptūnus mūrōs *magnōque* ēmōta tridentī
    fundāmenta quatit *tōtamque ā sēdibus urbem*
    ēruit. *Hīc Iūnō* Scaeās saevissima portās
    prīma tenet sociumque *furēns ā nāvibus agmen*
    ferrō accīncta *vocat.*
615 *Iam summās arcēs* Tritōnia, respice, Pallas
    īnsēdit nimbō effulgēns *et* Gorgone saevā.

---

accingō, ere, cīnxī, cīnctus gird (on), equip
effulgeō, ēre, lsī flash, glitter, gleam
ēmoveō, ēre, mōvī, mōtus move from
ēruō, ere uī, utus overthrow, tear up
fundāmentum, ī *n.* foundation, base
Gorgō, onis *f.* Gorgon
īnsīdō, ere, sēdī, sessus sit in (on), occupy
mūrus, ī *m.* (city) wall, battlement, rampart
Neptūnus, ī *m.* Neptune, god of the sea
nimbus, ī *m.* rainstorm, (storm)cloud
Pallas, adis *f.* Minerva, goddess of wisdom
    and the arts

porta, ae *f.* door, gate, entrance, exit
quatiō, ere, quassus shake, shatter
respiciō, ere, spexī, spectus look (back)
    at, regard
saevus, a, um fierce, harsh, stern
Scaeus, a, um Scaean (referring to the
    name of a gate at Troy)
socius, a, um allied, associated, friendly
tridēns, entis *m.* trident, symbol of
    Neptune as god of the sea
Trītōnius, a, um Tritonian (an epithet of
    Minerva)

> 610–18. Venus offers an itemized list of
> four Olympian gods (Neptune, Juno,
> Minerva, and Jupiter) who are deter-
> mined to bring the destruction of Troy
> to completion.

610–12. Neptune has long resented the
Trojans, because they did not offer him sat-
isfactory recompense for building the walls
of Troy for Priam's father Laomedon; now he
is poised to overturn the city with his trident
in revenge. **magnōque . . . tridentī:** abl. of
means.

612–14. Juno has long resented the Tro-
jans because of the judgment of Paris, who

favored Venus over her. **prīma:** Juno stands
in front of her Greek allies (**socium . . . ag-
men**) and leads their assault on Troy. On the
half-line, see the note on 1.534.

615–16. Pallas Minerva too resents the
Trojans as a result of the judgment of Paris.
respice: Venus directs Aeneas' attention
to the temple of Minerva that stood on the
citadel of Troy (described by Homer in *Iliad*
Book 6). **nimbō . . . et Gorgone saevā:** two
different abl. constructions with **effulgēns:**
nimbō is abl. of place where or separation
(*shining forth from a cloud*), and **Gorgone
saevā** is abl. of description. The head of the
Gorgon Medusa, terrible to look upon, deco-
rates Minerva's breastplate.

Ipse pater Danaīs animōs vīresque secundās
suﬃcit, *ipse deōs in* Dardana suscitat *arma.*
Ēripe, nāte, fugam finemque impōne *labōrī;*
620 nūsquam aberō *et* tūtum *patriō tē līmine* sistam."

---

absum, esse, āfuī be away, be distant, be
  lacking
Dardan(i)us, a, um Trojan, Dardanian
impōnō, ere, posuī, positus place upon,
  set to, impose (+ *dat.*)
nūsquam *adv.* nowhere, never
secundus, a, um following, favorable,
  obedient

sistō, ere, stetī, status stand, stop, stay
sufficiō, ere, fēcī, fectus supply, suffuse;
  be sufficient
suscitō (1) arouse, stir up, excite
tūtus, a, um protected, safe, secure

617–18. Venus' list culminates with Jupiter
himself (**ipse pater, ipse**). Unlike the other
gods mentioned here, he had long been sup-
portive of his favorites on both sides in the
war. The fact that he now throws his support
wholly onto the side of the Greeks indicates
to Venus that the end of Troy is near. **deōs:**
presumably the other gods over whom Jupiter
presides, i.e., all of them. **in:** *against.*

619. nāte: Venus brings her speech to a
close by using the same form of address with
which she began (594).

620. (in) patriō ... līmine: the ambiguous
phrase suggests first of all the Trojan dwell-
ing of Aeneas' father Anchises, but also antici-
pates his new home in Italy, the birthplace of
his ancestor, the early Trojan king Dardanus
(see 3.163–68).

Selections from
—BOOK 4—

teque isto corpore solvo (4.703)

Illustration for Book 4
"And free you from your body" by Thom Kapheim

Book 4.160–218

160 Intereā *magnō miscērī* murmure <u>caelum</u>
<u>incipit</u>, <u>i</u>nsequitur commixtā grandine <u>nimbus</u>,
et *Tyriī comitēs* passim *et* Troiāna iuventūs
Dardanius*que* nepōs Veneris dīversa *per* agrōs
tēcta metū *petiēre; ruunt dē* montibus amnēs.

165 Spēluncam *Dīdō* dux *et* Troiānus *eandem*
dēveniunt. *Prīma et Tellūs et* pronuba *Iūnō*
dant signum; *fulsēre ignēs et* cōnscius aethēr
cōnūbiīs *summōque* ulūlārunt vertice Nymphae.

---

aethēr, eris *m.* upper air, heaven, ether
ager, grī *m.* field, territory, land
amnis, is *m.* river, stream
commisceō, ēre, uī, mixtus mix, mingle
cōnscius, -a, -um *adj.* aware; privy to
cōnūbium, (i)ī *n.* marriage
Dardanius, a, um Dardanian, Trojan
dēveniō, īre, vēnī, ventus come (down), arrive (at)
dīversus, a, um separated, different
dux, ducis *m.* (*f.*) leader, guide, chief
fulg(e)ō, ēre (or **ere**), **lsī** shine, flash, gleam
grandō, inis *f.* hail(storm, stones)
incipiō, ere, cēpī, ceptus begin, undertake
īnsequor, ī, secūtus follow
intereā *adv.* meanwhile, (in the) meantime

iuventūs, ūtis *f.* youth, young men
metus, ūs *m.* fear, fright, anxiety
misceō, ēre, uī, mixtus mix, mingle, confuse
murmur, uris *n.* murmur, roar, rumble
nepōs, ōtis *m.* grandson; descendant
nimbus, ī *m.* rainstorm, (storm)cloud
Nympha, ae *f.* nymph, minor female
   divinity of the forests, waters, etc.
passim *adv.* everywhere, all about
prōnuba, ae *f.* matron of honor
signum, ī *n.* sign, signal, token, mark
spēlunca, ae *f.* cave, cavern, grotto
Troiānus, a, um Trojan, of Troy
ululō (1) howl, wail, shout, shriek
Venus, eris *f.* goddess of love; love
vertex, icis *m.* peak, summit, head, top

> 160–72. A sudden storm drives Aeneas and Dido into a cave for shelter during their hunting expedition.

163. nepōs Veneris = Ascanius.

166–68. Vergil here indicates the various features in a Roman wedding and represents Nature herself as performing these ceremonies. Earth and Heaven, parents of the universe, take the part of human parents in bringing the couple together; lightning (**ignēs**) represents the wedding torches (**taedae**); Juno performs the duty of the matron of honor (**prōnuba**), and the cries of the mountain nymphs take the place of the wedding song and festal cries.

Prīma Tellūs: Earth was called **prīma** as the oldest of the gods; as Mother Earth, the producer and nurse of life, she presided over marriage. **prōnuba:** the matron whose function it was to join the hand of the bride to that of the groom at the wedding.

167. dant signum: i.e., for the wedding. **ignēs** (*lightning*): instead of the marriage torches ordinarily employed at weddings. **cōnscius:** *witness* (to the marriage).

168. cōnūbiīs: *for the marriage*; poetic plural; the first **-i-** is pronounced as a consonant (i.e., as **-y-**), for the sake of the meter. **ululā(vē)runt:** instead of the marriage songs ordinarily sung at weddings, the nymphs make an eerie and ominous sound. **(in) vertice (montis).**

> *Ille diēs prīmus* lētī *prīmusque* malōrum
> 170 causa *fuit; neque* enim speciē *fāmāve movētur*
>   *nec iam* fūrtīvum Dīdō meditātur *amōrem:*
>   coniugium *vocat, hōc* praetexit *nōmine* culpam.

---

causa, ae *f.* cause, reason, occasion
coniugium, (i)ī *n.* wedlock, marriage
culpa, ae *f.* fault, offense, guilt, blame
enim *adv.* for, indeed, truly
fūrtīvus, a, um secret, stolen

lētum, ī *n.* death, destruction, ruin
malum, ī *n.* evil, misfortune, trouble
meditor, ārī, ātus meditate, design
praetexō, ere, uī, xtus fringe, cloak
speciēs, ēī *f.* appearance, sight, aspect

170–71. speciē fāmāve: *by* (regard for) *appearances or* (for) *her reputation.* **neque . . . movētur nec . . . Dīdō meditātur:** the subject of the two verbs is closer to the second of them.

172. hōc nōmine: abl. of means.

Extemplō Libyae magnās it Fāma per urbēs,
Fāma, malum quā nōn aliud vēlōcius ūllum:
175   mōbilitāte viget vīrēsque adquīrit eundō,
parva metū prīmō, mox sēsē attollit in aurās
ingrediturque solō et caput inter nūbila condit.
Illam Terra parēns īrā inrītāta deōrum
extrēmam, ut perhibent, Coeō Enceladōque sorōrem
180   prōgenuit pedibus celerem et pernīcibus ālīs,
mōnstrum horrendum, ingēns, cui quot sunt corpore plūmae,

---

adquīrō, ere, quīsīvī, sītus acquire, gain
āla, ae f. wing
attollō, ere lift, rear, raise
celer, eris, ere swift, speedy, quick
Coeus, ī m. one of the Titans, a giant, son of Earth
condō, ere, didī, ditus establish, hide
Enceladus, ī m. one of the Titans, a giant, son of Earth
extemplō adv. immediately, at once, suddenly
extrēmus, a, um final, last, furthest
horrendus, a, um awful, terrible, dire
ingredior, ī, gressus enter, proceed
inrītō (1) vex, enrage, provoke
Libya, ae f. country of North Africa
malum, ī n. evil, misfortune, trouble

metus, ūs m. fear, fright, anxiety
mōbilitās, ātis f. activity, motion, speed
mōnstrum, ī n. prodigy, portent, monster
mox adv. soon, presently
nūbila, ōrum n. clouds, cloudiness
parvus, a, um small, little
perhibeō, ēre, uī, itus present, say
pernīx, īcis active, nimble, swift
plūma, ae f. feather, plume
prīmō adv. at first, in the beginning
prōgignō, ere, genuī, genitus bring forth, bear
quot as many as
solum, ī n. ground, soil, earth
soror, ōris f. sister
vēlōx, ōcis swift, quick, rapid, fleet
vigeō, ēre, uī flourish, be strong, thrive

173–218. Rumor, a terrifying divinity, spreads gossip about the love affair, and finally carries the news to Iarbas, an African chieftain whose marriage proposal had been rejected by Dido. Iarbas reproaches his father, Jupiter Ammon, for not helping him.

174. **quā:** abl. with comparative; App. 327. **nōn (est).**

173–74. **Fāma...Fāma:** the repetition for emphasis of the same word in two contiguous lines is called EPANALEPSIS.

175. **eundō:** abl. of means, from the gerund of eō; App. 269.

176. **metū:** abl. of cause.

177. (in) **solō** = (in) **terrā.**

178. **deōrum:** objective gen. with īrā, abl. of means; App. 284. In anger at the Olympian gods for slaying her children, the Titans, Earth bore the giants, Rumor being one of them.

179. **ut perhibent:** Vergil often uses phrases like this to signal to his readers that he is alluding to an earlier work. In this case, he is recalling the cosmic myths of Hesiod's *Theogony*, where the battle of the Olympians and Titans is described.

181. **cui:** dat. of possession. **corpore:** abl. of specification.

181–83. Rumor is covered with feathers; and beneath each feather is an eye, a tongue, a mouth, and an ear.

tot vigilēs *oculī* subter (mīrābile *dictū*),
tot linguae, totidem *ōra* sonant, tot subrigit aurēs.
Nocte volat *caelī* mediō *terraeque per umbram*
185 strīdēns, *nec* dulcī dēclīnat *lūmina somnō;*
lūce sedet custōs *aut summī* culmine *tēctī*
turribus *aut altīs, et magnās* territat *urbēs,*
tam fictī prāvī*que* tenāx quam nuntia vērī.
Haec tum multiplicī populōs sermōne replēbat
190 gaudēns, *et* pariter facta *atque* īnfecta canēbat:
vēnisse Aenēān Troiānō *sanguine* crētum,
cui sē pulchra *virō* dignētur iungere Dīdō;

---

auris, is *f.* ear
canō, ere, cecinī, cantus sing (of), chant, tell, proclaim, prophesy
crētus, a, um grown, sprung
culmen, inis *n.* roof, summit, top, peak
custōs, ōdis *m.* *(f.)* guard(ian), sentinel
dēclīnō (1) turn aside, bend down, droop
dignor, ārī, ātus deem worthy, deign (+ *abl.*)
dulcis, e sweet, dear, fond
factum, ī *n.* deed, act, exploit
fictum, ī *n.* falsehood, fiction
gaudeō, ēre, gāvīsus sum rejoice, exult
īnfectus, a, um not done, false
iungō, ere, iūnxī, iūnctus join, yoke
lingua, ae *f.* tongue, language
medium, (i)ī *n.* middle, center
mīrābilis, e wonderful, marvelous
multiplex, icis manifold, multiple
nuntia, ae *f.* messenger
pariter *adv.* equally, alike
populus, ī *m.* people, nation

prāvum, ī *n.* wrong, perverse act
pulcher, chra, chrum beautiful, handsome, splendid, illustrious, noble
quam *adv.* how, than, as
repleō, ēre, ēvī, ētus fill, stuff
sedeō, ēre, sēdī, sessus sit (down), settle
sermō, ōnis *m.* conversation
sonō, āre, uī, itus (re)sound, roar
strīd(e)ō, ēre (or **ere), ī** hiss, whir, rustle
subrigō, ere, surrēxī, rēctus raise, rise
subter *adv.; prep* + *acc.* beneath, below
tam *adv.* so, as, such
tenāx, ācis tenacious, holding (to)
territō (1) frighten, terrify, alarm
tot so many, as many
totidem the same number, so many
Troiānus, a, um Trojan, of Troy
turris, is *f.* tower, turret
vērum, ī *n.* truth, right, reality
vigil, ilis wakeful, watchful, sleepless
volō (1) fly, flit, move with speed

---

182. oculī (sunt) subter (plūmās).

183. (Fāma) tot subrigit aurēs: *Rumor raises as many listening ears.*

184. caelī mediō terraeque: *between heaven and earth.* Note how the Latin word order imitates the meaning of the phrase.

185. strīdēns: with her wings as she flies, referring to the buzz of gossip. **lūmina (sua)** = **oculōs,** as often.

186–87. lūce: *by day,* abl. of time; App. 322. **(in) culmine aut (in) turribus.**

188. fictī prāvīque . . . vērī: gen. with **tenāx;** App. 287.

189. Haec = Fāma.

190. facta atque īnfecta: *fact and fiction,* lit., *things done and not done.* **canēbat:** followed by indir. stmt.

191. Troiānō sanguine: abl. of separation/origin with **crētum.**

192. virō = coniugī. iungere: complementary inf.; App. 259.

nunc hiemem *inter sē* luxū, quam *longa,* fovēre
rēgnōrum immemorēs turpī*que* cupīdine *captōs.*
195 *Haec* passim *dea* foeda *virum* diffundit *in ōra.*
Prōtinus *ad rēgem cursūs* dētorquet Iarbān
incendit*que animum dictīs atque* aggerat *īrās.*
Hic Hammōne ṣatuṣ raptā Garamantide nymphā
templa *Iovī* centum lātīs *immānia rēgnīs,*
200 centum ārāṣ *poṣuit* vigilem*que* ṣacrāverat *ignem,*
excubiās *dīvum* aeternās, pecudum*que* cruōre
pingue solum *et* variīs flōrentia *līmina* sertīs.

---

aeternus, a, um eternal, everlasting
aggerō (1) heap up, pile up, increase
centum hundred
cruor, ōris *m.* blood, gore
cupīdō, inis *f.* love, desire, longing
dētorqueō, ēre, rsī, rtus turn (away)
diffundō, ere, fūdī, fūsus scatter, spread
excubiae, ārum *f.* watch(fire), sentinel
flōreō, ēre, uī bloom, flourish, blossom
foedus, a, um foul, loathsome, filthy
foveō, ēre, fōvī, fōtus cherish, fondle
Garamantis, idis of the Garamantes, an
    African tribe
Hammōn, ōnis *m.* Hammon (or Ammon),
    god of North Africa, famous for his oracle
    and identified by the Romans with Jupiter
hiems, emis *f.* winter, storm
Iarbās, ae *m.* African chieftain, one of
    Dido's unsuccessful suitors
immemor, oris unmindful, forgetful

incendō, ere, ī, ēnsus kindle, burn, inflame
lātus, a, um wide, broad, spacious
luxus, ūs *m.* luxury, splendor, excess
nympha, ae *f.* nymph, minor female divinity
    of the forests, waters, etc.
passim *adv.* everywhere, all about
pecus, udis *f.* animal (of the flock)
pinguis, e fat, rich, fertile
prōtinus *adv.* continuously, immediately
quam *adv.* how, than, as
rapiō, ere, uī, ptus snatch (away), seize,
    ravish
sacrō (1) consecrate, hallow, dedicate
serō, ere, sēvī, satus sow, beget
sertum, ī *n.* wreath, garland
solum, ī *n.* ground, soil, earth
templum, ī *n.* temple, shrine, sanctuary
turpis, e shameful, disgraceful
varius, a, um varied, different, diverse
vigil, ilis watchful, wakeful, sleepless

---

193. (Dīdōnem et Aenēān) inter sē
fovēre hiemem quam longa (ea hiems sit).
inter sē fovēre: *were caressing one another.*
hiemem: *the whole long winter;* either acc. of
duration of time or dir. obj. of fovēre, i.e., *they
kept the winter warm.* inter sē is commonly
employed to denote reciprocal action. quam
longa (sit): *however long it may be.*

194. rēgnōrum: Carthage and Italy.
195. vir(ōr)um.
198. Hic: pronounce hicc (as if from the
earlier spelling of the word, hicce).

199–200. templa centum (posuit), cen-
tum ārās posuit: Latin commonly expresses
the verb with only the second of two such
clauses, English with the first. Cf. note on
170–71.

201. excubiās: in apposition with ignem;
the never-dying fire stands sentry in honor of
the gods, like the sacred fire of Vesta at Rome.

202. pingue: from the blood and the ani-
mal fat of many sacrifices. solum, līmina:
take either as obj. of sacrāverat (200), like
ignem, or supply erant.

Isque āmēns *animī et* rūmōre accēnsus amārō
dīcitur ante ārās media inter nūmina dīvum
205   *multa Iovem manibus* supplex ōrāsse supīnīs:
Vx.   "*Iuppiter* omnipotēns, *cui nunc* Maurūsia pictīs
gēns epulāta torīs Lēnaeum lībat *honōrem*,
aspicis *haec? An tē, genitor, cum* fulmina torquēs
nēquīquam horrēmus, çaecīque in nūbibus *ignēs*
210   terrificant *animōs et inānia murmura miscent?*
Fēmina, *quae nostrīs errāns in fīnibus urbem*
exiguam pretiō *posuit, cui lītus* arandum

---

an whether, or
accendō, ere, ī, ēnsus kindle, inflame
amārus, a, um bitter, unpleasant
āmēns, entis mad, crazy, frenzied
arō (1) plow, till, furrow
a(d)spiciō, ere, spexī, spectus see, behold
caecus, a, um blind, hidden, dark
epulor, ārī, ātus feast, banquet (+ *abl*.)
exiguus, a, um small, scanty, petty
fēmina, ae *f*. woman, female
fulmen, inis *n*. thunderbolt, lightning
horreō, ēre, uī shudder (at), quake
inānis, e empty, useless, vain, idle
Lēnaeus, a, um Lenaean, Bacchic, of
    Bacchus, god of wine
lībō (1) pour (as a libation), offer

Maurūsius, a, um Moorish
misceō, ēre, uī, mixtus mix, mingle
murmur, uris *n*. murmur, roar, rumble
nēquīquam *adv*. in vain, uselessly, idly
nūbēs, is *f*. cloud, fog, mist
omnipotēns, entis almighty, omnipotent
ōrō (1) pray (for), beseech, entreat
pingō, ere, pīnxī, pictus paint, embroider
pretium, (i)ī *n*. price, reward, value
rūmor, ōris *m*. rumor, report, gossip
supīnus, a, um flat, upturned
supplex, icis suppliant, humble
terrificō (1) frighten, terrify, alarm
torqueō, ēre, rsī, rtus twist, sway, hurl
torus, ī *m*. (banqueting) couch, bed

---

203. Is: Iarbas. **animī:** gen. of reference (a rare usage) with **āmēns**, or loc.; App. 287, 37, *c*.

204. media inter nūmina: *amid the divine presences*. **dīv(ōr)um:** modifying either **ārās** or **nūmina**.

205. multa Iovem: double acc. with **ōrāsse**.

206–7. Maurūsia . . . gēns: the people of Iarbas.

207. Lēnaeum . . . honōrem: i.e., wine (associated with Bacchus Lenaeus) poured in libation as a sign of honor.

208–10. Iarbas challenges Jupiter with the suggestion that all the god's thunder and lightning are just empty threats.

211. Fēmina: Dido; emphatic by position. **errāns:** Vergil is incorporating a clever multilingual etymological wordplay into this line. An ancient dictionary tells us that the name **Dīdō** is a Punic word equivalent to the Greek word **planēs** or **planētis**, meaning *wandering* or *wanderer*; thus, the phrase **fēmina errāns** is an explanation in Latin of Dido's Punic name. (Note that the English word *planet* comes from the same Greek word.)

212. pretiō: abl. of price; App. 336. She had not taken the place by force, but had been compelled to buy it, a confession of weakness from Iarbas' perspective.

cuique locī lēgēs *dedimus,* cōnūbia *nostra*
reppulit *ac* dominum *Aenēān in rēgna* recēpit.
215   *Et nunc ille* Paris *cum* sēmivirō comitātū,
Maeoniā mentum mitrā crīnem*que* madentem
subnexus, raptō potitur: *nos mūnera* templīs
_quippe *tuīs ferimus fāmamque* fovēmus inānem."

---

comitātus, ūs *m.* retinue, train, company
cōnūbium, (i)ī *n.* wedlock, marriage
crīnis, is *m.* long hair, locks, tresses
dominus, ī *m.* master, lord, ruler
foveō, ēre, fōvī, fōtus cherish, fondle
inānis, e empty, useless, vain, idle
lēx, lēgis *f.* law, jurisdiction, term
madeō, ēre, uī drip, be wet, reek
Maeonius, a, um Maeonian, Lydian,
    Asiatic
mentum, ī *n.* chin, beard

mitra, ae *f.* mitre, cap, turban
Paris, idis *m.* Trojan prince, eloped with
    Helen and thus caused the Trojan War
potior, īrī, ītus possess, gain (+ *abl.*)
quippe *adv.* to be sure, surely, indeed
raptum, ī *n.* plunder, prey, booty
recipiō, ere, cēpī, ceptus receive, recover
repellō, ere, reppulī, repulsus reject, repel
sēmivir, virī half-man, effeminate
subnectō, ere, nex(u)ī, nexus tie (under)
templum, ī *n.* temple, shrine, sanctuary

212–13. For the ELLIPSIS of **dedimus** in the first clause, see the note on 199–200.

214. dominum: in apposition with **Aenēān**; said with bitter disdain.

215. Paris: In stealing the woman Iarbas was planning to marry, Aeneas is like Paris, who stole Menelaus' wife Helen and so provoked the Trojan War. **sēmivirō:** the African chieftain despises the Trojans and so challenges their masculinity. This insult reflects an ancient bias against the peoples of the Near East, whose luxurious life was believed by the Greeks and Romans to be conducive to effeminate behavior. Iarbas may also be thinking of the castrated priests of Cybele, whose cult was based in Asia Minor, near Troy, and suggesting that Aeneas and the Trojans are similar.

216–17. mentum, crīnem: Gk. acc. of respect with **subnexus**, here used as a Gk. middle participle; App. 309, *a.* **madentem:** *dripping* (with perfume), another mark of effeminacy. **raptō:** abl. with **potior**; App. 342. **potitur:** with **-i-** irregularly short.

218. quippe: sarcastic. **fāmam fovēmus inānem:** *we keep alive a baseless belief* in your power and justice.

Book 4.259–361

Ut prīmum ālātīs ⟨tetigit⟩ māgālia plantīs,

260   *Aenēān* fundantem *arcēs ac tēcta* novantem

     ⟨cōnspicit⟩. *Atque illī* stēllātus iāspide fulvā

     ēnsis ⟨erat⟩ *Tyriōque* ⟨ardēbat⟩ mūrice laena

     dēmissa *ex umerīs,* dīves *quae mūnera Dīdō*

     ⟨fēcerat,⟩ *et* tenuī tēlās ⟨discrēverat⟩ *aurō.*

265   Continuō ⟨invādit⟩: "*Tū nunc* Karthāginis *altae*

     fundāmenta locās pulchram*que* uxōrius *urbem*

ālātus, a, um winged, furnished with wings
cōnspiciō, ere, spexī, spectus see, look at
continuō *adv.* immediately, at once
dēmittō, ere, mīsī, missus let down, send
   down, lower, drop
dī(ve)s, dī(vi)tis rich, wealthy
discernō, ere, crēvī, crētus separate
ēnsis, is *m.* sword, knife
fulvus, a, um yellow, tawny, blond
fundāmentum, ī *n.* foundation, base
fundō (1) found, build, establish
iāspis, idis *f.* jasper, a semiprecious stone
invādō, ere, sī, sus attack, address
Karthāgō, inis *f.* Carthage, a city of North
   Africa

laena, ae *f.* (woolen) mantle, cloak
locō (1) place, lay, establish, locate
māgālia, ium *n.* huts, hovels
mūrex, icis *m.* purple (dye), crimson,
   scarlet
novō (1) renew, make (new), build
planta, ae *f.* heel; sole of foot
pulcher, chra, chrum beautiful, handsome,
   noble, splendid, illustrious
stēllātus, a, um starred, star-spangled
tangō, ere, tetigī, tāctus touch, reach
tēla, ae *f.* web, textile
tenuis, e slight, thin, fine, delicate
uxōrius, a, um wife-ruled, uxorious,
   hen-pecked

259–95. Mercury delivers a message to Aeneas from Jupiter, reminding him about Italy. Aeneas is unsure how to inform Dido of his imminent departure.

259. māgālia: the word is not native to Latin, but is derived from Punic; its use here succinctly identifies Mercury's exotic destination, cf. 1.421.

261. iāspide: the initial i- is pronounced separately from -ā- (i.e., they do not combine to form a diphthong).

261–62. stēllātus ēnsis: the hilt was studded.

264. tenuī aurō: she had interwoven the warp of the fabric with fine gold thread.

266. uxōrius: used as a term of reproach.

exstruis? *Heu, rēgnī rērumque* oblīte *tuārum!*
Ipse deum tibi mē clārō dēmittit Olympō
rēgnātor, *caelum et terrās quī nūmine* torquet,
270   *ipse haec ferre iubet* celerēs mandāta *per aurās:*
Quid struis? *Aut quā* spē Libycīs teris ōtia *terrīs?*
Sī tē nūlla movet tantārum glōria *rērum*
[*nec super ipse tuā* mōlīris laude *labōrem,*]
Ascanium *surgentem et* spēs hērēdis Iūlī
275   respice, *cui rēgnum* Ītaliae Rōmāna*que tellūs*
dēbētur." *Tālī* Cyllēnius ōre locūtus
mortālēs vīsūs *mediō* sermōne reliquit
et procul in tenuem *ex oculīs* ēvānuit auram.

Ascanius, (i)ī *m.* son of Aeneas
celer, eris, ere swift, quick, speedy
clārus, a, um clear, bright, illustrious
Cyllēnius, (i)ī *m.* the Cyllenean; Mercury,
   born on Mt. Cyllene
dēbeō, ēre, uī, itus owe, be due, be destined
dēmittō, ere, mīsī, missus send down, let
   down
ēvānēscō, ere, nuī vanish, disappear
exstruō, ere, strūxī, strūctus build (up),
   rear
glōria, ae *f.* glory, renown, fame, pride
hērēs, ēdis *m.* heir, successor
Iūlus, ī *m.* Ascanius, son of Aeneas
laus, laudis *f.* praise, glory, merit
Libycus, a, um Libyan, of Libya, a country
   of North Africa
loquor, ī, locūtus speak, say, tell, talk

mandātum, ī *n.* command, order, behest
mōlior, īrī, ītus undertake, accomplish, do
mortālis, e mortal, human, earthly
oblīviscor, ī, ītus (+ *gen.*) forget
Olympus, ī *m.* Greek mountain, home of
   the gods; heaven
ōtium, (i)ī *n.* leisure, idleness, quiet
rēgnātor, ōris *m.* ruler, lord, director
respiciō, ere, spexī, spectus look (back)
   at, regard
Rōmānus, a, um Roman, of Rome
sermō, ōnis *m.* conversation, speech
spēs, eī *f.* hope, expectation
struō, ere, strūxī, strūctus build, contrive
tenuis, e slight, thin
terō, ere, trīvī, trītus rub, wear, waste
torqueō, ēre, rsī, rtus twist, hurl, sway
vīsus, ūs *m.* vision, view, aspect

---

267. oblīte: voc. of the participle of
oblīviscor. rēgnī rērumque: gen. with a verb
of forgetting; App. 288.

273. The line is virtually identical to
233, and was probably reproduced here by
an inattentive copyist; brackets are used by
editors to indicate that none of the major

primary manuscripts contains this line. Cf.
2.567–88.

274. Iūlī: either possessive gen. (i.e., the
hopes that Iulus has) or objective gen. (i.e.,
the hopes you have for Iulus).

277. mediō (in) sermōne: *in the middle (of
his) speech, abruptly;* App. 246.

At vērō Aenēās aspectū obmūtuit āmēns,

280   arrēctaeque horrōre comae *et vōx* faucibus haesit.

Ardet abīre fugā dulcēsque relinquere terrās,

attonitus *tantō* monitū *imperiōque deōrum.*

Heu quid agat? Quō nunc rēgīnam ambīre furentem

audeat adfātū? Quae prīma exordia sūmat?

285   *Atque animum nunc hūc* celerem *nunc* dīvidit illūc

_ *in partēsque rapit variās perque omnia versat.*

Haec alternantī potior sententia *vīsa est:*

Mnēsthea Sergestum*que vocat* fortem*que* Serestum,

---

abeō, īre, iī (īvī), itus depart
adfātus, ūs *m.* address, speech
alternō (1) change, alternate, waver
ambiō, īre, īvī (iī), itus go around;
  conciliate
āmēns, entis mad, frenzied, distraught
arrigō, ere, rēxī, rēctus erect, stand on end
a(d)spectus, ūs *m.* sight, appearance
attonitus, a, um thunderstruck, astounded
audeō, ēre, ausus sum dare, venture
celer, eris, ere swift, speedy, quick
coma, ae *f.* hair, locks, tresses
dīvidō, ere, vīsī, vīsus divide, distribute
dulcis, e sweet, dear, fond
exordium, (i)ī *n.* beginning,
  commencement
faux, faucis *f.* jaws, throat; gulf

fortis, e brave, strong, valiant
haereō, ēre, haesī, haesus cling (to), halt
  (+ *dat.*)
horror, ōris *m.* shudder(ing), horror, alarm
illūc *adv.* there, thither, to that place
Mnēstheus, eī (eos), *acc.* ea *m.* Trojan leader
monitus, ūs *m.* advice, warning
obmūtēscō, ere, tuī be dumb, stand
  speechless
potior, ius preferable, better
rapiō, ere, uī, ptus seize, snatch, rob
sententia, ae *f.* opinion, resolve, view
Serestus, ī *m.* Trojan leader
Sergestus, ī *m.* Trojan leader
sūmō, ere, mpsī, mptus take
varius, a, um various, different, diverse
versō (1) keep turning, roll, revolve

---

281. fugā: abl. of manner. **dulcēs relin-quere terrās (Carthāginis):** Vergil uses the adj. to evoke Aeneas' inner conflict—even in his eager haste (**ardet**) to obey Jupiter, Aeneas cannot help thinking of how happy he has been in Carthage.

283–84. agat, audeat, sūmat: delibera-tive subjunctives; App. 348. These questions vividly represent Aeneas' confusion. **furentem (amōre).**

285. animum celerem dīvidit: The image is Homeric; heroes in doubt are often described by Homer as "splitting" their thoughts as they debate alternatives.

286. rapit (animum), versat (animum).

287. (Aenēae) alternantī: whether he should inform Dido. The participle continues the imagery of the preceding lines.

classem aptent tacitī *sociōsque ad lītora* cōgant,
290 *arma parent et quae rēbus sit* causa novandīs
dissimulent; *sēsē* intereā, quandō optima *Dīdō*
nesciat *et tantōs* rumpī *nōn* spēret *amōrēs*,
temptātūrum aditūs *et quae* mollissima *fandī*
tempora, quis rēbus dexter modus. Ōcius *omnēs*
295 *imperiō laetī* pārent *et* iussa facessunt.

---

aditus, ūs *m.* approach, access
aptō (1) equip, make ready, furnish
causa, ae *f.* cause, reason, occasion
cōgō, ere, coēgī, coāctus muster, compel
dissimulō (1) conceal, dissimulate, pretend
  otherwise
facessō, ere, (īv)ī, ītus do, make, fulfill
intereā *adv.* meanwhile, (in the) meantime
iussum, ī *n.* command, behest, order
modus, ī *m.* manner, limit, method
mollis, e soft, yielding, easy, mild

nesciō, īre, īvī (iī) not know, be ignorant
novō (1) renew, make new, alter, build
ōcior, ius swifter, quicker; very swift
optimus, a, um best, finest
pāreō, ēre, uī, itus obey, yield (+ *dat.*)
quandō when, since, because
rumpō, ere, rūpī, ruptus break, burst
  (forth), utter
spērō (1) hope (for, to), expect, suppose
temptō (1) try, attempt, seek, test
tacitus, a, um silent, still, secret

289–91. (ut) aptent, cōgant, parent, dissimulent: indir. commands after **vocat**, which implies **et imperat** or something similar; App. 390. **rēbus novandīs:** an expression commonly used for taking a new step, including something as extreme as political revolution. **quae ... sit causa:** indir. quest.; App. 349.

291–93. sēsē temptātūrum (esse): implied indir. stmt., dependent on **vocat** (288), which implies **et dicit** or something similar;

App. 390. **nesciat:** subjunctive in a dependent clause in indir. stmt.; App. 390, *b*.

292. rumpī amōrēs: the expression is ambiguous: either Aeneas is counting on the likelihood that Dido will not reveal her true feelings publicly, or he thinks that nothing he can do can damage her love for him.

293–94. quae tempora (sint), quis modus (sit): indir. quests., objs. of **temptātūrum (esse)**; App. 349.

At rēgīna dolōs (*quis* fallere *possit* amantem?)
praesēnsit, mōtūs*que* excēpit *prīma futūrōs*
omnia tūta timēns. *Eadem* impia *Fāma furentī*
dētulit armārī *classem cursumque parārī.*

300   Saevit inops *animī tōtamque* incēnsa *per urbem*
bacchātur, quālis commōtīs excita *sacrīs*
Thyiās, *ubi audītō* stimulant trietērica Bacchō
orgia nocturnus*que vocat clāmōre* Cithaerōn.
Tandem hīs Aenēān compellat *vōcibus* ultrō:

---

amāns, antis *m.* (*f.*) lover
armō (1) arm, equip, furnish
bacchor, ārī, ātus rush wildly, rave
Bacchus, ī *m.* (god of) wine
Cithaerōn, ōnis *m.* Greek mountain near
Thebes, on which the rites of Bacchus
were celebrated
commoveō, ēre, mōvī, mōtus move, stir,
shake, agitate
compellō (1) address, accost, speak to
dēferō, ferre, tulī, lātus carry down, report
dolus, ī *m.* deceit, stratagem, fraud
excipiō, ere, cēpī, ceptus catch, receive,
take (up)
exciō, īre, īvī, itus arouse, excite, stir
fallō, ere, fefellī, falsus deceive, cheat,
mock

impius, a, um wicked, accursed, disloyal
incendō, ere, ī, ēnsus inflame, burn
inops, opis needy, destitute, bereft (of)
mōtus, ūs *m.* movement, emotion
nocturnus, a, um of the night, nocturnal
orgia, ōrum *n.* mystic rites, rituals
praesentiō, īre, sēnsī, sēnsus perceive first,
suspect
quālis, e of what sort, (such) as
saeviō, īre, īvī (iī), ītus rage, storm
stimulō (1) spur, goad, prick, incite
Thyias, adis *f.* Bacchant, a woman devotee
of the worship of Bacchus
timeō, ēre, uī fear, dread
trietēricus, a, um triennial
tūtus, a, um protected, safe, secure
ultrō *adv.* further, voluntarily

> 296–330. Dido, suspecting the truth,
> reproaches Aeneas and, with tears and
> prayers, attempts to prevail on him to
> remain.

296. possit: deliberative subjunctive;
App. 348.

298. tūta: used concessively, i.e., (no matter how) *safe*, with **omnia. eadem:** refers to
the first appearance of Fama (173). **furentī
(Dīdōnī).**

300. animī: gen. with adj. **inops;** App. 287.

302. trietērica: every two years, counted
as three in the ancient system of inclusive
reckoning.

302–3. Thyias: the letters -yi- form a diphthong (pronounced *we*). The Bacchic revels
celebrated every two years on Mt. Cithaeron,
near Thebes, are depicted in their most terrifying aspect in Euripides' tragedy *Bacchae.*
When the **sacra** (ritual objects the precise
identity of which remain unknown) were
brought out of the temple, the female worshippers of Bacchus ran wild, dressed themselves in fawn skins, and joined the Bacchic
revels, where they brandished **thyrsī** (*wands*),
and danced to the accompaniment of clashing
cymbals. **audītō Bacchō:** abl. abs.; *as the cry
'Bacchus' is heard.* The worshippers shouted
'*iō Bacche*' and '*Euoe Bacche.*' **stimulant (illam), vocat (illam).**

305   "Dissimulāre etiam spērāstī, perfide, *tantum*
      posse nefās tacitus*que meā* dēcēdere *terrā?*
      Nec tē noster amor nec tē data dextera quondam
      nec moritūra *tenet* crūdēlī fūnere *Dīdō?*
      Quīn etiam hībernō mōlīri *sīdere classem*
310   *et mediīs* properās Aquilōnibus *īre per* altum,
      crūdēlis? *Quid, sī nōn arva* aliēna *domōsque*
      ignōtās *peterēs, et Troia antīqua manēret,*
      Troia per undōsum *peterētur classibus aequor?*
      Mēne fugis? Per ego hās lacrimās dextramque tuam tē
315   (quandō *aliud mihi iam miserae* nihil *ipsa relīquī*),
      per cōnūbia *nostra, per* inceptōs hymenaeōs,
      sī bene *quid dē tē* meruī, *fuit aut tibi* quicquam

---

aliēnus, a, um belonging to another, other's, alien, foreign
altum, ī *n.* the deep (sea); heaven
Aquilō, ōnis *m.* (north) wind
bene *adv.* well, rightly, securely, fully
cōnūbium, (i)ī *n.* wedlock, marriage
crūdēlis, e cruel, bloody, bitter
dēcēdō, ere, cessī, cessus depart
dissimulō (1) conceal, dissimulate, pretend otherwise
etiam *adv.* also, even, besides, yet, still
fūnus, eris *n.* funeral, death, disaster
hībernus, a, um wintry, of the winter
hymenaeus, ī *m.* wedding (hymn), so called after Hymen, god of marriage
ignōtus, a, um unknown, strange

incipiō, ere, cēpī, ceptus begin, undertake
mereō, ēre, uī, itus deserve, earn, merit
mōlior, īrī, ītus prepare, attempt, do
morior, ī, mortuus die, perish
nefās *n. indecl.* impiety, unspeakable thing, crime
nihil, nīl nothing, not at all
perfidus, a, um treacherous, perfidious
properō (1) hasten, hurry, speed
quandō when, since, if ever, because
quīn why not, but that, in fact
quisquam, quicquam anyone, anything
spērō (1) hope (for, to), expect, suppose
tacitus, a, um silent, noiseless, secret
undōsus, a, um billowing, wavy

---

305. Dissimulāre: Dido's first word echoes the instructions Aeneas has just given his men (291).

305–6. etiam spērā(vi)stī, perfide, (tē) posse dissimulāre tantum nefās?

307. data dextera: the clasping of right hands was a Roman symbol of marriage, seen frequently in sculpture.

307–8. Note the combination of ANAPHORA and TRICOLON CRESCENS (i.e., the use of three parallel phrases or clauses, balanced so that each is slightly longer than the one preceding it).

309. hībernō sīdere = METONYMY for **tempore**. The ancients regularly suspended

navigation during the winter months. **mōlīrī:** some manuscripts read **mōlīris** (2ⁿᵈ person sing.) instead of the inf.

311–13. Quid sī, etc.: you wouldn't sail now, even if you were going back to secure homes in Troy, and were not (as you are) sailing away to strange foreign lands (**arva aliēna**). **Troia peterētur (hībernō sīdere):** the conclusion of the pres. contrary-to-fact conditions, **sī peterēs** and **sī manēret**; App. 382.

314–19. Mē: emphatic by position, obj. of **fugis. Per ego,** etc.: when used in an oath, **per** is best translated *by.* **per lacrimās et per dextram. tē:** obj. of **ōrō.**

dulce *meum,* miserēre *domūs lābentis et* istam,
ōrō, *sī quis* adhūc precibus *locus,* exue *mentem.*

320   *Tē* propter Libycae *gentēs* Nomadum*que* tyrannī
ōdēre, īnfēnsī *Tyriī; tē* propter *eundem*
exstīnctus pudor *et, quā sōlā sīdera* adībam,
fāma prior. *Cui mē* moribundam dēseris hospes
(*hoc solum nōmen* quoniam *dē coniuge* restat)?

325   *Quid* moror? An *mea* Pygmaliōn *dum moenia* frāter
dēstruat *aut captam dūcat* Gaetūlus Iarbās?

---

adeō, īre, iī (īvī), itus approach
adhūc *adv.* to this point, till now
an whether, or
dēserō, ere, uī, rtus desert, forsake
dēstruō, ere, strūxī, strūctus destroy
dulcis, e sweet, dear, pleasant, delightful
exsting(u)ō, ere, īnxī, īnctus extinguish,
   blot out, destroy, ruin
exuō, ere, uī, ūtus bare, doff, discard
frāter, tris *m.* brother
Gaetūlus, a, um of the Gaetuli, an African
   tribe
hospes, itis *m. (f.)* stranger, guest, host
Iarbās, ae *f.* African prince, one of Dido's
   suitors
īnfēnsus, a, um hostile, bitter
iste, ta, tud that (of yours)

Libycus, a, um of Libya, a country of North
   Africa
misereor, ērī, itus pity, commiserate
   (+ *gen.*)
moribundus, a, um dying, about to die
moror, ārī, ātus delay, tarry, hinder
Nomas, adis *m.* tribe of North Africa
ōdī, isse hate, detest, loathe
ōrō (1) to pray (for), entreat, beseech
prex, precis *f.* prayer, entreaty, vow
prior, ius soon, former, first, prior
propter on account of, near (+ *acc.*)
pudor, ōris *m.* shame, modesty, honor
Pygmaliōn, ōnis *m.* brother of Dido
quoniam since, because
restō, āre, stitī remain, be left
tyrannus, ī *m.* ruler, chieftain, tyrant

---

318. miserēre: imperat. **domūs:** gen. with
misereor; App. 289.

319. **sī quis** (indef.) **locus** (sit).

320. **Tē propter:** ANASTROPHE.

320–21. **gentēs et tyrannī ōdēre (mē).**
ōdēre = ōdērunt. īnfēnsī (mihi sunt) Tyriī:
the native chieftains, as well as her own peo-
ple, resented her kindly attitude toward Ae-
neas and the Trojans, who were foreigners,
and her rejection of their offers of alliance
through marriage.

322. **et (fāma) quā:** abl. of means. **sīdera
adībam:** *I was approaching the stars,* i.e., earn-
ing immortality through fame. (**exstīncta
est) fāma (mea):** *(my) reputation.*

323. **moribundam = moritūram.**

324. **hoc nōmen = hospes. dē coniuge =
dē nōmine coniugis.**

325. **Quid** (= **cūr) moror (mortem
meam). An (moror):** *am I waiting?* **dum
dēstruat, dūcat:** anticipatory subjunctives
with **dum;** App. 374.

Saltem *sī qua mihī dē tē* suscepta *fuisset*
ante fugam subolēs, *sī quis mihi* parvulus aulā
lūderet *Aenēās, quī tē* tamen *ōre referret,*
330 *nōn* equidem omnīnō *capta ac* dēserta *vidērer."*

---

aula, ae *f.* hall, palace, court
dēserō, ere, uī, rtus desert, forsake
equidem *adv.* indeed, truly, surely
lūdō, ere, sī, sus play, sport, mock
omnīnō *adv.* altogether, completely, utterly

parvulus, a, um tiny, very small, little
saltem *adv.* at least, at any rate
subolēs, is *f.* offspring, progeny, child
suscipiō, ere, cēpī, ceptus take up, beget, bear
tamen *adv.* however, nevertheless, but

---

327. suscepta: an allusion to the Roman custom of placing a newborn child on the ground before the father, who picked it up if he wished to acknowledge and rear it as his own.

327–30. sī fuisset, sī lūderet, … vidērer: mixed contrary-to-fact condition; App. 382, *d.*

328. parvulus: this is the only appearance of a diminutive adj. in the *Aeneid.* The rareness of such an emotional form of expression probably reflects how pathetic it is meant to sound coming from Dido.

329. referret: subjunctive in a rel. clause of characteristic; App. 389; i.e., "the sort of child who could remind me of you."

Dīxerat. Ille Iovis monitīs immōta *tenēbat*
lūmina et obnixus *cūram sub* corde premēbat.
Tandem pauca *refert: "Ego tē, quae plūrima fandō*
ēnumerāre valēs, numquam, *rēgīna*, negābō
335   prōmeritam, *nec mē* meminisse pigēbit Elissae
dum memor *ipse meī, dum* spīritus *hōs* rēgit artūs.
Prō *rē* pauca loquar. *Neque ego hanc* abscondere fūrtō
spērāvī (*nē* finge) *fugam, nec coniugis* umquam
praetendī taedās *aut haec in* foedera *vēnī.*
340   *Mē sī fāta meīs* paterentur *dūcere vītam*

---

abscondō, ere, (di)dī, ditus hide
artus, ūs *m.* joint, limb, member, body
cor, rdis *n.* heart, spirit, feelings
Elissa, ae *f.* Dido
ēnumerō (1) recount, enumerate
fingō, ere, fīnxī, fictus fashion, pretend,
    imagine, form, mold
foedus, eris *n.* treaty, agreement, pact
fūrtum, ī *n.* stealth, theft, trick
immōtus, a, um unmoved, unshaken
loquor, ī, locūtus speak, say, tell, talk
meminī, isse remember, recall (+ *gen.*)
memor, oris mindful, remembering (+ *gen.*)
monitum, ī *n.* advice, warning
negō (1) deny, refuse, say no (not)
numquam *adv.* never, at no time
obnītor, ī, sus (obnixus) struggle

patior, ī, passus suffer, endure, allow
paucus, a, um little, few, scanty
piget, ēre, uit it displeases
praetendō, ere, ī, ntus hold before, use as
    screen
premō, ere, pressī, pressus (re)press, crush
prō instead of, on behalf of, for, before
    (+ *abl.*)
prōmereor, ērī, itus deserve, render
    service, merit, earn
regō, ere, rēxī, rēctus rule, direct, guide
spērō (1) hope (for, to), expect, suppose
spīritus, ūs *m.* breath, spirit, life, soul
taeda, ae *f.* (bridal) torch, pinewood torch
umquam *adv.* ever, at any time
valeō, ēre, uī, itus be strong, be able, fare
    well

331–61. Aeneas replies that he is not fol-
lowing his own desires but the plans of the
gods and the stern decrees of fate.

331. Dīxerat (Dīdō). monitīs: abl. of
cause with **tenēbat**.

332. lūmina = **oculōs. premēbat** =
reprimēbat: repressing all outward indica-
tions of his feelings.

**333–35. Ego, rēgīna, numquam negābō
tē prōmeritam (esse dē mē) plūrima quae:**
answer to Dido's **sī meruī** of 317. **valēs** =
potes. Elissae = **Dīdōnis;** gen. with **meminī;**
App. 288.

336. dum memor (sum) meī.

337. Prō rē: *in defense of my course of action.*
The expression is legalistic.

338. nē finge: poetic negative imperat., =
nōlī fingere; App. 256, *a.*

339. praetendī taedās: the phrase has a
double meaning: lit., *I never held the marriage
torches before [you],* i.e., in a marriage proces-
sion; and *I never held out the prospect* (or *made
a pretense) of marriage.* **haec in foedera:** i.e.,
of marriage.

340. paterentur: pres. contrary-to-fact
condition; App. 382.

auspiciīs *et* sponte *meā* compōnere *cūrās,*
urbem Troiānam *prīmum* dulcēs*que meōrum*
reliquiās colerem, *Priamī tēcta alta manērent,*
et recidīva *manū posuissem* Pergama *victīs.*

345 *Sed nunc Ītaliam magnam* Grȳnēus Apollō,
Ītaliam Lyciae *iussēre* capessere sortēs;
hic amor, haec patria *est. sī tē* Karthāginis *arcēs*
Phoenissam Libycae*que* aspectus dētinet *urbis,*
quae tandem Ausoniā *Teucrōs* cōnsīdere *terrā*

350 invidia *est? Et nos* fās extera *quaerere rēgna.*
Mē patris Anchīsae, quotiēns ūmentibus *umbrīs*
nox operit *terrās,* quotiēns astra ignea *surgunt,*
admonet *in somnīs et* turbida terret imāgō;

---

admoneō, ēre, uī, itus advise, warn
Apollō, inis *m.* god of light, music, and prophecy
a(d)spectus, ūs *m.* sight, appearance
astrum, ī *n.* star, constellation
Ausonius, a, um Ausonian, Italian
auspicium, (i)ī *n.* auspices, authority
capessō, ere, īvī, ītus (try to) seize, reach
colō, ere, uī, cultus cultivate, dwell (in), cherish, honor
compōnō, ere, posuī, positus put together, settle, calm, quiet
cōnsīdō, ere, sēdī, sessus sit (down), settle
dētineō, ēre, uī, tentus hold back, detain
dulcis, e sweet, dear, fond
exterus, a, um outside, foreign
fās *n. indecl.* right, justice, divine law
Grȳnēus, a, um of Grynium, a town in Asia Minor, with an oracle of Apollo
igneus, a, um fiery, flaming

imāgō, inis *f.* image, likeness, ghost
invidia, ae *f.* grudge, envy, jealousy
Karthāgō, inis *f.* Carthage, a city of North Africa
Libycus, a, um Libyan, of Libya, a country of North Africa
Lycia, ae *f.* country of Asia Minor
operiō, īre, uī, rtus cover, hide
patria, ae *f.* homeland, country
Pergama, ōrum *n.* (citadel of) Troy
Phoenissa, ae *f.* Phoenician woman, Dido
quotiēns how often, as often as
recidīvus, a, um revived, renewed
reliquiae, ārum *f.* remnants, relics, leavings
sors, rtis *f.* lot, fate, portion, oracle
spōns, spontis *f.* wish, will, desire
terreō, ēre, uī, itus frighten, terrify
Troiānus, a, um Trojan, of Troy
turbidus, a, um troubled, agitated
ūmēns, entis moist, dewy, damp

343–44. colerem, manērent, posuissem: apodoses in the contrary-to-fact condition; App. 382. **victīs (Teucrīs):** dat. of reference.

346. Lyciae sortēs = sortēs Lyciī Apollinis.

347. hic: pronounce **hicc** (the full form was originally **hicce**), making a long syllable; App. 107, 3, *c.* **hic (est) amor, haec patria est:** both refer to Italy, each pron.

being attracted into the gender of its predicate noun; App. 240, *a.*

349–50. quae invidia est (tibi). Teucrōs cōnsīdere is the subject and **invidia** the predicate of **est.**

350. Et: *also, too* (as well as for you). **fās (est).**

351–53. patris Anchīsae: gen. with **imāgō.**

mē puer Ascanius *capitisque* iniūria cārī,

355   *quem rēgnō* Hesperiae fraudō *et* fātālibus *arvīs.*

Nunc etiam interpres *dīvum Iove missus ab ipsō*
(testor utrumque *caput*) celerēs mandāta *per aurās*
dētulit: *ipse deum* manifestō *in lūmine vīdī*
intrantem mūrōs *vōcemque hīs* auribus hausī.

360   Dēsine *mēque tuīs* incendere *tēque* querēlis;
Ītaliam nōn sponte *sequor."*

Ascanius, (i)ī *m.* son of Aeneas
auris, is *f.* ear
cārus, a, um dear, beloved, fond
celer, eris, ere swift, quick, speedy
dēferō, ferre, tulī, lātus carry down, report
dēsinō, ere, sīvī (iī), situs cease, desist
etiam *adv.* also, even, besides, furthermore
fātālis, e fated, fatal, destined
fraudō (1) defraud, deprive, cheat
hauriō, īre, hausī, haustus drink (in), drain
Hesperia, ae *f.* Hesperia, Italy; lit., the western place

incendō, ere, ī, ēnsus inflame, kindle, burn
iniūria, ae *f.* wrong, injury, injustice
interpres, etis *m. (f.)* interpreter, agent
intrō (1) enter, penetrate
mandātum, ī *n.* command, mandate
manifestus, a, um clear, manifest
mūrus, ī *m.* (city) wall, battlement
querēla, ae *f.* complaint, lament
spōns, spontis *f.* wish, will, desire
testor, ārī, ātus call to witness, swear by, testify
uterque, utraque, utrumque each (of two), both

---

354. mē puer Ascanius (movet): (the thought of) *my son Ascanius urges me on.* **capitis cārī = Ascanī**; obj. gen., *the wrong* (I am doing) *to Ascanius;* App. 284.

355. rēgnō, arvīs: abl. of separation.
356. interpres dīv(ōr)um: Mercury.
357. utrumque = et meum et tuum.
361. sponte (meā).

Book 4.659–705

Dīxit, et ōs impressa torō "Moriēmur inultae,
660   *sed moriāmur" ait.* "Sīc, sīc iuvat īre sub umbrās.
Hauriat *hunc oculīs ignem* crūdēlis *ab altō*
Dardanus, *et nostrae sēcum ferat ōmina mortis."*
Dīxerat, atque illam media inter tālia ferrō
conlāpsam aspiciunt *comitēs,* ēnsem*que* cruōre
665   spūmantem sparsās*que manūs. It clāmor ad alta*
ātria: concussam bacchātur *Fāma per urbem.*
Lāmentīs gemitū*que et* fēmineō ululātū

---

a(d)spiciō, ere, spexī, spectus see, behold
altum, ī *n.* the deep (sea); heaven
ātrium, ī *n.* hall, court, atrium
bacchor, ārī, ātus rave, rush wildly
concutiō, ere, cussī, cussus shake, shatter
conlābor, ī, lāpsus fall in a heap, faint
crūdēlis, e cruel, harsh, bloody
cruor, ōris *m.* blood, gore
Dardan(i)us, a, um Trojan, Dardanian
ēnsis, is *m.* sword, knife
fēmineus, a, um feminine, of women
gemitus, ūs *m.* groan, roar, lament

hauriō, īre, hausī, haustus drain, drink (in)
imprimō, ere, pressī, pressus press (upon),
    imprint
inultus, a, um unavenged, unpunished
iuvō, āre, iūvī, iūtus help, please
lāmenta, ōrum *n.* lamentation, shriek
morior, ī, mortuus die, perish
ōmen, inis *n.* portent, omen, sign
spargō, ere, rsī, rsus scatter, sprinkle
spūmō (1) foam, froth, spray
torus, ī *m.* couch, bed
ululātus, ūs *m.* wail, shout

659–705. Dido's passion reaches its inevitable conclusion, and her tormented soul departs from her body.

659. ōs: obj. of the middle participle **impressa**; a farewell kiss.

660. Sīc, sīc: the repetition has been thought by some to suggest Dido's repeated stabs, though it need not be taken quite so literally.

661–62. Hauriat, ferat: jussive or volitive subjunctive; App. 254. **Dardanus = Aenēās. ōmina:** i.e., her death will bring him continual sorrow and misfortune.

663. ferrō: abl. of means or place where (*upon the sword*).

667. fēmineō ulutātū: the HIATUS between the two words emphasizes the eerie sound made by the women.

tēcta fremunt, resonat *magnīs* plangōribus aethēr,
nōn aliter quam *sī* immissīs ruat hostibus *omnis*

670 Karthāgō *aut antīqua* Tyros, *flammaeque furentēs*
culmina *perque* hominum volvantur *perque deōrum.*
Audiit exanimis trepidōque exterrita *cursū*
unguibus *ōra* soror foedāns *et pectora* pugnīs
per mediōs ruit, ac morientem *nōmine* clāmat:

675 *"Hoc illud,* germāna, *fuit? Mē* fraude *petēbās?*
Hoc rogus iste *mihi, hoc ignēs āraeque parābant?*
Quid prīmum dēserta querar? *Comitemne* sorōrem
sprēvistī moriēns? *Eadem mē ad fāta vocāssēs:*

---

aethēr, eris *m.* upper air, sky, ether
aliter *adv.* otherwise, differently
clāmō (1) shriek, cry (out), call (on)
culmen, inis *n.* roof, peak, summit, top
dēserō, ere, uī, rtus desert, forsake
exanimis, e breathless, lifeless
exterreō, ēre, uī, itus terrify, frighten
foedō (1) pollute, defile, disfigure
fraus, fraudis *f.* deceit, guile, fraud
fremō, ere, uī, itus shout, roar, groan
germāna, ae *f.* sister
homō, inis *m.* (*f.*) man, human, mortal
hostis, is *m.* (*f.*) enemy, foe, stranger
immittō, ere, mīsī, missus let in, send in
iste, ta, tud that (of yours)

Karthāgō, inis *f.* city of North Africa
morior, ī, mortuus die, perish
plangor, ōris *m.* wailing, beating (of breast)
pugnus, ī *m.* fist
quam *adv.* how, than, as
queror, ī, questus complain, (be)wail
resonō (1) (re)sound, roar
rogus, ī *m.* funeral pyre
soror, ōris *f.* sister
spernō, ere, sprēvī, sprētus scorn, reject
trepidus, a, um trembling, excited
Tyrus (os), ī *f.* city of Phoenicia, birthplace
of Dido
unguis, is *m.* nail, claw

---

669. quam sī ruat: the protasis of a po-
tential (future-less-vivid) condition used as
a clause of comparison; App. 383.
669–71. The SIMILE recalls the fall of Troy
depicted in Book 2.
670. Tyros: nom. sing., a Gk. form;
App. 67.
671: culmina: obj. (twice) of **per. homi-
num, deōrum:** i.e., homes of the residents
and temples of the gods.
672. cursū: abl. of manner.

673. ōra foedāns et pectora: as an expres-
sion of grief.
675–76. Hoc, hoc: pronounce **hocc** (from
the original form, **hocce**), making a long syl-
lable. **Hoc (fuit) illud (quod parābās):** *was this*
(your own death) *that which you were planning?*
677. Quid querar: deliberative quest.;
App. 348.
678–79. vocā(vi)ssēs, tulisset: optative
subjunctive, expressing a wish; App. 253.

īdem ambās *ferrō* dolor *atque eadem* hōra *tulisset.*
680 *Hīs* etiam strūxī *manibus patriōsque vocāvī*
vōce deōs, sīc tē ut positā*, crūdēlis, abessem?
Exstīnxtī *tē mēque*, soror, populum*que patrēsque*
Sīdoniōs *urbemque tuam. Date*, vulnera lymphīs
abluam *et*, extrēmus *sī quis super* hālitus *errat,*
685 *ōre* legam." *Sīc fāta* gradūs ēvāserat *altōs,*
sēmianimem*que* sinū germānam amplexa fovēbat
cum gemitū *atque ātrōs* siccābat veste cruōrēs.
Illa gravēs *oculōs* cōnāta attollere rūrsus
dēficit; īnfixum strīdit *sub pectore* vulnus.

---

abluō, ere, uī, ūtus wash (off)
absum, esse, āfuī be away, be distant
ambō, ae, ō both
amplector, ī, plexus embrace, enfold
attollō, ere lift, rear, raise
cōnor, ārī, ātus attempt, try, endeavor
crūdēlis, e cruel, bloody, hardhearted
cruor, ōris *m.* blood, gore
dēficiō, ere, fēcī, fectus fail, faint
dolor, ōris *m.* grief, pain, passion, anger
etiam *adv.* also, even
ēvādō, ere, sī, sus go forth (from), pass over
exstinguō, ere, īnxī, īnctus blot out, destroy, extinguish
extrēmus, a, um final, last, extreme
foveō, ēre, fōvī, fōtus fondle, cherish
gemitus, ūs *m.* groan, roar, lament
germāna, ae *f.* sister

gradus, ūs *m.* step, gait, pace, stride
gravis, e heavy, grievous, serious
hālitus, ūs *m.* breath, exhalation
hōra, ae *f.* hour, season, time
īnfīgō, ere, xī, xus fix, pierce, fasten
legō, ere, lēgī, lēctus choose, gather, catch
lympha, ae *f.* water
populus, ī *m.* people, nation
rūrsus, um *adv.* again, anew, back(ward)
sēmianimis, e half-dead, dying
siccō (1) dry, stanch
Sīdonius, a, um Sidonian, of Sidon, a city of Phoenicia
sinus, ūs *m.* fold; bosom; bay; hollow
strīd(e)ō, ēre, ī hiss, gurgle, rustle
struō, ere, strūxī, strūctus build, plan
vestis, is *f.* cloth(ing), garment, robe
vulnus, eris *n.* wound, deadly blow

---

680. strūxī (tuum rogum).
681. tē positā: abl. abs. **ut abessem:** purpose; App. 359.
682. Exstīnx(is)tī.
683. Date: Anna turns to Dido's attendants to request help in preparing the corpse.
684. (ut) abluam: purpose clause. **super:** adv.

685. ōre legam: it was a Roman custom to catch with a kiss the last breath of a dying relative or friend. **fāta:** perf. participle of deponent verb **for, fārī**; modifies the subject of the sentence, Anna. **gradūs:** of the funeral pyre.
686. sēmianimem: treat the first -i- as a consonant, and pronounce **sēmyănĭmēmquĕ** here.
689. strīdit: from the gurgling blood.

690   Ter *sēsē* attollēns cubitō*que* adnixa levāvit,
          ter revolūta torō *est oculīsque errantibus altō*
          quaesīvit caelō lūcem ingemuit*que* repertā.
          Tum Iūnō omnipotēns *longum* miserāta dolōrem
          difficilēs*que* obitūs Īrim dēmīsit Olympō
695   *quae* luctantem *animam* nexōs*que* resolveret artūs.
          Nam quia *nec fātō* merita *nec morte* perībat,
          sed misera ante diem subitō*que* accēnsa furōre,
          nōndum *illī* flāvum Prōserpina vertice crīnem
          abstulerat Stygiō*que caput* damnāverat Orcō.

accendō, ere, ī, ēnsus inflame, burn
adnītor, ī, sus (nixus) lean on, struggle
artus, ūs *m.* joint, limb, member
attollō, ere lift, rear, raise
auferō, ferre, abstulī, ablātus take away
crīnis, is *m.* hair, locks, tresses
cubitum, ī *n.* elbow, arm
damnō (1) condemn, sentence, doom, devote
dēmittō, ere, mīsī, missus send down, let go, drop, lower
difficilis, e difficult, hard, painful
dolor, ōris *m.* grief, pain, passion, anger
flāvus, a, um yellow, tawny, blond
furor, ōris *m.* madness, frenzy, passion
ingemō, ere, uī groan, roar, lament
Īris, (id)is *f.* goddess of the rainbow, messenger of Juno
levō (1) lift, lighten, raise, relieve
luctor, ārī, ātus struggle, wrestle
mereō, ēre, uī, itus deserve, earn, merit

miseror, ārī, ātus pity, commiserate
nectō, ere, nexuī, nexus weave, fasten, bind
nōndum *adv.* not yet
obitus, ūs *m.* death, downfall, ruin
Olympus, ī *m.* high Greek mountain, home of the gods; heaven
omnipotēns, entis almighty, omnipotent
Orcus, ī *m.* (god of) the lower world, Hades
pereō, īre, iī (īvī), itus perish, die
Prōserpina, ae *f.* Pluto's queen, goddess of the lower world
quia because
reperiō, īre, repperī, repertus find
resolvō, ere, ī, solūtus loose(n), free, pay
revolvō, ere, ī, volūtus roll over, revolve
Stygius, a, um Stygian, of the Styx, a river in Hades
subitus, a, um sudden, unexpected
ter three times
torus, ī *m.* (banqueting, funeral) couch, bed
vertex, icis *m.* top, peak, head, summit

690. cubitō: abl. of means with **adnītor.**
691. (in) torō.
692. repertā (lūce): abl. abs.
695. nexōs (animae). quae resolveret: rel. clause of purpose; App. 388. For the thought see the note on 385.

696. fātō: natural death was supposed to be occasioned by a decree of the gods. **merita nec morte:** note the postponement of the conjunction.
698. illī: dat. of reference. **Prōserpina:** she was supposed to cut a lock from the head of the dying, as a sort of offering to the gods of the lower world.

700 Ergō Īris croceīs *per caelum* rōscida pennīs
mīlle *trahēns* variōs adversō sōle colōrēs
dēvolat *et* suprā *caput* astitit. *"Hunc ego* Dītī
sacrum iussa ferō tēque istō *corpore* solvō":
Sīc ait et dextrā crīnem secat, *omnis et* ūnā
705 dīlāpsus calor *atque in ventōs vīta* recessit.

---

adversus, a, um opposite, facing
a(d)stō, āre, stitī stand (ready, by)
calor, ōris *m.* heat, warmth, glow
color, ōris *m.* color
crīnis, is *m.* hair, locks, tresses
croceus, a, um yellow, saffron, ruddy
dēvolō (1) fly down
dīlābor, ī, lāpsus glide away, depart
Dīs, Dītis *m.* Pluto, god of the lower world
ergō *adv.* therefore, then, consequently
Īris, (id)is *f.* goddess of the rainbow,
    messenger of Juno

iste, ta, tud that (of yours)
mīlle; *pl.* **mīlia, ium** *n.* thousand
penna, ae *f.* wing, feather
recēdō, ere, cessī, cessus depart, withdraw
rōscidus, a, um dewy
secō, āre, uī, ctus cut, cleave, slice
sōl, sōlis *m.* sun; day
solvō, ere, ī, solūtus loose(n), free, pay
suprā above, over (+ *acc.*)
ūnā *adv.* together, at the same time
varius, a, um varied, different, diverse

---

701. The rainbow. **adversō sōle:** abl. abls. denoting cause.

702–3. Hunc (crīnem). ego . . . iussa (ā Iūnōne). istō = **tuō,** as often.

705. in ventōs: the soul was identified with the breath, **anima, spīritus** (cf. the English word *spirit*) and at death vanished into the air.

Selections from
—BOOK 6—

Funeris heu tibi causa fui? (6.458)

Illustration for Book 6
"Was I the cause?" by Thom Kapheim

Book 6.295–332

295   *Hinc via Tartareī quae fert Acherontis ad undās.*
       Turbidus hīc caenō vastāque vorāgine gurges
       aestuat atque omnem Cōcytō ēructat harēnam.
       Portitor hās horrendus aquās et flūmina servat
       terribilī squālōre Charōn, cui plūrima mentō
300   *cānitiēs inculta iacet, stant lūmina flammā,*

Acherōn, ontis *m.* river of Hades
aestuō (1) boil, seethe, rage
aqua, ae *f.* water
caenum, ī *n.* mud, filth, slime
cānitiēs, ēī *f.* grayness, gray hair
Charōn, ontis *m.* ferryman of souls of the
   dead across the river Styx
Cōcytus, ī *m.* river of Hades
ēructō (1) vomit, belch (forth)
flūmen, inis *n.* river, stream, flood
gurges, itis *m.* whirlpool, abyss, gulf
harēna, ae *f.* sand, beach

horrendus, a, um horrifying, dire,
   awesome
iaceō, ēre, uī, itus lie (low, outspread)
incultus, a, um wild, unkempt, shaggy
mentum, ī *n.* chin, beard
portitor, ris *m.* ferryman
squālor, ōris *m.* filth, squalor
Tartareus, a, um of or concerning Tartarus,
   abode of the wicked and impious in Hades
terribilis, e dreadful, terrible
turbidus, a, um wild, turbid, thick
vorāgō, inis *f.* whirlpool, whirling water

295–332. Seeking his father Anchises,
Aeneas enters the underworld with the
guidance of the Sybil. They now approach
the river Styx.

295. Hinc: Aeneas has just passed through
the entrance to Hades and has seen all the
monsters dwelling there. **via (est). Acheron-
tis:** the name of the river is derived from the
Gk. verb meaning *grieve*.

296–97. caenō: abl. of specification.
vastāque vorāgine: abl. of specification or
description. **Cōcytō:** dat. of direction; App.
306. The name of the river, derived from the
Gk. verb meaning *lament*, is ONOMATOPOETIC.

298–99. terribilī squālōre: abl. of speci-
fication or description with **horrendus. cui:**
dat. of reference, here close to dat. of posses-
sion. **mentō:** abl. of place where.

300. stant lūmina flammā: *his fixed gaze
is lit with fire.*

sordidus *ex umerīs* nōdō dēpendet amictus.
Ipse ratem contō subigit *vēlīsque ministrat*
et ferrūgineā subvectat *corpora* cumbā,
iam senior, *sed* crūda *deō* viridis*que* senectūs.

305   *Hūc omnis* turba *ad* rīpās effūsa *ruēbat,*
       mātrēs atque virī dēfūncta*que corpora vītā*
       magnanimum hērōum, *puerī* innūptae*que* puellae,
       impositī*que* rogīs iuvenēs *ante ōra parentum:*
       quam *multa in silvīs* autumnī frīgore *primō*
310   *lāpsa* cadunt folia, *aut ad terram* gurgite *ab altō*

---

amictus, ūs *m.* cloak, robe
autumnus, ī *m.* autumn, fall
cadō, ere, cecidī, cāsus fall, fail, sink, die
contus, ī *m.* pole, pike
crūdus, a, um raw, fresh; bloody
cumba, ae *f.* skiff, boat
dēfungor, ī, fūnctus perform, finish (+ *abl.*)
dēpendeō, ēre hang (down), depend
effundō, ere, fūdī, fūsus pour out
ferrūgineus, a, um rusty (in color), dusky
folium, (i)ī *n.* leaf, foliage
frīgus, oris *n.* cold, frost, chill
gurges, itis *m.* whirlpool, abyss, gulf
hērōs, ōis *m.* hero, mighty warrior
imponō, ere, posuī, positus place upon, set to, impose (+ *dat.*)
innūptus, a, um unmarried, virgin

iuvenis, is *m.* (*f.*) youth, young man or woman
magnanimus, a, um great-souled
ministrō (1) tend, serve, supply
nōdus, ī *m.* knot, node; fold, coil
puella, ae *f.* girl
quam how, than, as
ratis, is *f.* raft, ship, boat
rīpa, ae *f.* bank, shore
rogus, ī *m.* and **rogum, ī** *n.* funeral pyre
senectūs, ūtis *f.* old age
senior, ōris *m.* old (aged) man, sire
sordidus, a, um dirty, filthy, squalid
subigō, ere, ēgī, āctus push, force; subdue
subvectō (1) bear, convey, transport
turba, ae *f.* mob, crowd
viridis, e green, fresh, vigorous

---

301. nōdō: abl. of means or manner.

302–3. contō: abl. of means with **subigit. vēlīs:** abl. of means with **ministrat. ferrūgineā cumbā:** abl. of means with **subvectat.**

304. deō: dat. of possession.

305–8. mātrēs . . . virī . . . corpora . . . hērōum, puerī . . . puellae, . . . iuvenēs: six separate nouns are used to capture the inclusivity of Hades: all of the dead are here, and there are many of them. Each group of three

creates a TRICOLON CRESCENS. **mātrēs:** mothers are singled out, but the noun can also be used more generally of women. **vītā:** abl. with **dēfūncta;** App. 342. **magnanim(ōr)um.**

309–12. A double SIMILE. The comparison of the dead souls to leaves and birds brings out their lightness and motility, and also hints at the chill permeating the underworld. **quam multa:** *as many as.* **frīgore prīmō:** abl. of time or cause.

quam *multae* glomerantur avēs, *ubi* frīgidus annus
trāns pontum fugat *et terrīs* immittit aprīcīs.
Stābant ōrantēs *primī* trānsmittere cursum
tendēbantque manūs rīpae ulteriōris amōre.

315 Nāvita *sed tristis nunc hōs nunc* accipit illōs,
ast *aliōs* longē summōtōs arcet harēnā.
Aenēās mīrātus enim *mōtusque* tumultū
"Dīc," ait, "ō virgō, *quid vult* concursus ad amnem?
Quidve petunt animae? *Vel quō* discrīmine rīpās

320 hae linquunt, *illae rēmīs* vada līvida verrunt?"

---

amnis, is *m.* river, stream, torrent
annus, ī *m.* year
aprīcus, a, um sunny, sun-loving
arceō, ēre, uī keep off, defend, restrain
avis, is *f.* bird, fowl
concursus, ūs *m.* throng, crowd
discrīmen, inis, *n.* distinction; crisis
enim *adv.* for, indeed, truly
frīgidus, a, um cold, chill, frigid
fugō (1) put to flight, rout
glomerō (1) roll together, gather, collect
harēna, ae *f.* sand, beach
immittō, ere, mīsī, missus let in, send
   in(to), loose(n), give freely (+ *dat.*)
linquō, ere, līquī, lictus leave, desert
līvidus, a, um blue, dark, livid

longē *adv.* far (off, from), at a distance
mīror, ārī, ātus wonder at, admire
nāvita, ae, *m.* sailor, boatman
ōrō (1) beseech, pray (for), entreat
pontus, ī *m.* sea, waves
quam how, than, as
rīpa, ae *f.* bank, shore
summoveō, ēre, mōvī, mōtus remove
trāns across, beyond (+ *acc.*)
trānsmittō, ere, mīsī, missus cross, send
   across
tumultus, ūs *m.* tumult, uprising, clamor
ulterior, ius farther, further, beyond
vadum, ī *n.* shallow(s), shoal, depth(s)
verrō, ere, verrī, versus sweep (over)
virgō, inis *f.* girl, maid(en)

---

313. ōrantēs prīmī (esse). (sē) trānsmittere: poetic use of the infinitive with **ōrō** instead of an indir. command (**ut/nē** + subjunctive), = **ut trānsmitterent. cursum:** acc. with **trāns(mittere)**; App. 308, *a*.

314. rīpae ulteriōris: objective gen. **amōre:** abl. of cause.

315. nunc hōs nunc accipit illōs: ANAPHORA and ASYNDETON underscore Charon's constant vigilance when faced with the unceasing approach of souls.

316. harēnā: abl. of separation with **arcet**.
317. tumultū: abl. of means.
318. quid vult concursus ad amnem: *how does the gathering at the river want [to be understood]?*, i.e., what does it mean?
319. quō discrīmine: abl. of means.
320. hae ... illae: Aeneas points to the different groups of souls. **rēmīs:** abl. of means.

Ollī sīc breviter *fāta* *est* longaeva sacerdōs:
"*Anchīsā* generāte, *deum* certissima prōlēs,
Cōcȳtī stāgna *alta vidēs* Stygiam*que* palūdem,
dī cuius iūrāre timent *et* fallere *nūmen.*
325   *Haec omnis, quam cernis,* inops inhumāta*que* turba *est*;
portitor *ille* Charōn; *hī, quōs* vehit *unda,* sepultī.
Nec rīpās *datur* horrendās *et* rauca fluenta
trānsportāre prius quam *sēdibus* ossa quiērunt.

---

breviter *adv.* shortly, briefly, concisely
certus, a, um fixed, sure, certain, reliable
Charōn, ontis *m.* ferryman of souls of the dead across the river Styx
Cōcȳtus, ī *m.* river of Hades
fallō, ere, fefellī, falsus deceive, cheat, mock, beguile, escape the notice (of)
fluentum, ī *n.* stream, flood
generō (1) beget, bear
horrendus, a, um horrifying, dire, awesome
inhumātus, a, um unburied
inops, opis needy, destitute, bereft (of)
iūrō (1) take an oath, swear, conspire
longaevus, a, um aged, very old
os, ossis *n.* bone
palūs, ūdis *f.* swamp, marsh

portitor, ōris *m.* ferryman
prius *adv.* former(ly), sooner, first, before
prōlēs, is *f.* progeny, offspring
quam *adv.* how, than, as
quiēscō, ere, quiēvī, quiētus rest, calm, cease
raucus, a, um hoarse, sounding, clanging
rīpa, ae *f.* bank, shore
sacerdōs, dōtis *m.* (*f.*) priest(ess)
sepeliō, īre, īvī, sepultus bury, inter
stagnum, ī *n.* still waters, depth
Stygius, a, um Stygian, of the Styx, a river in Hades
timeō, ēre, uī fear, dread, be anxious
trānsportō (1) carry across, transport
turba, ae *f.* mob, crowd
vehō, ere, vēxī, vectus carry, convey

---

321. Ollī: an archaic dat., = **illī.**
322. Anchīsā: abl. of separation with **generāte. de(ōr)um.**
323. Stygiam . . . palūdem: i.e., the river Styx, the name of which is derived from the Gk. verb meaning *hate.*
324. cuius . . . nūmen: nūmen is a special acc. used in the formula for oath-taking: *the Styx, [on] the divine power of which the gods fear to swear and to deceive.* **iūrāre timent et fallere:** the gods are fearful of swearing on the Styx if they in fact intend to deceive the person(s) before whom they swear.

326. portitor ille Charōn (est). sepultī (sunt).
327. Nec . . . datur (Charontī). rīpās . . . et . . . fluenta: acc. with **trāns(portāre),** App. 308, *a.*
328. prius quam: the combination creates the conjunction *before,* although the two words can be separated by HYPERBATON; when juxtaposed, they are sometimes written as one word (**priusquam**). **sēdibus:** abl. of place where. **quiē(vē)runt.**

Centum *errant* annōs volitant*que haec lītora circum;*
330   *tum* dēmum admissī stāgna exoptāta revīsunt."
Cōnstitit *Anchīsā* satus *et* vestīgia pressit
multa putāns sortem*que animō* miserātus inīquam.

---

admittō, ere, mīsī, missus admit
annus, ī *m.* year, season
centum *indecl.* hundred
cōnsistō, ere, stitī, stitus stand (fast), rest, stop, settle
dēmum *adv.* at length, finally
exoptō (1) choose, desire, hope (for)
inīquus, a, um unfair, unjust, hostile
miseror, ārī, ātus pity, commiserate

premō, ere, pressī, pressus (re)press
putō (1) think, suppose, consider
revīsō, ere revisit, see again, return to
serō, ere, sēvī, satus sow, beget
sors, sortis *f.* lot, destiny, portion, oracle
stagnum, ī *n.* still waters, depth
vestīgium, (i)ī *n.* track, (foot)print, step, trace
volitō (1) fly, speed, flit, flutter

---

329. haec lītora circum: ANASTROPHE for **circum haec lītora.**
331. Anchīsā: abl. of separation with **satus.** **(com)pressit** or **(re)pressit.**

332. animō: abl. of place where.

Book 6.384–425

Ergō iter inceptum peragunt fluviō*que* propinquant.
385   Nāvita *quōs iam* inde *ut* Stygiā prōspexit *ab undā*
per tacitum nemus *īre pedemque* advertere rīpae,
sīc prior adgreditur *dictīs atque* increpat ultrō:
" Quisquis *es*, armātus *quī nostra ad* flūmina *tendis*,
fāre age, quid veniās, iam istinc *et* comprime gressum.
390   *Umbrārum hic locus est, somnī noctisque* sopōrae:

---

adgredior, ī, gressus attack, address,
     approach
advertō, ere, advertī, adversus turn to,
     heed
armō (1) arm, equip, furnish
comprimō, ere, pressī, pressus (re)press
ergō *adv.* therefore, then, consequently
flūmen, inis *n.* river, stream, flood
fluvius, (i)ī *m.* river, stream
gressus, ūs *m.* step, walk, course, gait
istinc from there (where you are)
iter, itineris *n.* way, road, journey, route
incipiō, ere, cēpī, ceptus begin, undertake
increpō, āre, uī, itus reprove, chide
inde *adv.* thence, afterward, thereupon
nāvita, ae *m.* sailor, boatman

nemus, oris *n.* grove, wood
peragō, ere, ēgī, āctus accomplish, finish,
     traverse
prior, ius sooner, former, first, prior
propinquō (1) approach, draw near (+ *dat.*)
prospiciō, ere, spexī, spectus look out
     on, see
quisquis, quidquid (quicquid) *indef. pron.;*
     quisquis, quodquod *indef. adj.* whoever,
     whatever
rīpa, ae *f.* bank, shore
sopōrus, a, um sleepy, causing slumber
Stygius, a, um Stygian, of the Styx, a river
     in Hades
tacitus, a, um silent, noiseless, secret
ultrō *adv.* further, voluntarily

384–425. After encountering the soul of
his unburied helmsman Palinurus and
promising him burial, Aeneas proceeds in
the company of the Sibyl.

385. Nāvita: Charon. **quōs = eōs** (i.e.,
Aeneas and the Sibyl), subject of **īre** and **ad-**
vertere in the indir. stmt. following **prōspexit.**
ut . . . prōspexit: temporal clause; App. 368.

386. rīpae: dat. of direction.
388. Quisquis es: although Charon sees
two figures approaching, he addresses only
the one whose presence is not expected.
armātus quī: ANASTROPHE.
389. fāre: imperat. **age:** a second imperat.
that emphasizes the first: *come now, speak.*
quid veniās: indir. quest.

corpora vīva nefās Stygiā vectāre carīnā.
Nec vērō Alcīdēn mē sum laetātus *euntem*
accēpisse lacū, *nec* Thēsea Pīrithoümque,
dīs quamquam genitī *atque* invictī *vīribus essent.*

395   Tartareum *ille manū* custōdem *in* vincla petīvit
ipsius ā soliō *rēgis trāxitque* trementem;
hī dominam Dītis thalamō dēdūcere adortī."

---

adorior, īrī, ortus attempt, attack
Alcīdēs, ae *m.* patronymic (meaning
   "descendant of Alceus") for Hercules, son
   of Jupiter and Alcmena
carīna, ae *f.* keel; ship, boat
custōs, ōdis *m.* guard(ian), sentinel
dēdūcō, ere, dūxī, ductus lead off, abduct
Dīs, Dītis *m.* Pluto, god of Hades
domina, ae *f.* mistress, queen
gignō, ere, genuī, genitus bear, produce,
   beget
invictus, a, um unconquered, invincible
lacus, ūs *m.* lake, marsh
laetor, ārī, ātus rejoice, exult
nefās *n. indecl.* impiety, unspeakable thing,
   crime
Pīrithoüs, ī *m.* Greek hero who descended
   to Hades with his friend Theseus to carry
   off Proserpina

quamquam although, and yet, however
solium, (i)ī *n.* throne, seat
Stygius, a, um Stygian, of the Styx, a river
   in Hades
Tartareus, a, um of or concerning
   Tartarus, abode of the wicked and
   impious in Hades
thalamus, ī *m.* marriage chamber,
   bedroom
Thēseus, eī (eos) *acc.* ea *m.* mythical
   king of Athens who, among his other
   exploits, descended to Hades with his
   friend Pirithoüs to carry off Proserpina
tremō, ere, tremuī tremble, quiver,
   shake
vectō (1) convey, carry, bear
vērō *adv.* truly, indeed, but
vinc(u)lum, ī *n.* chain, bond, cable
vīvus, a, um living, natural, alive

---

391. nefās (est).

392. Nec . . . sum laetātus: LITOTES. According to Servius, Charon was punished when he helped another hero cross the Styx; he is not eager to be punished again. **Alcīdēn . . . euntem** = Hercules, whose name cannot be used in dactylic hexameter ($- \cup -$). As one of Hercules's celebrated twelve labors, he descended to Hades and carried off Cerberus, the three-headed dog of Pluto, which guarded the entrance to the infernal regions.

393. lacū: abl. of place where. **Thēsea Pīrithoümque:** Theseus went to the underworld together with his friend Pirithoüs, hoping to carry off Proserpina; instead, he was caught and trapped there by Hades, who imprisoned him in a stone seat. In some versions of this tale, when Hercules came to the

underworld he rescued Theseus and brought him back to the surface of the earth; but Vergil will later locate Theseus (and, presumably, Pirithoüs) still trapped in the underworld (6.617–20).

394. quamquam . . . essent: concessive clause; the indicative is usual with **quamquam**, and the subjunctive here suggests the influence of patterns common with other concessive conjs. **vīribus:** abl. of specification.

395. ille: *the former,* i.e., Hercules. **in vinc(u)la petīvit = petīvit ut vinclīs caperet. custōdem:** Cerberus.

396. ipsius . . . rēgis: Pluto.

397. hī: *the latter,* i.e., Theseus and Pirithoüs. **dominam:** Proserpina. **Dītis:** possessive gen. modifying either **dominam** or **thalamō. adortī (sunt).**

Quae contrā breviter *fāta est* Amphrȳsia *vātēs*:
"*Nūllae hīc* īnsidiae *tālēs* (absiste *movērī*),
400   *nec vim tēla ferunt*; licet *ingēns* iānitor antrō
aeternum lātrāns exsanguēs terreat *umbrās*,
casta licet patruī *servet* Prōserpina *līmen*.
Trōius *Aenēās*, pietāte īnsignis *et armīs*,
ad genitōrem īmās Erebī dēscendit *ad umbrās*.
405   *Sī tē nūlla movet tantae* pietātis imāgō,
at rāmum *hunc*" (aperit rāmum *quī* veste latēbat)
"agnōscās." Tumida *ex īrā tum* corda resīdunt;

---

absistō, ere, stitī cease, stop
aeternus, a, um eternal, everlasting
agnōscō, ere, nōvī, itus recognize
Amphrȳsius, a, um Amphrysian,
  of Amphrysus, a river in Thessaly
  frequented by Apollo
antrum, ī *n.* cave, cavern, grotto
aperiō, īre, uī, ertus open, disclose,
  reveal
breviter *adv.* shortly, briefly, concisely
castus, a, um pure, holy, chaste
contrā opposite, facing, against (+ acc.);
  adv. opposite, facing, in reply
cor, cordis *n.* heart, spirit, feelings
dēscendō, ere, dēscendī, dēscēnsus
  descend
Erebus, ī *m.* underworld, Hades
exsanguis, e bloodless, lifeless, pale
iānitor, ōris *m.* doorkeeper

imāgō, inis *f.* likeness, image, ghost, soul,
  form
īnsidiae, ārum *f.* snare, ambush, treachery
īnsignis, e distinguished, marked, splendid
lateō, ēre, uī lie hid, hide, lurk, escape the
  notice (of)
latrō (1) bark, howl, bay
licet, ēre, uit, itum it is permitted
patruus, ī *m.* paternal uncle
pietās, ātis *f.* loyalty, devotion, (sense of)
  duty
Prōserpina, ae *f.* wife of Pluto and queen
  of the underworld
rāmus, ī *m.* branch, bough, limb
resīdō, ere, sēdī sit down
terreō, ēre, uī, itus frighten, terrify
Trōius, a, um Trojan
tumidus, a, um swollen, swelling
vestis, is *f.* garment, cloth(ing), robe

---

398. Quae = haec. Amphrȳsia vātēs: through a learned reference to the river Amphrysus, Vergil associates the Sibyl with Apollo. The Amphrysus is a river in Thessaly; on its shores Apollo is said to have shepherded the flocks of the mortal Admetus.

399. Nūllae ... īnsidiae (sunt).

400–402. licet ... (ut) terreat ... (ut) servet: the omission of **ut** with **licet** is frequent.

aeternum: cognate acc. with **lātrāns**; translate adverbially. **patruī:** Proserpina is married to Pluto, brother of her father, Jupiter.

406. rāmum: the golden bough; earlier in Book 6, the Sibyl had instructed Aeneas to find this and he had plucked it and brought it back to her (136–48, 187–211).

407. agnōscās: subjunctive used for a polite command instead of imperat.

nec plūra hīs. Ille admīrāns venerābile *dōnum*
fātālis virgae *longō* post *tempore vīsum*
410   caeruleam advertit *puppim* rīpae*que* propinquat.
Inde *aliās animās, quae per* iuga *longa* sedēbant,
dēturbat laxat*que* forōs; *simul accipit* alveō
ingentem Aenēān. Gemuit *sub* pondere cumba
sūtilis *et multam accēpit* rīmōsa palūdem.
415   *Tandem* trāns fluvium incolumēs *vātemque virumque*
īnformī līmō glaucā*que* expōnit *in* ulvā.
Cerberus *haec ingēns* lātrātū *rēgna* trifaucī
personat adversō recubāns *immānis in* antrō.

---

admīror, ārī, ātus wonder (at), admire
adversus, a, um opposite, facing
advertō, ere, advertī, adversus turn to,
  heed
alveus, ī *m.* hollow; boat; trough
antrum, ī *n.* cave, cavern, grotto
caeruleus, a, um dark (blue)
Cerberus, ī *m.* monstrous three-headed
  dog in Hades
cumba, ae *f.* skiff, boat
dēturbō (1) drive off, dislodge
expōnō, ere place out, (cause to) disembark
fātālis, e fatal, deadly, fated, fateful
fluvius, (i)ī *m.* river, stream
forus, ī *m.* gangway, deck (of a boat)
gemō, ere, uī, itus groan (for), lament
glaucus, a, um gray, grayish-green,
  gleaming
incolumis, e safe, unharmed, intact
inde *adv.* thence, afterward, thereupon
informis, e shapeless, hideous

iugum, ī *n.* yoke, (mountain) ridge
lātrātus, ūs *m.* bark(ing), howl(ing)
laxō (1) loosen, free, open, release
limus, ī *m.* slime, mud, mire
palūs, ūdis *f.* swamp, marsh
personō (1) sound through, make (re)
  sound
pondus, eris *n.* weight, burden
post after, behind (+ *acc.*); *adv.* afterward,
  next
propinquō (1) draw near, approach (+ *dat.*)
recubō, āre recline, lie
rīmōsus, a, um leaky, full of cracks
rīpa, ae *f.* bank, shore
sedeō, ēre, sēdī, sessus sit, settle
sūtilis, e sewn, with seams
trāns across, beyond (+ *acc.*)
trifaux, faucis three-throated
ulva, ae *f.* sedge, marsh grass
venerābilis, e venerable, causing awe
virga, ae *f.* staff, wand, twig

---

408. Nec plūra (dicta sunt *or* **dixērunt).**
hīs: abl. of comparison.

411. iuga: the word usually denotes a long
ridge or spine, but here indicates the *benches*
on Charon's boat.

412. alveō: SYNIZESIS allows this word to
be read as a spondee.

414. sūtilis: the boat is sewn together from
animal skins or tree bark.

415. līmō glaucāque . . . in ulvā: both
nouns are objs. of **in** (ANASTROPHE).

Cui vātēs horrēre *vidēns iam* colla colubrīs
420   melle sopōrātam *et* medicātīs frūgibus offam
obicit. *Ille* famē rabidā tria guttura pandēns
corripit obiectam, *atque immānia* terga resolvit
fūsus humī *tōtōque ingēns* extenditur antrō.
Occupat *Aenēās* aditum custōde sepultō
425   ēvādit*que* celer rīpam inremeābilis *undae.*

---

aditus, ūs *m.* approach, entrance, access
antrum, ī *n.* cave, cavern, grotto
celer, eris, ere swift, speedy, quick
collum, ī *n.* neck
coluber, brī *m.* snake, serpent
corripiō, ere, uī, reptus seize, snatch up
custōs, ōdis *m. (f.)* guard(ian), keeper
ēvādō, ere, ēvāsī, ēvāsus go forth (from),
    escape, pass over, traverse
extendō, ere, extendī, extensus (or
    extentus) stretch out, extend, increase
famēs, is *f.* hunger
frūx, frūgis *f.* fruit, grain
guttur, uris *n.* throat, gullet
horreō, ēre, uī bristle, shudder, tremble
humus, ī *f.* ground, soil, earth
inremeābilis, e from which there is no
    return, irretraceable

medicō (1) drug, medicate
mel, mellis *n.* honey
obicio, ere, iēcī, iectus present, place
    before
occupō (1) seize (beforehand), occupy
offa, ae *f.* morsel, cake
pandō, ere, pandī, passus spread, open,
    loosen
rabidus, a, um raving, mad, frenzied
resolvō, ere, resolvī, resolūtus loose(n),
    free, pay, unravel
rīpa, ae *f.* bank, shore
sepeliō, īre, sepelīvī (iī), sepultus bury,
    inter
sopōrō (1) make drowsy, drug
tergum, ī *n.* back, body, rear
trēs, tria three

---

419. horrēre: inf. in indir. stmt. after
vidēns; its subject is **colla**.
420. melle, medicātīs frūgibus: both abl.
of means.
421. obicit: the Sibyl's swift action is re-
flected by ENJAMBMENT. Note the length
of the first syllable of **obicit**: although the
vowel **o**- is short by nature here, the syllable
is lengthened by the consonantal vowel with
which the stem of the verb begins: **ob(i)icit**

< **ob** + **iaciō. famē rabidā:** abl. of cause or
description.
422. obiectam (offam).
423. humī: locative. **tōtō . . . antrō:** abl.
of place where.
424. custōde sepultō: abl. abs. The meta-
phorical use of **sepelīre** is humorous here.
425. inremeābilis: a rare word, coined
by Vergil; it is based on the verb **remeāre,** *to
come or go back.*

Book 6.450–476

450 *Inter quās* Phoenissa recēns *ā vulnere Dīdō*
errābat silvā in magnā; quam Trōius hērōs
ut prīmum iuxtā *stetit* agnōvit*que per umbrās*
obscūram, quālem *prīmō quī surgere* mēnse
aut videt aut vīdisse putat per nūbila lūnam,
455 *dēmīsit lacrimās* dulcī*que* adfātus *amōre est:*
"Īnfēlīx Dīdō, vērus *mihi* nuntius ergō

---

adfor, ārī, ātus address, accost
agnōscō, ere, nōvī, nitus recognize
dēmittō, mittere, mīsī, missus send down,
    let fall, drop, lower
dulcis, e sweet, dear, fond
ergō *adv.* therefore, then, consequently
hērōs, ōis *m.* hero, mighty warrior
iuxtā near, next, close to (+ *acc.*)
lūna, ae *f.* moon, moonlight
mēnsis, is *m.* month

nūbilum, ī *n.* cloud, cloudiness
nuntius, (i)ī *m.* messenger, message
obscūrus, a, um dark, obscure, dim
Phoenissa, ae *f.* Phoenician (woman), Dido
putō (1) think, suppose, consider
quālis, e (such) as, of what sort
recēns, entis recent, fresh
Trōius, a, um Trojan, of Troy
vērus, a, um true, real, genuine
vulnus, eris *n.* wound, deadly blow

450–76. Among those who have died for love Aeneas sees the shade of Dido. He attempts to defend his sudden departure from Carthage, but she scornfully turns away and returns to Sychaeus, her first husband.

450. Inter quās: Dido is the last in a list of mythical females about whose sad deaths we are reminded as Aeneas observes them in the underworld. Translate **quās** as a demonstrative, *these women*. **recēns ā vulnere:** *recentī vulnere* (*with a fresh wound*) would be more natural in English; but Vergil wants to emphasize not only the freshness of Dido's

wound, but also her very recent arrival in the underworld.

451. quam: with **iuxtā** and understood with **agnōvit** in 452.

453–54. This SIMILE comparing Dido to the elusive new moon merits comparison to that with which we (and Aeneas) were introduced to her at 1.498–502.

455. amōre: abl. of manner.

456. nuntius: we may well wonder how this message was delivered to Aeneas; it has not been mentioned before. At the beginning of Book 5, Vergil tells us only that the Trojans see flames in Carthage as they sail off, and that thoughts of what a woman scorned may do lead them to ominous suspicions.

vēnerat exstinctam *ferrōque* extrēma *secūtam?*
Fūneris *heu tibi* causa *fuī? Per sīdera* iūrō,
per superōs et sī qua fidēs *tellūre sub īmā est,*

460   invītus, *rēgīna, tuō dē lītore* cessī.
Sed mē iussa *deum, quae nunc hās īre per umbrās,*
per loca senta situ cōgunt *noctemque* profundam,
imperiīs ēgēre suīs; nec crēdere quīvī
hunc tantum tibi mē discessū *ferre* dolōrem.

465   Siste gradum *tēque* aspectū *nē* subtrahe *nostrō.*
Quem fugis? Extrēmum *fātō quod tē* adloquor *hoc est."*
Tālibus Aenēās ardentem *et* torva tuentem
lēnībat *dictīs animum lacrimāsque* ciēbat.
Illa solō fixōs *oculōs* āversa *tenēbat*

---

adloquor, ī, locūtus address, accost
a(d)spectus, ūs *m.* sight, vision, aspect
āvertō, ere, ī, rsus turn away, avert
causa, ae *f.* cause, reason, occasion
cēdō, ere, cessī, cessus yield, depart
cieō, ēre, cīvī, citus stir (up), (a)rouse
cōgō, ere, coēgī, coāctus force (together)
crēdō, ere, didī, ditus believe, trust (+ *dat.*)
discessus, ūs *m.* departure, separation
dolor, ōris *m.* grief, pain, passion, anger
exstinguō, ere, īnxī, īnctus quench,
    destroy, extinguish
extrēma, ōrum *n.* end, death, funeral
extrēmus, a, um final, last, utmost
fidēs, eī *f.* faith, honor, pledge
fīgō, ere, xī, xus fasten, fix, pierce

fūnus, eris *n.* funeral, death, disaster
gradus, ūs *m.* step, gait, pace, stride
invītus, a, um unwilling, reluctant
iūrō (1) swear (by), take oath
iussum, ī *n.* command, order, behest
lēniō, īre, īvī, ītus soften, soothe, calm
profundus, a, um deep, profound, vast
queō, quīre, īvī (iī), ītus be able, can
sentus, a, um rough, thorny
sistō, ere, stetī, status stay, stop
situs, ūs *m.* position; neglect; decay
solum, ī *n.* ground, earth, soil
subtrahō, ere, trāxī, tractus withdraw
torvus, a, um fierce, grim, lowering
tueor, ērī, itus (tūtus) look (at), watch

**457. (tē) exstinctam (esse). extrēma (=
mortem) secutam (esse).**
    461. iussa de(ōr)um: see 4.237 and 270.
    466. Extrēmum: *this is the last (word,* or
speech) I shall address to you. **quod:** cognate
acc. **hoc:** pronounce **hocc,** making a long syl-
lable. **hoc est:** it is unusual, to say the least, to
conclude a line with two monosyllables; their
appearance here, though perhaps inelegant, is
certainly emphatic.
    467. torva: neut. acc. pl. used adverbi-
ally, probably in imitation of the similar Gk.
construction.

467–68. tuentem … animum: the expres-
sion is unusually contorted—how can one's
mind or *anger* be imagined as *watching?* Vergil
implies that Dido is effectively consumed by
her anger—it is all that remains of her.
    468. lēnībat = lēniēbat, which could not
be used in hexameter ($- \cup - \cup$). It has a co-
native meaning here, *he tried to soothe;* App.
351, 2, *a.*

470 *nec* magis inceptō vultum sermōne *movētur*
     quam *sī* dūra silex *aut stet* Marpēsia cautēs.
     Tandem corripuit *sēsē atque* inimīca refūgit
     in nemus umbriferum, *coniūnx ubi* prīstinus *illī*
     respondet *cūrīs* aequat*que* Sychaeus *amōrem.*
475 *Nec* minus *Aenēās* cāsū concussus inīquō
     prōsequitur *lacrimīs* longē *et* miserātur *euntem.*

---

aequō (1) equal(ize), match, level
cāsus, ūs *m.* chance, (mis)fortune
cautēs, is *f.* rock, cliff, crag
concutiō, ere, cussī, cussus shake, shatter,
   agitate
corripiō, ere, uī, reptus snatch (up, away)
dūrus, a, um hard(y), harsh, stern
incipiō, ere, cēpī, ceptus begin, undertake
inimīcus, a, um hostile, unfriendly
inīquus, a, um unjust, harsh, uneven
longē *adv.* (from) afar, at a distance
magis *adv.* more, rather
Marpēs(s)ius, a, um of Marpe(s)sus, a
   mountain on the island of Paros famous
   for its white marble

minus *adv.* less
miseror, ārī, ātus pity, commiserate
nemus, oris *n.* (sacred) grove, forest
prīstinus, a, um ancient, former
prōsequor, ī, secūtus follow, attend
quam *adv.* how, than, as
refugiō, ere, fūgī flee (away), shun
respondeō, ēre, ī, ōnsus answer;
   sympathize with
sermō, ōnis *m.* conversation, speech
silex, icis *m.* (*f.*) flint, rock, crag
Sychaeus, ī *m.* deceased husband of Dido
umbrifer, era, erum shady
vultus, ūs *m.* countenance, face, aspect

---

470. vultum: acc. of respect; App. 311.
sermōne: the word is ironic, since it suggests conversation; yet Dido does not respond.
471. Marpēsia cautēs: Marpessus on the Greek island of Paros was renowned as a source of fine marble for sculpture.

473. umbriferum: the double meaning is active here: the underworld is filled with both gloom and the shades of the dead. **ubi:** the conjunction has been postponed. **illī:** dat. of reference.
475. cāsū (Dīdōnis).
476. prōsequitur et miserātur (eam).

Book 6.847–899

"Excūdent *aliī* spīrantia mollius aera
(crēdō equidem), vīvōs *dūcent dē* marmore vultūs,
ōrābunt causās melius, *caelīque* meātūs
850   dēscrībent radiō *et surgentia sīdera dīcent:*
tū regere *imperiō* populōs, Rōmāne, mementō

---

aes, aeris *n.* bronze
causa, ae *f.* cause, case (at law)
crēdō, ere, didī, ditus believe, suppose
dēscrībō, ere, psī, ptus mark out, map
equidem *adv.* indeed, truly, surely
excūdō, ere, ī, sus hammer out, fashion
marmor, oris *n.* marble
meātus, ūs *m.* course, path, motion
melior, ius better, superior, finer
meminī, isse remember (+ *gen.*)

molliter *adv.* softly, gently, gracefully
ōrō (1) pray (for), entreat, plead, argue
populus, ī *m.* people, nation
radius, (i)ī *m.* rod, spoke, compass
regō, ere, rēxī, rēctus rule, guide, direct
Rōmānus, a, um Roman, of Rome
spīrō (1) breathe, blow, live, quiver
vīvus, a, um living, alive, natural
vultus, ūs *m.* countenance, face, aspect

847–99. Anchises, displaying to Aeneas a parade of Roman heroes in the underworld, pauses to reflect on Rome's destiny as a military and political power. The two culminating figures in the parade are the elder Marcellus and the younger Marcellus, to the latter of whom Anchises devotes a lengthy and emotional description. Their tour of the underworld concludes with a review of the tasks still awaiting Aeneas. Aeneas and the Sibyl then depart; Aeneas and his companions set sail once more.

told in the *Aeneid* as a whole. This instance of PROLEPSIS is worth considering from several perspectives: from the point of view of both Anchises and Aeneas, the events and characters foretold do not yet exist except as a promise of the fates; from the point of view of Vergil and his readers, these events and characters are already reflections of the past. **aliī:** the implied reference here is to the Greeks, whose accomplishments in sculpture, rhetoric, and the sciences are guaranteed by Anchises' prescience. **spīrantia aera:** bronze statues so lifelike that they seem to breathe.

847–48. sculptors, orators.

849–50. astronomers. **dīcent = vocābunt.**

847. Excūdent: Anchises uses the future tense repeatedly in this passage, to describe the great moments in the history of a people which does not yet exist. The entire passage is proleptic—that is, it looks forward in time and outside the frame of the rest of the tale

851. Rōmāne: addressed to the Roman people in general, and to Aeneas in particular—he represents the people whose nation and identity do not yet exist, but are assured by the fates.

(*hae tibi erunt* artēs), pāci*que* impōnere mōrem,
parcere subiectīs *et* dēbellāre superbōs."
    Sīc pater Anchīsēs, atque haec mīrantibus addit:
855 "Aspice, *ut* īnsignis spoliīs Mārcellus opīmīs
    ingreditur *victorque virōs* superēminet *omnēs*.
    Hic rem Rōmānam *magnō* turbante tumultū
    sistet eques, sternet Poenōs Gallum*que* rebellem,

---

addō, ere, didī, ditus add
a(d)spiciō, ere, spexī see, look at
ars, artis *f.* skill
dēbellō (1) exhaust through war, crush
eques, itis *m.* cavalryman, knight, man of
    equestrian rank
Gallus, a, um Gallic, Gaul
impōnō, ere, posuī, positus place on,
    impose, establish
ingredior, ī, gressus step, stride, enter
īnsignis, e distinguished, marked,
    noteworthy
Mārcellus, ī *m.* 1. Marcus Claudius
    Marcellus, d. 208 BCE; famous Roman
    consul, served in both 1st and 2nd Punic
    Wars; 2. Marcus Claudius Marcellus,
    42–23 BCE; son of Octavia, sister of
    Augustus, and first husband of Augustus'
    daughter Julia
mīror, ārī, ātus wonder (at), admire

mōs, mōris *m.* custom, usage, rule, law
opīmus, a, um rich, splendid, sumptuous;
    spolia opīma "spoils of honor," won
    when a Roman general with his own hand
    slew the general of the enemy
parcō, ere, pepercī (parsī), parsus spare
    (+ *dat.*)
pāx, pācis *f.* peace, quiet, repose
Poenus, a, um Phoenician, Carthaginian
rebellis, e rebellious, insurgent
Rōmānus, a, um Roman, of Rome
sistō, ere, stetī, status stop, stand
spolium, (i)ī *m.* spoil, booty, plunder
sternō, ere, strāvī, strātus lay low, strew
subiciō, ere, iēcī, iectus vanquish
superbus, a, um proud, haughty
superēmineō, ēre tower above
tumultus, ūs *m.* tumult, uprising, clamor
turbō (1) confuse, shake, disturb

---

852. hae: attracted into the gender of the
predicate; App. 240, *a*. **pācī:** some editors
prefer **pācis**, gen., instead of the dat. printed
here; but **pācī** makes much better sense with
impōnere, while **pācis** is not supported by
the manuscripts.

854. (Aenēae et Sibyllae) mīrantibus.

855. spoliīs opīmīs: the technical term
in Latin for arms and other booty taken on
the field of battle by the victorious from the
vanquished general, whom he has slain with
his own hand. These were won before by Ro-
mulus early in his kingship and by Cossus in
428 BCE (the latter of these is mentioned at
841), and finally by the elder Marcellus in
222 BCE. When Augustus came to power, he
decreed that, since he had **imperium** and was

effectively commander-in-chief, only he and
his successors could claim the honor hence-
forth. **Mārcellus:** M. Claudius Marcellus,
who served in the First Punic War, was an
outstanding general in the Second Punic War
and was an ancestor of the younger Marcellus
described below.

857. tumultū: the war with the Gauls in
Italy, in which the elder Marcellus had killed
Viridomarus, leader of the Gauls, at Clastidi-
um (222 BCE), and stripping him of his armor
had obtained the third and last **spolia opīma**
(the **tertia arma capta** of 859).

858. eques: *(though but) a man of eques-
trian rank*, though the term also serves as a
reminder that the battle of Clastidium was
waged by cavalry.

tertia*que arma patrī* suspendet *capta* Quirīnō."

860   *Atque hīc Aenēās* (ūnā *namque īre vidēbat*
       ēgrēgium formā iuvenem *et* fulgentibus *armīs,*
       sed frōns *laeta* parum *et* dēiectō *lūmina* vultū)
       "*Quis, pater, ille, virum quī sīc* comitātur *euntem?*
       Fīlius, anne aliquis *magnā dē* stirpe nepōtum?

865   *Quī* strepitus circā *comitum! Quantum īnstar in ipsō!*
       Sed nox ātra caput trīstī circumvolat *umbrā."*
       Tum pater Anchīsēs lacrimīs ingressus obortīs:
       "*Ō gnāte, ingentem* lūctum *nē quaere tuōrum;*

---

aliquis, quid some(one), any(one)
an(ne) *interrog.* whether, or
circā *adv.* around, about
circumvolō (1) fly around, fly about
comitor, ārī, ātus accompany, attend, escort, follow
dēiciō, ere, iēcī, iectus cast down
ēgregius, a, um extraordinary, distinguished
fīlius, (i)ī *m.* son
forma, ae *f.* form, beauty, shape
frōns, frontis *f.* front, forehead, brow
fulg(e)ō, ēre, lsī shine, gleam, glitter
ingredior, ī, gressus stride, begin, enter
īnstar *n. indecl.* likeness, weight, dignity

iuvenis, is *m. (f.)* youth, young (man, woman)
lūctus, ūs *m.* grief, mourning, sorrow
nepōs, ōtis *m.* grandson; descendant
oborior, īrī, ortus arise, spring up
parum *adv.* slightly, too little, not
quantus, a, um so (much, great, many), as
Quirīnus, ī *m.* the deified Romulus as god of war
stirps, pis *f.* stock, lineage
strepitus, ūs *m.* uproar, noise
suspendō, ere, ī, ēnsus hang up
tertius, a, um third
ūnā *adv.* together, at the same time
vultus, ūs *m.* countenance, face, aspect

---

859. suspendet: Vergil introduces another technical term, here part of the vocabulary for making a dedication of spoils to a god by hanging them in (or on) the temple. **Quirīnō:** the name comes as something of a surprise, since the **spolia opīma** were traditionally dedicated not to Quirinus but to Jupiter Feretrius. It is not wise to suppose, however, as some editors have done, that Vergil was confused; it is far more likely that this alteration serves a purpose here—perhaps to bring special honor to Romulus, who as the first winner of **spolia opīma** began the tradition of dedication of Jupiter Feretrius; since upon his death Romulus was deified as Quirinus, Vergil may well intend to remind us here of both divinities associated with the ritual.

860. Aenēās (dīcit). ūnā (cum Mārcellō).

862. frōns (erat). et lūmina (erant) dēiectō vultū: abl. of description, = **et lūmina (erant) dēiecta. lūmina** = **oculī,** as often.

863. virum: i.e., the elder Marcellus. **ille:** the younger M. Claudius Marcellus born in 42 BCE, i.e., the son of Augustus' sister Octavia and husband of Augustus' daughter Julia; Augustus had chosen him to be his successor, but he died in 23 BCE.

864. nepōtum (nostrōrum).

865. strepitus: indicating the future fame and popularity of the younger Marcellus.

867. ingressus (est).

868–86. Ancient tradition reports that these lines were recited by Vergil to Augustus and Octavia, the mother of Marcellus. Octavia is said to have fainted upon hearing the poet's tribute to her son.

868. gnāte: archaic spelling of **nāte.**

ostendent *terrīs hunc* tantum *fāta neque* ultrā
870   *esse sinent.* Nimium *vōbīs* Rōmāna propāgō
vīsa potēns, superī, propria *haec sī dōna fuissent.*
Quantōs *ille virum magnam* Māvortis *ad urbem*
campus aget gemitūs! *Vel quae,* Tiberīne, *vidēbis*
fūnera, *cum* tumulum praeterlābēre recentem!
875   *Nec puer* Īliacā quisquam *dē gente* Latīnōs
in tantum spē tollet avōs, nec Rōmula *quondam*
ūllō sē tantum tellūs iactābit alumnō.
Heu pietās, *heu* prīsca fidēs invicta*que bellō*
dextera! Nōn illī sē quisquam impūne *tulisset*

---

alumnus, ī *m.* nursling, (foster) child
avus, ī *m.* grandfather; ancestor
fidēs, eī *f.* trust, fidelity, pledge
fūnus, eris *n.* funeral, death, disaster
gemitus, ūs *m.* groan(ing), wail(ing)
iactō (1) toss, vaunt, boast
Īliacus, a, um Ilian, Trojan
impūne *adv.* unpunished, with impunity
invictus, a, um unconquered, invincible
Latīnus, a, um Latin, of Latium
Māvors, rtis *m.* Mars, god of war
nimium *adv.* too (much), too great(ly)
ostendō, ere, ī, ntus show, display
pietās, ātis *f.* loyalty, devotion, sense of
   duty, righteousness, nobility
potēns, entis powerful, mighty
praeterlābor, ī, lāpsus glide by

prīscus, a, um ancient, primitive
propāgō, inis *f.* offshoot, offspring
proprius, a, um one's own, special, secure
quantus, a, um how (great, much, many), as
quisquam, quaequam, quidquam any(one,
   thing)
recēns, entis recent, fresh, new
Rōmānus, a, um Roman, of Rome
Rōmulus, a, um of Romulus, Roman
sinō, ere, sīvī, situs permit, allow
spēs, eī *f.* hope, expectation
tantum *adv.* so much, so great(ly), only
Tiberīnus, ī *m.* (god of) the Tiber, river on
   which Rome is situated
tumulus, ī *m.* mound, tomb
ultrā *adv.* beyond, farther

---

869. neque ultrā: Marcellus was only nineteen at the time of his death.

871. vīsa (esset): apodosis in a past contrary-to-fact condition; App. 382. **sī fuissent:** protasis in a past contrary-to-fact condition. **haec dōna:** Marcellus.

872. vir(ōr)um. Māvortis: modifies both **urbem**, since Rome was founded by Romulus, a son of Mars, and **campus** (873), since the part of the city through which the funeral procession would have gone was the flat, open land just north of the ancient city center, known as the **campus Martius** (*field of Mars*). It is on this plain that the populace of Rome would have gathered to witness the funeral.

873. Tiberīne: Anchises addresses the divinity inhabiting the Tiber, anticipating the sympathy that he, in anthropomorphic form, can offer.

874. tumulum: the magnificent mausoleum of Augustus, begun by the emperor in 28 BCE (and probably barely finished at the time of Marcellus' death). Marcellus was the first of what would eventually be many members of the Julio-Claudian clan to be buried here. **praeterlābēre = praeterlābēris.**

876. spē: *by the hope* (of his future greatness).

879. illī = Mārcellō: dat. with **obvius** (880). **tulisset:** apodosis of a contrary-to-fact condition, with the condition itself (the **sī**-clause) implied. If expressed, it would be something like *if he had lived long enough.*

880   obvius armātō, seu *cum pedes īret in* hostem
       seu spūmantis *equī foderet* calcāribus armōs.
       Heu, miserande *puer, sī* quā *fāta* aspera rumpās—
       tū Mārcellus *eris. Manibus date* līlia plēnīs
       purpureōs spargam flōrēs *animamque* nepōtis
885   *hīs* saltem accumulem *dōnīs, et fungar inānī*
       mūnere." Sīc tōtā passim regiōne vagantur
       āeris *in campīs* lātīs *atque omnia* lūstrant.
       Quae postquam *Anchīsēs nātum per* singula *dūxit*

---

accumulō (1) heap up; pile up; honor
āēr, āeris *m.* air, mist, fog
armō (1) arm, equip, furnish
armus, ī *m.* shoulder, flank, side
asper, era, erum rough, harsh, fierce
calcar, āris *n.* spur, goad
flōs, ōris *m.* flower, blossom, bloom
fodiō, ere, fōdī, fossus dig, pierce, spur
fungor, ī, fūnctus perform, fulfil (+ *abl.*)
hostis, is *m.* enemy, foe, stranger
inānis, e empty, useless, unavailing
lātus, a, um wide, broad, spacious
līlium, (i)ī *n.* lily
lūstrō (1) purify; survey; traverse
Mārcellus, ī *m.* 1. Marcus Claudius
   Marcellus, d. 208 BCE; famous Roman
   consul, served in both 1st and 2nd Punic
   Wars; 2. Marcus Claudius Marcellus,
   42–23 BCE; son of Octavia, sister of
   Augustus, and first husband of Augustus'
   daughter Julia

miseror, ārī, ātus pity, commiserate
nepōs, ōtis *m.* grandson; descendant
obvius, a, um meeting (+ *dat.*)
passim *adv.* everywhere, all about
pedes, itis *m.* foot soldier, infantry
plēnus, a, um full, filled, complete
postquam after (that), when
purpureus, a, um purple, crimson,
   bright
quā *adv.* where(by), wherever, in any
   (some) way
regiō, ōnis *f.* district, region, quarter
rumpō, ere, rūpī, ruptus break, burst
   (forth)
saltem *adv.* at least, at any rate
singulī, ae, a each, one by one
sīve, seu or if, whether, or
spargō, ere, rsī, rsus scatter, sprinkle
spūmō (1) foam, froth, spray
vagor, ārī, ātus wander, roam, rove

---

882. sī rumpās: protasis of a future- less-
vivid condition, the apodosis of which is not
expressed; App. 381. The exact interpretation
of this and the following verse has been long
debated. What exactly is Anchises saying?
Some have understood him to mean that the
young man before him will come to merit the
name Marcellus, or will be a "real" Marcellus,
only if he manages to overcome his sad fate;
but many now think it more likely that we
are to imagine here an outburst on Anchises'
part, breaking off with an APOSIOPESIS as he
is overcome by emotion at the sight of the
youth. Anchises is then saying, "You will (i.e.,

must) be Marcellus; oh, if only you were to
break your harsh fate somehow!" **quā (viā).**
883. date: Anchises addresses Aeneas and
the Sibyl; but we may also imagine that
through Anchises Vergil himself is address-
ing his readers.
884–85. purpureōs: a color indicative of
both distinguished rank and deserved honor.
spargam, accumulem, fungar: understand
either as volitive subjunctives; App. 254, or
as subjunctives in a sequence of indir. com-
mands after **date**, with **ut** implied.
   **886. vagantur (Anchīsēs et Aenēās et
Sibylla).**

incendit*que animum fāmae venientis amōre,*
890 exim *bella virō* memorat *quae* deinde gerenda,
Laurentēs*que* docet populōs *urbemque* Latīnī,
et quō quemque modō *fugiatque feratque labōrem.*
Sunt geminae Somnī portae, *quārum* altera *fertur*
cornea, *quā* vērīs facilis *datur* exitus *umbrīs,*
895 altera candentī perfecta nitēns elephantō,
sed falsa *ad caelum mittunt* īnsomnia Mānēs.
Hīs ibi *tum nātum Anchīsēs* ūnā*que* Sibyllam
prōsequitur *dictīs* portā*que* ēmittit eburnā;
ille viam secat *ad nāvēs sociōsque* revīsit.

---

alter, era, erum one (of two), other (of two), second
candēns, entis shining, white, gleaming
corneus, a, um of horn
deinde *adv.* thence, next, thereupon
doceō, ēre, uī, ctus teach (about), tell
eburnus, a, um (of) ivory
elephantus, ī *m.* elephant, ivory
ēmittō, ere, mīsī, missus send forth
exim, exin(de) *adv.* from there, next, thereupon
exitus, ūs *m.* exit, outlet, egress
facilis, e easy, favorable, ready
falsus, a, um false, deceitful, mock
gerō, ere, gessī, gestus bear, wage
ibi *adv.* there, then
incendō, ere, ī, ēnsus inflame, kindle
īnsomnium, (i)ī *n.* dream, vision
Latīnus, ī *m.* early king of Italy, whose daughter, Lavinia, married Aeneas

Laurēns, entis of Laurentum, a city near Rome
Mānēs, ium *m.* (souls of) the dead, Hades
memorō (1) recount, (re)call, relate
modus, ī *m.* manner, measure, limit
nitēns, entis gleaming, bright, shining
perficiō, ere, fēcī, fectus finish, make
populus, ī *m.* people, nation
porta, ae *f.* door, gate, entrance, exit
prōsequor, ī, secūtus follow, escort
quisque, quaeque, quidque (quodque) each, every(one)
revīsō, ere revisit, see again
secō, āre, uī, ctus cut, cleave
Sibylla, ae *f.* ancient Italian prophetess
Somnus, ī *m.* Sleep, Slumber personified as a divinity
ūnā *adv.* together, at the same time
vērus, a, um true, real, genuine, honest

---

890. virō: dat. of agent with pass. periphrastic construction; App. 302. **gerenda (sint).**
892. fugiat, ferat: subjunctives in indir. quest., introduced by **docet . . . quōmodō.**
quō . . . modō: normally written as either one or two words; the intrusion of **quemque** here creates a true TMESIS.
893. fertur (esse) = **dīcitur (esse).** Again Vergil implies that the two gates from the

underworld are part of a tradition already known to his readers: in this case, first and foremost from Homer, who describes the two Gates of Dreams in *Odyssey* 19.562–67.
895. candentī elephantō: abl. of material; App. 324. The association of ivory with deception is based in part on a play on words: the Greek verb *elephairesthai* means "to deceive."
896. sed: i.e., through this gate.
899. ille: Aeneas.

Mausoleum of Augustus (Marcellus was the first to be buried here).
Photograph by Barbara Weiden Boyd

A Selected Bibliography

No bibliography of Virgil's *Aeneid* can hope to be complete or even comprehensive. I have simply focused, therefore, on recent work available in English and of particular relevance to the selections contained in this textbook. Most of the works cited are from the last 30 years; exceptions are works of particular relevance and/or lasting impact. And of course, most are in English; but I have been unable to exclude a small number of works in Italian whose influence continues to be profound. While these are likely to be above and beyond the ability and interest of even the most avid student Vergilian, teachers with modest everyday Italian should be able to use these books and articles to their profit, and to share many of them with their students. I also remind my readers to avail themselves of the Vergilian bibliography that appears in *Vergilius* (the annual publication of the Vergilian Society) and of the selective but handy bibliography online at http://www.vroma.org/~bmcmanus/werner_vergil.html. Finally, I hope that in the next edition of this listing I will be able to add the *Virgil Encyclopedia* currently being edited by J. Ziokowski and R. Thomas and scheduled to be published by Blackwell in 2012: it promises to be a rich resource for teachers and scholars of Vergil at all levels.

Texts and Commentaries

Austin, R.G., ed. *P. Vergili Maronis Aeneidos Liber Primus.* Oxford, 1971.

———, ed. *P. Vergili Maronis Aeneidos Liber Secundus.* Oxford, 1964.

———, ed. *P. Vergili Maronis Aeneidos Liber Quartus.* Oxford, 1955.

———, ed. *P. Vergili Maronis Aeneidos Liber Sextus.* Oxford, 1977.

Horsfall, N., ed. *Virgil, Aeneid 2: A Commentary.* Leiden and Boston, 2008.

Pease, A.S., ed. *P. Vergili Maronis Aeneidos Liber Quartus.* Cambridge, MA, 1935.

Traina, A., ed. *Virgilio:L'utopia e la storia (Il libro xii dell'Eneide e antologia delle opere).* Turin, 1997.

Williams, R.D., ed. *The Aeneid of Virgil.* Two volumes. London, 1972.

General Studies of and Collections of Essays on the AENEID

Anderson, W.S. and L.N. Quartarone, eds. *Approaches to Teaching Vergil's Aeneid.* New York, 2002.

Harrison, S.J., ed. *Oxford Readings in Vergil's Aeneid.* Oxford and New York, 1990.

Heinze, R. *Vergil's Epic Technique,* trans. H. and D. Harvey and F. Robertson. Bristol, 1993. (A valuable translation of the time-honored classic.)

Horsfall, N. *A Companion to the Study of Virgil.* Mnemosyne Supplement 151. Leiden and New York, 1995.

Martindale, C., ed. *The Cambridge Companion to Virgil.* Cambridge, 1997.

Perkell, C., ed. *Reading Vergil's Aeneid: An Interpretive Guide.* Norman, OK, 1999.

Quinn, S., ed. *Why Vergil? A Collection of Interpretations.* Wauconda, IL, 2000.

Ross, D.O. *Virgil's Aeneid: A Reader's Guide.* Malden, MA, 2007.

Smith, R.A. *Virgil.* Malden, MA, 2011.

Harrison, Perkell, Quinn, Anderson-Quartarone, and Martindale are available in paperback, and should be on every Vergil teacher's shelf; Heinze, Horsfall, Ross, and Smith should be within easy reach in the closest college or university library.

Essays Focusing on the Passages in this Textbook

Brenk, F.E. "*Avorum Spes et Purpurei Flores*: The Eulogy for Marcellus in *Aeneid* VI." *American Journal of Philology* 107 (1986) 218–28.

Casali, S. "The King of Pain: Aeneas, Achates and *achos* in *Aeneid* 1." *Classical Quarterly* 58 (2008) 181–89.

Dyer, R.R. "Vergil's *Fama*: A New Interpretation of *Aeneid* 4.173ff." *Greece & Rome* 36 (1989) 28–32.

Dyson, J. "Dido the Epicurean." *Classical Antiquity* 15 (1996) 203–21.

————. "Jupiter's *Aeneid*: *Fama* and *Imperium*." *Classical Antiquity* 28 (2009) 279-327.

Egan, R. "A Reading of the Helen Episode in *Aeneid* 2." *Echos du monde classique* 40 (1996) 379–95.

Feeney, D.C. "History and Revelation in Vergil's Underworld." *Proceedings of the Cambridge Philological Society* 32 (1986) 1–24.

Goold, G.P. "Servius and the Helen Episode." *Harvard Studies in Classical Philology* 74 (1970) 101–68.

Harrison, S.J. "Vergil on Kingship: The First Simile of the *Aeneid*." *Proceedings of the Cambridge Philological Society* 34 (1988) 55–59.

Hexter, R. "What Was the Trojan Horse Made Of?: Interpreting Vergil's *Aeneid*." *Yale Journal of Criticism* 3 (1990) 109–31.

Murgia, C. "More on the Helen Episode." *California Studies in Classical Antiquity* 4 (1971) 203–17.

————. "The Date of the Helen Episode." *Harvard Studies in Classical Philology* 101 (2003) 405–26.

Perkell, C. "Ambiguity and Irony: The Last Resort?" *Helios* 21 (1994) 63–74.

Shackleton Bailey, D.R. "*Tu Marcellus eris*." *Harvard Studies in Classical Philology* 90 (1986) 199–205.

Tarrant, R.J. "Aeneas and the Gates of Sleep." *Classical Philology* 77 (1989) 51–55.

Tracy, S.V. "Laocoon's Guilt." *American Journal of Philology* 108 (1987) 451–54.

Volk, K. "A New Reading of *Aeneid* 6.847-853." *Materiali e discussioni per l'analisi dei testi classici* 61 (2008) 71–84.

Warden, J. "*Ripae ulterioris amore*: Structure and Desire in *Aeneid* 6." *Classical Journal* 95 (2000) 349–61.

Weber, C. "The Allegory of the Golden Bough." *Vergilius* 41 (1995) 3–34.

Works for Further Reading and Research

ON THE *AENEID*

Adler, E. *Vergil's Empire: Political Thought in the Aeneid*. Lanham, MD, 2003.

Barchiesi, A. *La traccia del modello: effetti omerici nella narrazione virgiliana*. Pisa, 1984.

Boyle, A. "The Canonic Text: Virgil's *Aeneid*." In A. Boyle, ed., *Roman Epic*, 79–107. London and New York, 1993.

Cairns, F. *Virgil's Augustan Epic.* Cambridge, 1989.

Clausen, W. *Virgil's Aeneid and the Tradition of Hellenistic Poetry.* Berkeley and Los Angeles, 1987.

———. *Virgil's Aeneid: Decorum, Allusion, and Ideology.* Munich and Leipzig, 2002. (A revised reworking of the same author's earlier book [see preceding]; much new material is included.)

Conte, G.B. *The Rhetoric of Imitation: Genre and Poetic Memory in Virgil and Other Latin Poets*, ed. C.P. Segal. Ithaca, NY and London, 1986.

Corte, F. della, et al., eds. *Enciclopedia Virgiliana.* Six volumes. Rome, 1984–91.

Dyson, J. *King of the Wood: The Sacrificial Victor in Virgil's Aeneid.* Norman, OK, 2001.

Feeney, D.C. *The Gods in Epic.* Oxford, 1991.

Gillis, D. *Eros and Death in the Aeneid.* Rome, 1983.

Hardie, P.R. *Virgil's Aeneid: Cosmos and Imperium.* Oxford, 1986.

Horsfall, N.M. "The Aeneas Legend from Homer to Virgil." In J.N. Bremmer and N.M. Horsfall, *Roman Myth and Mythography*, 12–24. BICS Supplement 52. London, 1987.

Lyne, R.O.A.M. *Further Voices in Vergil's Aeneid.* Oxford, 1987.

———. *Words and the Poet: Characteristic Techniques of Style in Vergil's Aeneid.* Oxford, 1989.

Mackie, C.J. *The Characterisation of Aeneas.* Edinburgh, 1988.

O'Hara, J.J. *Death and the Optimistic Prophecy in Vergil's Aeneid.* Princeton, 1990.

———. *True Names: Vergil and the Alexandrian Tradition of Etymological Wordplay.* Ann Arbor, 1996.

Panoussi, V. *Greek Tragedy in Vergil's Aeneid: Ritual, Empire, and Intertext.* Cambridge, 2009.

Petrini, M. *The Child and the Hero: Coming of Age in Catullus and Vergil.* Ann Arbor, 1997.

Powell, A. *Virgil the Partisan: A Study in the Re-integration of Classics.* Swansea, 2008.

Putnam, M.C.J. *Virgil's Aeneid: Interpretation and Influence.* Chapel Hill and London, 1995.

Reed, J.D. *Virgil's Gaze: Nation and Poetry in the Aeneid.* Princeton, 2007.

Smith, R.A. *The Primacy of Vision in Vergil's Aeneid.* Austin, TX, 2005.

Stahl, H.-P., ed. *Vergil's Aeneid: Augustan Epic and Political Context.* London, 1997.

Syed, Y. *Vergil's Aeneid and the Roman Self. Subject and Nation in Literary Discourse.* Ann Arbor, 2004.

ON THE AUGUSTAN CONTEXT

Galinsky, G.K. *Augustan Culture: An Interpretive Introduction.* Princeton, 1996.

———, ed. *The Cambridge Companion to the Age of Augustus.* Cambridge, 2005.

Gurval, R. *Actium and Augustus: The Politics and Emotions of Civil War.* Ann Arbor, 1995.

Miller, J.F. *Apollo, Augustus, and the Poets.* Cambridge, 2009.

White, P. *Promised Verse: Poets in the Society of Augustan Rome.* Cambridge, MA and London, 1993.

Zanker, P. *The Power of Images in the Age of Augustus.* Ann Arbor, 1988.

ON THE SURVIVAL OF VERGIL

Farrell, J. and M.C.J. Putnam, eds. *A Companion to Vergil's Aeneid and Its Tradition.* Malden, MA, 2010.

Martindale, C., ed. *Virgil and His Influence.* Bristol, 1984.

Wilson-Okamura, D.S. *Virgil in the Renaissance.* Cambridge, 2010.

Wright, D.H. *The Vatican Vergil: A Masterpiece of Late Antique Art.* Princeton, 1993.

———. *The Roman Vergil and the Origins of Medieval Book Design.* Toronto, 2001.

Ziolkowski, J. and M.C.J. Putnam, eds. *The Virgilian Tradition: The First Fifteen Hundred Years.* New Haven, 2008.

Ziolkowski, T. *Virgil and the Moderns.* Princeton, 1993.

APPENDIX A

Vergil's Meter: The Dactylic Hexameter

Vergil used dactylic hexameter, the meter of epic poetry, to compose the *Aeneid*. Homer (8th century BCE) established the epic character of dactylic hexameter by using it to compose the *Iliad* and the *Odyssey*; many other early Greek epic poems, now lost, were composed in the same meter. Beginning in the third century BCE, Latin poets began to experiment with adapting dactylic hexameter to their language. This was no easy task—Greek has a much larger vocabulary, including many more words with multiple short syllables, than does Latin, and is therefore better suited than Latin to dactylic hexameter. Vergil is generally considered by scholars and other admirers to have been the first to bring dactylic hexameter to perfection in Latin; in fact, many believe that he was the first *and* last Latin poet to do so. Whether this is true or not, there is no better introduction to Latin meter than through Vergil; and, strained and odd-sounding though the results may be at first, it is in fact possible with practice to get a reasonable idea of how Latin poetry might have sounded 2,000 years ago. It is important to make this attempt both for its own sake and because much ancient poetry, including the *Aeneid*, was intended to be heard; and a well-read excerpt can be quite powerful.

The term **dactylic hexameter** is derived from Greek. **Hexameter** means "six measures" (**hex**, "six"; **metron**, "measure"). A **dactyl** is a measure consisting of one long and two short syllables; the name **dactyl** comes from the Greek word for "finger" (**daktylos**), since with its two joints a finger can be imagined as consisting of one longer and two shorter sections. A line of dactylic hexameter consists of five dactylic measures (or, as they are commonly called, "feet") followed by a final measure of two syllables, the first of which is always long. Any of the five dactyls can be replaced by a **spondee** (a measure consisting of two long syllables). The pattern of long and short syllables in dactylic hexameter looks like this (*Aen.* 1.1–11):

– ∪ ∪| – ∪ ∪| – –|– –| – ∪ ∪ |– ×
ARMA virumque canō, Troiae quī prīmus ab ōrīs

–∪∪|– –|– ∪ ∪| – –|– ∪ ∪ | – ×
Ītaliam fātō profugus Lāvīniaque vēnit

– ∪ ∪ | – – | – – | – – |– ∪ ∪ |– ×
lītora, multum ille et terrīs iactātus et altō

– ∪ ∪| – –|– ∪ ∪| – –|– ∪ ∪ |– ×
vī superum, saevae memorem Iūnōnis ob īram,

– ∪ ∪| – –|– – |– – | – ∪ ∪ | – ×
5   multa quoque et bellō passus, dum conderet urbem

– – |– ∪ ∪|– ∪∪|– ∪ ∪ | – ∪ ∪|– ×
īnferretque deōs Latiō; genus unde Latīnum

– –|– ∪ ∪| – –| – – | – ∪∪| – ×
Albānīque patrēs atque altae moenia Rōmae.

– ∪ ∪|– –|– ∪ ∪|– – | – ∪ ∪ | – ×
Mūsa, mihī causās memorā, quō nūmine laesō

– ∪ ∪|– –|– ∪ ∪|– – | – ∪ ∪ | – ×
quidve dolēns rēgīna deum tot volvere cāsūs

– – | – ∪∪|– ∪ ∪| – ∪ ∪|– ∪ ∪| – ×
10 īnsignem pietāte virum, tot adīre labōrēs

– ∪ ∪|– –| – ∪ ∪| – –|– ∪ ∪ |– ×
impulerit. Tantaene animīs caelestibus īrae?

Note that the final syllable in a line is always indicated by ×. It can be either long or short; its Latin name, **syllaba anceps**, means "ambiguous" or "undecided syllable."

Most lines of hexameter consist of a combination of dactyls and spondees. The variety of combinations available would have kept the spoken verse from sounding monotonous. Note, however, that lines consisting entirely of spondees are very rare, and that Vergil uses a spondee in the fifth foot only on rare occasions. Such lines (i.e., those with a fifth-foot spondee) are called "spondaic lines," or **spondeiazontes** (singular, **spondeiazon**). Lines consisting entirely of dactyls are relatively unusual as well, although they are not as rare as spondaic lines.

Latin meter is **quantitative**. Every syllable in a Latin word has a quantity, either "long" or "short." Syllable length is determined a) by nature or b) by position. See items 14–24 in the online Grammatical Appendix located at www.bolchazy.com/extras/vergilgrammaticalappendix.pdf for general guidelines on how to determine the length of a syllable.

Some special features of the Latin hexameter should be noted:

Elision – when one word ends with a vowel, diphthong, or -m, and the following word begins with a vowel or h-, the first vowel or diphthong is elided, i.e., blended, with the second. The length of the resulting combination syllable will generally be whatever the length of the second syllable originally was. There are examples of elision above in lines 3, 5, 7, and 11.

Hiatus – see the list of rhetorical and stylistic devices below.

Consonantal vowels – when used in combination with other vowels (e.g., *Iuppiter, coniunx, genua*), the vowels -i- and -u- can sometimes serve as consonants, pronounced as -j- and -w-, respectively. As such, they do not create diphthongs with the vowels next to them, and they can lengthen a preceding short syllable if combined with another consonant. There is an example above in line 2, *Laviniaque*, where the second -i- is treated as a consonant.

Synizesis – see the list of rhetorical and stylistic devices below.

Hypermetric lines – occasionally a hexameter ends with a syllable that can elide with the first syllable of the next line. This final syllable is not needed to complete the metrical pattern of the line in which it appears.

APPENDIX B

Glossary of Rhetorical Terms, Figures of Speech, and Metrical Devices Mentioned in the Notes

Alliteration is the repetition of the same letter or sound, usually at the beginning of a series of words, as at *Aen.* 1.124, *Interea **magno misceri murmure pontum.* **Alliteration** is often used in combination with **Onomatopoiea** (see below), as in this example.

Anaphora is the repetition of a word or words at the beginning of successive clauses. E.g., *Aen.* 1.421–22, **Miratur** *molem Aeneas, ...,* / **miratur** *portas.* In Vergil, **Anaphora** is often used in combination with **Asyndeton** (see below), as in this example.

Anastrophe is the inversion of the normal order of words, as at *Aen.* 4.320, **te propter**.

Aposiopesis ("a falling silent") is a breaking off in the middle of a sentence, the syntax of which is never resumed. E.g., *Aen.* 1.135, **Quos ego—sed motos praestat componere fluctus**, when Neptune decides to suppress his wrath, at least temporarily.

Apostrophe is a sudden break from the previous narrative for an address, in the second person, of some person or object, absent or present. E.g., *Aen.* 1.94–96, **O terque quaterque beati, /quis ante ora patrum Troiae sub moenibus altis / contigit oppetere!**, addressed to the Trojans who fell at Troy.

Asyndeton is the omission of conjunctions, as at *Aen.* 6.315, **nunc hos nunc accipit illos.**

Ecphrasis is an extended and elaborate description of a work of art, a building, or a natural setting. E.g., *Aen.* 1.159–69, describing the cave of the nymphs at Carthage.

this should be easy.

Ellipsis is the omission of one or more words which must be logically supplied in order to create a grammatically complete expression. E.g., *Aen.* 1.543, *sperate deos memores*, where the verb **futuros esse** must be supplied to complete the sense of the line.

Enallage is the transference of an epithet from the word to which it strictly belongs to another word connected with it in thought. E.g., *Aen.* 6.390, **somni noctisque soporae**, where the epithet **soporae** in fact describes not night itself but the drowsiness associated with sleep and night.

(N.B.: this definition is sometimes mistakenly given in textbooks and notes for a related but not identical figure of speech, **Hypallage**. The figure of speech sometimes called **Hypallage** is identical to **Metonymy** [see below].)

Enjambment is the continuation of a unit of thought beyond the end of one verse and into the first few feet of the next. E.g., *Aen.* 6.420–21, *melle soporatam et medicatis frugibus offam* / **obicit**, where **obicit** completes the meaning of the preceding line; a strong pause follows immediately thereafter.

Epanalepsis is the repetition of a word (often a proper name, and often in successive lines of verse) for dramatic and/or emotional effect. (It sometimes appears in combination with **Anaphora** and **Asyndeton** [see above for both terms].) E.g., *Aen.* 602–3, **divum** *inclementia,* **divum** / *has evertit opes . . .*

Euphemism is the avoidance of a direct, sometimes blunt manner of speaking in favor of a more subtle and sometimes diluted form of expression. E.g., *Aen.* 6.457, the circumlocution **extrema** *secutam* instead of the explicit **mortuam**.

Hendiadys is the expression of an idea by means of two nouns connected by a conjunction instead of by a noun and a modifying adjective, or by one noun modified by another. E.g., *Aen.* 1.54, **vinclis et carcere =** **vinclis carceris.**

Hiatus is the avoidance in meter of elision between one word ending in a vowel and another beginning with a vowel (or h). E.g., *Aen.* 4.667, **femineo ululatu**. Here as often the metrical device enhances **Onomatopoiea** (see below).

Hyperbaton is the distanced placement of two (or more) words which are logically meant to be understood together. E.g., *Aen.* 2.589–91, *cum mihi* **se**, *non ante oculis tam clara, videndam* / **obtulit** *et pura per noctem in luce*

refulsit / alma parens, where the subject + verb + object combination **se obtulit et refulsit alma parens** is dislocated, and added emphasis is thus given to each word.

Hyperbole is exaggeration for rhetorical effect. E.g., *Aen.* 1.103, *fluctusque ad sidera tollit.*

Hysteron proteron is the reversal of the natural or logical order of ideas. E.g., *Aen.* 1.69, **submersas . . . obrue puppes**, where, contrary to logic, Juno instructs Aeolus to flood the Trojan ships *after* they have been sunk.

Litotes is understatement, often enhanced by the use of the negative. E.g., *Aen.* 6.392, *nec . . . me sum laetatus.*

Metonymy is the substitution of one word for another which it suggests. E.g., *Aen.* 4.309, *hiberno* **sidere** = *hiberno* **tempore**.

Onomatopoeia is the use of words the sound of which suggests the sense. E.g., *Aen.* 1.105, **insequitur cumulo praeruptus aquae mons**.

Pathetic fallacy is the attribution of human emotion to inanimate objects. E.g., *Aen.* 4.667–68, *Lamentis gemituque et femineo ululatu /* **tecta fremunt**, where the roaring is in fact done not by the dwelling but by those whose cries fill it. When used with adjectives, **Pathetic fallacy** is a special type of **Transferred epithet** (see below).

Pleonasm is exceptional (and usually unnecessary) fullness of expression, typical of archaic Latin style. E.g., *Aen.* 4.203, **amens animi**.

Polyptoton is the repetition of a noun or pronoun in different cases at the beginning of successive phrases or clauses. E.g., *Aen.* 1.106–7, **Hi** *summo in fluctu pendent;* **his** *unda dehiscens / terram inter fluctus aperit* . . . **Polyptoton** is a form of **Anaphora**, and often is found with **Asyndeton** (see above).

Polysyndeton is an overabundance of conjunctions, as at *Aen.* 1.85–86, *una Euru***sque** *No***tus**que *ruunt creber***que** *procellis / Africus …*

Rhetorical question is a question that anticipates no real answer. E.g., *Aen.* 2.577–78 (Aeneas to himself): **Scilicet haec Spartam incolumis patriasque Mycenas / aspiciet, partoque ibit regina triumpho?**

Prolepsis is the inclusion in the main story of references to events which in fact will occur after the dramatic time of the poem, and to the people and circumstances involved in these later events. E.g., *Aen.* 6.847–50, **Excudent ... ducent ... orabunt ... describent ... dicent**, all used to describe the Romans who will be descended from Aeneas and who are not themselves characters in the *Aeneid.*

Simile is a figure of speech which likens or asserts an explicit comparison between two different things. E.g., *Aen.* 6.451–54, [Dido] **quam . . . / obscuram, qualem primo qui surgere mense / aut videt aut vidisse putat per nubile lunam.**

 Synchysis is interlocking word order; many variations on the pattern *abAB* exist. E.g., *Aen.* 4.700, **Iris croceis . . . roscida pennis.**

Synecdoche is the use of a part for the whole, or the reverse. E.g., *Aen.* 4.354, **capitis . . .** *iniuria* **cari,** where **capitis cari** is used to indicate a person.

Synizesis is a metrical effect whereby two contiguous vowels within the same word and normally pronounced separately are slurred into one syllable. E.g., *Aen.* 1.120, **Ilionei,** where the last two vowels, normally pronounced as a short vowel followed by a long, become one long vowel.

Tmesis ("splitting") is the separation into two parts of a word normally written as one, often for a (quasi-)visual effect. E.g., *Aen.* 2.218–19, *bis collo squamea* **circum / terga dati,** where **circum** + **dati** = **circumdati;** the word **terga** is literally "surrounded" by the two parts of **circumdati.**

 Transferred Epithet is an epithet which has been transferred from the word to which it strictly belongs to another word connected with it in thought. E.g., *Aen.* 1.123, **inimicum** *imbrem* = **inimici dei** *imbrem.*

(See also **Enallage** [above], an ancient name for the same stylistic feature.)

Tricolon crescens is the accumulation of three parallel phrases or clauses, each of which is at least one syllable longer than that preceding it. E.g., *Aen.* 4.307–8, **Nec te noster amor** [6 syllables] **nec te data dextera quondam** [9 syllables] / **nec moritura tenet crudeli funere Dido?** [15 syllables]. **Tricolon crescens** is often found in combination with **Anaphora** and **Asyndeton** (see above).

Zeugma is the joining of two words by a modifying or governing word which strictly applies to only one of them. E.g., *Aen.* 12.898, *limes agro positus* **litem** *ut* **discerneret arvis,** where zeugma occurs in the use of the verb **discerneret** with both **litem** and **arvis:** the boundary stone *settles* disagreements by *dividing* the fields.

Vocabulary

A

Abās, antis *m.* a Trojan leader

abdō, ere, didī, ditus hide, put away, bury

abeō, īre, iī (īvī), itus depart

abluō, ere, uī, ūtus wash (off)

abripiō, ere, uī, reptus carry off, snatch away

abscondō, ere, (di)dī, ditus hide

absistō, ere, stitī cease, stop

absum, esse, āfuī be away, be distant, be lacking

absūmō, ere, sūmpsī, sūmptus take away, diminish, use up, consume

accēdō, ere, cessī, cessus approach, reach

accendō, ere, ī, ēnsus inflame, kindle, enrage, burn

accingō, ere, cīnxī, cīnctus gird (on), equip

accumbō, ere, cubuī, cubitus recline (at) (+ *dat.*)

accumulō (1) heap up; pile up; honor

Achātēs, ae *m.* faithful comrade of Aeneas

Achillēs, is (eī, ī) *m.* central character of Homer's *Iliad*, first among the Greek chieftains in the Trojan War

Achīvus, a, um Achaean, Greek

aciēs, ēī *f.* edge; eye(sight); battle line, army

acūtus, a, um sharp, pointed, keen

addō, ere, didī, ditus add

adeō *adv.* to such an extent, so (much)

adeō, īre, iī (īvī), itus approach, encounter

adfātus, ūs *m.* address, speech

adfor, fārī, fātus address, accost, speak to

adgredior, ī, gressus attack, address, approach

adhūc *adv.* to this point, till now

aditus, ūs *m.* approach, entrance, access

adloquor, ī, locūtus address, accost

admīror, ārī, ātus wonder (at), admire

admittō, ere, mīsī, missus admit

admoneō, ēre, uī, itus advise, warn

adnītor, ī, sus (nixus) lean (against, on), struggle, strive

adnō (1) swim, to, swim up to

adorior, īrī, ortus attempt, attack

adōrō (1) worship, adore, honor

adquīrō, ere, quīsīvī, sītus acquire, gain

a(d)spectō (1) *see* **aspectō**

a(d)spectus, ūs *m. see* **aspectus**

a(d)spiciō, ere, spexī, spectus *see* **aspiciō**

a(d)stō, āre, stitī *see* **astō**

adsurgō, ere, surrēxī, surrēctus rise

adultus, a, um grown, adult

adveniō, īre, vēnī, ventus arrive, reach

adversus, a, um opposite, facing

advertō, ere, ī, rsus turn to, heed

adytum, ī *n.* inner shrine, sanctuary

Aeacidēs, ae *m.* descendant of Aeacus, Achilles, Greek chieftain

aeger, gra, grum sick, weary, wretched

Aeneadae, (ār)um *m.* descendants (followers) of Aeneas

Aeolia, ae *f.* one of the Liparian Islands near Sicily

Aeolus, ī *m.* god of the winds

aequaevus, a, um of equal age

aequō (1) (make) equal(ize), match, level, even

āēr, āeris, *acc.* **āera,** *m.* air, mist, fog

aes, aeris *n.* bronze (implement), trumpet

aestās, ātis *f.* summer

aestus, ūs *m.* flood, tide, boiling, surge; heat

aetās, ātis *f.* age, time

aeternus, a, um eternal, everlasting

aethēr, eris, *acc.* **era** *m.* upper air, sky, ether, heaven

aetherius, a, um of the upper air, high in the air, airy, ethereal

Āfricus, ī *m.* (southwest) wind

ager, agrī *m.* field, territory, land

agger, eris *m.* mound, heap, dike, dam, bank

aggerō (1) heap up, pile up, increase

agnōscō, ere, nōvī, nitus recognize

Aiāx, ācis *m.* Greek leader, who in the sack of Troy had taken Priam's daughter, Cassandra, by force from the sanctuary of Minerva

āla, ae *f.* wing, (group of) hunters

ālātus, a, um winged, furnished with wings

Albānus, a, um Alban, of Alba Longa in central Italy, mother city of Rome

Alcīdēs, ae *m.* patronymic (meaning "descendant of Alceus") for Hercules, son of Jupiter and Alcmena

Alētēs, ae *m.* Trojan leader

aliēnus, a, um belonging to another, other's, alien, foreign

aliquis (quī), qua, quid (quod) some(one), any(one)

aliquis, quid some(one), any(one)

aliter *adv.* otherwise, differently

alligō (1) bind, hold (to)

almus, a, um nourishing, kind(ly)

alter, era, erum one (of two), other (of two), second

alternō (1) change, alternate, waver

altum, ī *n.* the deep (sea); heaven

alumnus, ī *m.* nursling, (foster) child

alveus, ī *m.* hollow; boat; trough

alvus, ī *f.* belly, body

amāns, antis *m. (f.)* lover

amārus, a, um bitter, unpleasant

ambiō, īre, īvī (iī), itus go around; conciliate

ambō, ae, ō both

āmēns, entis mad, crazy, frenzied, insane, distracted

amictus, ūs *m.* cloak, robe

amnis, is *m.* river, stream, torrent

Amphrȳsius, a, um Amphrysian, of Amphrysus, a river in Thessaly frequented by Apollo

amplector, ī, plexus embrace, encompass, enfold

an *interrog.* or, whether

an(ne) *interrog.* whether, or

ancora, ae *f.* anchor

anguis, is *m. (f.)* snake, serpent

annus, ī *m.* year, season

Antheus, eī, *acc.* **ea,** *m.* Trojan leader, comrade of Aeneas

antrum, ī *n.* cave, cavern, grotto

aperiō, īre, uī, ertus open, disclose, reveal

apertus, a, um open, clear

apis, is *f.* bee

Apollō, inis *m.* god of light, music, and prophecy

appāreō, ēre, uī, itus appear

aprīcus, a, um sunny, sun-loving

aptō (1) equip, make ready, furnish

aqua, ae *f.* water

Aquilō, ōnis *m.* (north) wind

Ārae, ārum *f.* the Altars, a ledge of rocks between Sicily and Africa

arboreus, a, um branching, tree-like

arceō, ēre, uī keep off, defend, restrain

arcus, ūs *m.* bow

Argī, ōrum *m.* Argos, city of southern Greece, home of Diomedes, a Greek chieftain against Troy; center of the worship of Juno

Argīvus, a, um Argive, Greek

Argolicus, a, um Argive, Greek

āridus, a, um dry

armentum, ī *n.* herd, flock, drove, cattle

armō (1) arm, equip, furnish

armus, ī *m.* shoulder, flank, side

arō (1) plow, till, furrow

arrigō, ere, rēxī, rēctus erect, raise, prick up, stand on end, rear

ars, artis *f.* skill

artus, ūs *m.* joint, limb, member, body

Ascanius, (i)ī *m.* son of Aeneas

ascendō, ere, ī, ēnsus ascend, mount

asper, era, erum rough, harsh, fierce

aspectō (1) look at, see, face, behold

aspectus, ūs *m.* sight, appearance, vision, aspect

aspiciō, ere, spexī, spectus see, behold, look (at)

astō, āre, stitī stand (on, at, near, by) (+ *dat.*)

ast *conj.* (= **at**) but

astrum, ī *n.* star, constellation

ātrium, ī *n.* hall, court, atrium

attollō, ere lift, rear, raise

attonitus, a, um thunderstruck, astounded

audeō, ēre, ausus sum dare, venture

auferō, auferre, abstulī, ablātus carry away, remove, take off, take away

aula, ae *f.* hall, palace, court

auris, is *f.* ear

Ausonius, a, um Ausonian, Italian

auspicium, (i)ī *n.* auspices, authority

Auster, trī *m.* (south) wind

autem *adv.* but, however, moreover

autumnus, ī *m.* autumn, fall

auxilium, (i)ī *n.* aid, help, assistance

āvehō, ere, vēxī, vectus carry, convey (away)

āvellō, ere, āvellī or **āvulsī, āvulsus** tear (off, from)

āvertō, ere, ī, rsus keep off, turn aside, turn away, avert

avis, is *f.* bird, fowl

avus, ī *m.* grandfather; ancestor

B

bacchor, ārī, ātus rush wildly, rave, rage

Bacchus, ī *m.* (god of) wine

barba, ae *f.* beard, whiskers

barbarus, a, um foreign, strange, barbarous, uncivilized

beātus, a, um happy, blessed, fortunate

bene *adv.* well, rightly, securely, fully

bīgae, ārum *f.* two-horse chariot

birēmis, is *f.* bireme, galley (with two banks of oars)

bis twice

bonus, a, um good, kind(ly), useful

brevis, e short, shallow

breviter *adv.* shortly, briefly, concisely

C

cadō, ere, cecidī, cāsus fall, fail, sink, die, subside

cadus, ī *m.* jar, urn

caecus, a, um blind, dark, hidden

caelestis, e divine, heavenly

caelicola, ae *m./f.* divinity, deity

caeruleus, a, um dark (blue)

Caīcus, ī *m.* comrade of Aeneas

calcar, āris *n.* spur, goad

cālīgō, āre, āvī be dark, darken

calor, ōris *m.* heat, warmth, glow

candēns, entis shining, white, gleaming

canō, ere, cecinī, cantus sing (of), chant, prophesy, proclaim

capessō, ere, īvī, ītus (under)take, perform, (try to) seize, reach

Capys, yos, *acc.* **Capyn,** *m.*
comrade of Aeneas

carcer, eris *m.* prison, enclosure

careō, ēre, uī, itus be free from,
lack (+ *abl.*)

carīna, ae *f.* keel; ship, boat

carus, a, um dear, beloved, fond

Cassandra, ae *f.* Trojan
prophetess, punished by Apollo
and so never believed

castus, a, um pure, holy, chaste

cāsus, ūs *m.* chance, (mis)fortune

caterva, ae *f.* band, troop, crowd

causa, ae *f.* cause, reason,
occasion, case (at law)

cautēs, is *f.* rock, cliff, crag

caverna, ae *f.* hollow, cavity, cave

cavus, a, um hollow, vaulted

cēdō, ere, cessī, cessus yield,
depart

celer, eris, ere swift, speedy, quick

cella, ae *f.* cell, storeroom

celsus, a, um high, lofty, towering

centum *indecl.* hundred

Cerberus, ī *m.* monstrous three-
headed dog in Hades

Cereālis, e of Ceres, (goddess of)
grain

Cerēs, eris *f.* (goddess of) grain

certō (1) strive, fight, vie, contend

certus, a, um fixed, sure, certain,
reliable

cervīx, īcis *f.* neck

cervus, ī *m.* stag, deer

Charōn, ontis *m.* ferryman of
souls of the dead across the river
Styx

cieō, ēre, cīvī, citus (a)rouse, stir
(up)

cingō, ere, cīnxī, cīnctus
encircle, surround, gird

cinis, eris *m.* ashes (of the dead),
embers

circā *adv.* around, about

circumstō, āre, stetī surround,
stand around

circumvolō (1) fly around, fly
about

Cithaerōn, ōnis *m.* Greek
mountain near Thebes, on
which the rites of Bacchus were
celebrated

citō *adv.* quickly, soon

cīvis, is *m.* (*f.*) citizen, compatriot

clāmō (1) shriek, cry (out), call
(on)

clārus, a, um clear, bright,
illustrious

claudō, ere, sī, sus (en)close, shut
(in)

claustrum, ī *n.* bolt, fastening,
barrier

clipeus, ī *m.* (or **clipeum, ī** *n.*)
round shield, buckler

Cōcȳtus, ī *m.* river of Hades

coepī, isse, ptus begin, commence

Coeus, ī *m.* one of the Titans, a
giant, son of Earth

cognōmen, inis *n.* (sur)name,
cognomen, nickname

cōgō, ere, coēgī, coāctus bring
together, force, muster, compel

colligō, ere, lēgī, lēctus collect,
gather

collis, is *m.* hill

collum, ī *n.* neck

colō, ere, uī, cultus cultivate,
dwell (in), cherish, honor

colōnus, ī *m.* colonist, settler

color, ōris *m.* color

coluber, brī *m.* snake, serpent

columna, ae *f.* column, pillar

cōma, ae *f.* hair, locks, tresses

comitātus, ūs *m.* retinue, train, company

comitō (1) accompany, attend, escort, follow

comitor, ārī, ātus accompany, attend, escort, follow

commendō (1) entrust, commit

commisceō, ēre, uī, mixtus mix, mingle

commissum, ī *n.* fault, crime

commoveō, ēre, mōvī, mōtus move, stir, shake, agitate, disturb

commūnis, e (in) common, joint, mutual

compāgēs, is *f.* joint, seam, fastening

compellō (1) address, accost, speak to

compellō, ere, pulī, pulsus drive, compel, force

compōnō, ere, posuī, pos(i)tus compose, construct, calm, quiet, put together, settle

comprimō, ere, pressī, pressus (re)press

conciliō (1) win over, unite

conclāmō (1) cry, shout, exclaim

conclūdō, ere, sī, sus (en)close

concrētus, a, um grown together, hardened, matted

concursus, ūs *m.* throng, crowd

concutiō, ere, cussī, cussus shake, shatter, agitate

condō, ere, didī, ditus found, establish; hide, bury

cōnfiteor, ērī, fessus confess, reveal

coniugium, (i)ī *n.* wedlock; husband, wife, marriage

conlābor, ī, lāpsus fall in a heap, faint, collapse

cōnor, ārī, ātus attempt, try, endeavor

cōnscendō, ere, ī, ēnsus mount, climb, ascend, embark

cōnscius, -a, -um *adj.* aware; privy to

cōnsīdō, ere, sēdī, sessus sit (down), settle

cōnsistō, ere, stitī, stitus stand (fast), rest, stop, settle

cōnspectus, ūs *m.* sight, view

cōnspiciō, ere, spexī, spectus see, look at, behold

contendō, ere, ī, ntus strive, contend; bend, draw tight; shoot, aim, hasten

contineō, ēre, uī, tentus hold together, restrain, check

contingō, ere, tigī, tāctus touch, befall

continuō *adv.* immediately, at once

contorqueō, ēre, rsī, rtus hurl, twirl

contra opposite, facing, against, in reply (+ *acc.*); *adv.* opposite, facing, in reply

contus, ī *m.* pole, pike

cōnūbium, (i)ī *n.* right of intermarriage, marriage

convertō, ere, ī, rsus turn (around), reverse

coörior, īrī, ortus (a)rise

cōpia, ae *f.* abundance, plenty, forces

cor, cordis *n.* heart, spirit, feelings

cōram *adv.* before the face, face to face, openly

corneus, a, um of horn

cornū, ūs *n.* horn, tip, end

corripiō, ere, uī, reptus seize, snatch up

corrumpō, ere, rūpī, ruptus spoil, ruin

coruscus, a, um waving, quivering, flashing

crēber, bra, brum frequent, repeated, crowded

crēdō, ere, didī, ditus believe, (en)trust (+ *dat.*), suppose

crētus, a, um grown, sprung

Creūsa, ae *f.* wife of Aeneas, lost during the sack of Troy

crīnis, is *m.* hair, locks, tresses

croceus, a, um yellow, saffron, ruddy

crūdēlis, e cruel, bloody, bitter, harsh

crūdus, a, um raw, fresh; bloody

cruentus, a, um bloody, cruel

cruor, ōris *m.* blood, gore

cubitum, ī *n.* elbow, arm

culmen, inis *n.* roof, peak, summit, top

culpa, ae *f.* fault, blame, weakness, guilt, offense

culpō (1) blame, censure, reprove

cumba, ae *f.* skiff, boat

cumulus, ī *m.* heap, mass, pile

cupīdō, inis *f.* love, desire, longing

cūr why? for what reason?

currus, ūs *m.* chariot, car

curvus, a, um curved, winding, bent

cuspis, pidis *f.* point, spear, lance

custōs, ōdis *m.* (*f.*) guard(ian), keeper, sentinel

Cyclōpius, a, um Cyclopean, of the Cyclopes, huge one-eyed giants of Sicily

Cyllēnius, (i)ī *m.* the Cyllenean, i.e., Mercury, born on Mt. Cyllene in Arcadia; *adj.*, **Cyllēnius, a, um** Cyllenean, of Mt. Cyllene in Arcadia, birthplace of Mercury

Cȳmothoē, ēs *f.* a sea nymph

D

damnō (1) condemn, sentence, doom, devote

Dardan(i)us, a, um Trojan, Dardanian

Dardania, ae *f.* Troy, citadel of Dardanus

Dardanidēs, ae *m.* Dardanian, Trojan

dēbellō (1) exhaust through war, crush

dēbeō, ēre, uī, itus owe, be due, be destined

dēcēdō, ere, cessī, cessus depart

dēclīnō (1) turn aside, bend down, droop

dēcurrō, ere, (cu)currī, cursus run (down), hasten

decus, oris *n.* ornament, glory, dignity, beauty

dēdūcō, ere, dūxī, ductus lead
forth, lead down, launch, lead
off, abduct

dēfendō, ere, ī, fēnsus ward off,
protect

dēferō, ferre, tulī, lātus carry
(down), report

dēfessus, a, um weary, tired, worn

dēficiō, ere, fēcī, fectus fail, faint,
be lacking

dēfungor, ī, fūnctus perform,
finish (+ *abl.*)

dehinc *adv.* then, thereupon

dehīscō, ere, hīvī yawn, gape,
open (up), split

dēiciō, ere, iēcī, iectus throw
(down), cast down, dislodge

deinde *adv.* thence, next,
thereupon

Dēiopēa, ae *f.* a nymph

dēlūbrum, ī *n.* shrine, temple,
sanctuary

dēmittō, ere, mīsī, missus send
down, let down, drop, lower,
derive

dēmum *adv.* at length, finally

dēnique *adv.* finally, at last (esp.
at the end of a list), in short, in
a word

dēpascor, ī, pāstus feed on, devour

dēpendeō, ēre hang (down),
depend

dēscendō, ere, ī, ēnsus descend

dēscrībō, ere, psī, ptus mark out,
map

dēserō, ere, uī, rtus desert,
forsake

dēsinō, ere, sīvī (iī), situs cease,
desist (+ *dat.*)

dēsistō, ere, stitī, stitus cease
(from), desist

dēstruō, ere, strūxī, strūctus
destroy

dēsuper *adv.* from above

dētineō, ēre, uī, tentus detain,
hold back

dētorqueō, ēre, rsī, rtus turn
(away)

dētrūdō, ere, sī, sus push off,
dislodge

dēturbō (1) drive off, dislodge

dēveniō, īre, vēnī, ventus come
(down), arrive (at)

dēvolō (1) fly down

dī(ve)s, dī(vi)tis rich, wealthy
(+ *gen.*)

dicō (1) consecrate, assign,
proclaim, dedicate

difficilis, e difficult, hard, painful

diffugiō, ere, fūgī flee apart,
scatter

diffundō, ere, fūdī, fūsus scatter,
spread

dignor, ārī, ātus deem worthy,
deign (+ *abl.*)

dīlābor, ī, lāpsus glide away,
depart

dīmittō, ere, mīsī, mīssus send
out, scatter, dismiss

dīripiō, ere, uī, reptus plunder,
ravage, tear from

dis(s)iciō, ere, iēcī, iectus scatter,
disperse

Dīs, Dītis *m.* Pluto, god of Hades

discernō, ere, crēvī, crētus divide,
separate; dissolve (a dispute)

discessus, ūs *m.* departure,
separation

discrīmen, inis *n.* crisis, danger

dis(s)iciō, ere, iēcī, iectus scatter, disperse

dispellō, ere, pulī, pulsus drive apart, disperse, scatter

dissimulō (1) conceal, dissimulate, pretend otherwise, hide, disguise

distendō, ere, ī, ntus distend, stretch

dīvellō, ere, ī (or **vulsī**), **vulsus** tear apart

dīversus, a, um scattered, various, separated, different, diverse

dīvidō, ere, vīsī, vīsus divide, separate, distribute

doceō, ēre, uī, ctus teach (about), tell

doleō, ēre, uī, itus suffer, grieve (at), be angry (at, with), resent

dolor, ōris *m.* grief, pain, passion, anger, suffering

dolus, ī *m.* deceit, wiles, trick, fraud, scheme, stratagem

domina, ae *f.* mistress, queen

dominus, ī *m.* master, lord, ruler

dorsum, ī *n.* back, ridge, reef

dracō, ōnis *m.* dragon, serpent

ductor, ōris *m.* leader, chieftain, guide

dulcis, e sweet, dear, fond, pleasant, delightful

duo, ae, o two

duplex, icis double, both

dūrō (1) harden, endure

dūrus, a, um hard(y), harsh, rough, stern

dux, ducis *m./f.* leader, conductor, guide, chief

E

eburnus, a, um (of) ivory

ecce see! look! behold!

ēdūcō, ere, dūxī, ductus lead out, raise, lead forth

efferō, ferre, extulī, ēlātus carry (out), raise, lift up, carry forth

efficiō, ere, fēcī, fectus make, form

effodiō, ere, fōdī, fossus dig out, excavate

effugiō, ere, fūgī flee (from), escape

effulgeō, ēre, lsī flash, glitter, gleam

effundō, ere, fūdī, fūsus pour out

ēgredior, ī, gressus go out, disembark

ēgregius, a, um extraordinary, distinguished

ei alas! ah!

ēiciō, ere, iēcī, iectus cast out, eject

elephantus, ī *m.* elephant, ivory

Elissa, ae *f.* Dido

ēmittō, ere, mīsī, missus send forth, shoot, hurl

ēmoveō, ēre, mōvī, mōtus move from

Enceladus, ī *m.* one of the Titans, a giant, son of Earth

enim *adv.* for, indeed, truly, surely

ēnsis, is *m.* sword, knife

ēnumerō (1) recount, enumerate

epulae, ārum *f.* banquet, feast

epulor, ārī, ātus feast, banquet (+ *abl.*)

eques, itis *m.* cavalryman, knight, man of equestrian rank

equidem *adv.* indeed, truly, surely

Erebus, ī *m.* underworld, Hades

ergō *adv.* therefore, then, consequently

Erīnys, yos *f.* Fury, Curse (personified)

error, ōris *m.* error, wandering, deceit, trick

ēruō, ere, uī, utus overthrow, tear up

Eryx, ycis *m.* Eryx, a mountain in western Sicily named after a son of Venus (and half-brother of Aeneas) who settled there

etiam *adv.* also, even, besides, yet, still

etsī although, even if

Eurus, ī *m.* (east) wind

ēvādō, ere, sī, sus go forth (from), escape, pass over, traverse

ēvānēscō, ere, nuī vanish, disappear

ēvertō, ere, ī, rsus overturn, destroy

exanimis, e breathless, lifeless; also, **exanimus, a, um** breathless, lifeless

exardēscō, ere, arsī, arsus blaze (up)

excidium, (i)ī *n.* destruction, overthrow

excīdō, ere, ī, sus cut out, destroy; fall from, perish

exciō, īre, īvī, itus arouse, excite, stir

excipiō, ere, cēpī, ceptus catch, receive, take (up)

excitō (1) arouse, stir up, excite

excubiae, ārum *f.* watch(fire), sentinel

excūdō, ere, ī, sus hammer out, fashion

excutiō, ere, cussī, cussus cast out, shake off

exerceō, ēre, uī, itus drive, exercise, perform, be busy, train

exhālō (1) breathe out, exhale

exigō, ere, ēgī, āctus drive out, complete, pass; determine, discover

exiguus, a, um small, scanty, petty

exim, exin(de) *adv.* from there, next, thereupon

exitus, ūs *m.* exit, issue, end

exoptō (1) choose, desire, hope (for)

exordium, (i)ī *n.* beginning, commencement

expediō, īre, īvī (iī), ītus bring out, prepare

expendō, ere, ī, pēnsus expiate, pay (for)

experior, īrī, pertus try, experience

expleō, ēre, ēvī, ētus fill (out), fulfil

explōrō (1) explore, search (out), examine

expōnō, ere place out, (cause to) disembark

exprōmō, ere, mpsī, mptus express, bring forth

exsanguis, e bloodless, lifeless, pale

exspectō (1) await (eagerly), expect

exspīrō (1) breathe out, exhale

exsting(u)ō, ere, īnxī, īnctus extinguish, blot out, destroy, ruin

exstruō, ere, strūxī, strūctus build (up), rear

extemplō *adv.* immediately, at once, suddenly, straightaway

extendō, ere, extendī, extensus (or **extentus**) stretch out, extend, increase

exterreō, ēre, uī, itus terrify, frighten

exterus, a, um outside, foreign

extrēma, ōrum *n.* end, death, funeral

extrēmus, a, um final, last, furthest, farthest

exuō, ere, uī, ūtus bare, doff, discard

exūrō, ere, ussī, ustus burn (up)

exuviae, ārum *f.* spoils, booty, relics, mementos; slough

F

fabricō (1) fashion, make

facessō, ere, (īv)ī, ītus do, make, fulfill

faciēs, ēī *f.* appearance, face, aspect

facilis, e easy, favorable, ready

factum, ī *n.* deed, act, exploit

fallō, ere, fefellī, falsus deceive, cheat, mock, beguile, escape the notice (of)

falsus, a, um false, deceitful, mock

famēs, is *f.* hunger

fandus, a, um to be uttered, right, just

fās *n. indecl.* right, justice, divine will, divine law

fastīgium, (i)ī *n.* top, roof, summit

fātālis, e fatal, deadly, fated, fateful

fatīscō, ere split, open, gape

faux, faucis *f.* jaws, throat; gulf

fax, facis *f.* firebrand, torch

fēmina, ae *f.* woman, female

fēmineus, a, um feminine, of women

feriō, īre strike, smite, beat, kill

ferrūgineus, a, um rusty (in color), dusky

ferus, ī *m.* beast, monster

ferv(e)ō, ēre, (ferbu)ī glow, boil; be busy

fēstus, a, um festal, festival, pertaining to a holiday

fētus, a, um teeming, pregnant, filled

fētus, ūs *m.* offspring, brood, shoot

fictum, ī *n.* falsehood, fiction

fidēs, eī *f.* faith, belief, trust(worthiness), honor, pledge, fidelity; **Fidēs, eī** *f.* Faith, Honor (personified)

fīdūcia, ae *f.* confidence, trust

fīdus, a, um faithful, trustworthy, safe

fīgō, ere, fīxī, fīxus fix, fasten, pierce

fīlius, (i)ī *m.* son

fingō, ere, fīnxī, fictus fashion, pretend, imagine, form, mold, shape

fīō, fierī, factus become, be made, arise

flammō (1) inflame, burn, fire, kindle

flāvus, a, um yellow, tawny, blond

flectō, ere, flexī, flexus bend, move, turn, guide

fleō, ēre, ēvī, ētus weep, lament, mourn

flētus, ūs *m.* weeping, tears, lament

flōreō, ēre, uī bloom, flourish, blossom

flōreus, a, um flowery

flōs, ōris *m.* flower, blossom, bloom

fluentum, ī *n.* stream, flood

flūmen, inis *n.* river, stream, flood

fluvius, (i)ī *m.* river, stream

fodiō, ere, fōdī, fossus dig, pierce, spur

foedō (1) befoul, defile, pollute; mar, mangle, disfigure

foedus, a, um foul, loathsome, filthy

foedus, eris *n.* treaty, agreement, pact

folium, (i)ī *n.* leaf, foliage

fōmes, itis *m.* tinder, fuel, shaving

forma, ae *f.* form, beauty, shape

fors(it)an *adv.* perhaps, possibly, perchance

fortis, e strong, brave, valiant

fortūnātus, a, um fortunate, blessed

forus, ī *m.* gangway, deck (of a boat)

foveō, ēre, fōvī, fōtus cherish, fondle

fraglāns, antis fragrant, sweet-smelling

fragor, ōris *m.* crash, uproar

frangō, ere, frēgī, frāctus break, crush, shatter

frāter, tris *m.* brother

fraudō (1) defraud, deprive, cheat

fraus, fraudis *f.* deceit, guile, fraud

fremō, ere, uī, itus murmur, lament, groan, roar, rage

frēnō (1) curb, check, restrain

fretum, ī *n.* strait, sound, channel, narrow sea

frīgidus, a, um cold, chill, frigid

frigus, oris *n.* cold, frost, chill

frondeus, a, um leafy

frōns, frontis *f.* front, forehead, brow, face

frūx, frūgis *f.* fruit, grain

fūcus, ī *n.* drone

fugō (1) put to flight, rout

fulg(e)ō, ēre (or **ere**), **lsī** shine, flash, gleam, glitter

fulmen, inis *n.* thunderbolt, lightning

fulvus, a, um tawny, yellow, blond

fūmus, ī *m.* smoke, vapor, fog, fume

fundāmentum, ī *n.* foundation, base

fundō (1) found, establish, make fast

fungor, ī, fūnctus perform, fulfil (+ *abl.*)

fūnis, is *m.* rope, cable

fūnus, eris *n.* funeral, death, disaster

furiae, ārum *f.* furies, madness, frenzy

furiō (1) madden, frenzy, infuriate

furor, ōris *m.* madness, frenzy, rage, passion, fury; **Furor, ōris** *m.* Madness, Rage, Frenzy (personified)

fūrtīvus, a, um secret, stolen

fūrtum, ī *n.* stealth, theft, trick

G

Gaetūlus, a, um of the Gaetuli, a tribe of North Africa

galea, ae *f.* helmet

Gallus, a, um Gallic, Gaul

Ganymēdēs, is *m.* son of Laōmedon, first king of Troy; carried off by Jupiter's eagle and made cupbearer to the gods

Garamantis, idis of the Garamantes, an African tribe

gaudeō, ēre, gāvisus sum (semideponent) rejoice, exult

gaza, ae *f.* wealth, treasure

gemitus, ūs *m.* groan(ing), wail(ing), lament, moan

gemō, ere, uī, itus groan (for), lament

generō (1) beget, bear

germāna, ae *f.* sister

gerō, ere, gessī, gestus bear, carry (on), wage

gestō (1) bear, wear, carry

gignō, ere, genuī, genitus bear, produce, beget

glaeba, ae *f.* a lump of earth, clod

glaucus, a, um gray, grayish-green, gleaming

glomerō (1) roll together, gather, collect

glōria, ae *f.* renown, glory, fame, pride

Gorgō, onis *f.* Gorgon

gradus, ūs *m.* step, gait, pace, stride

Graius, a, um Greek

grandaevus, a, um aged, old

grandō, inis *f.* hail(storm, stones)

grātus, a, um welcome, pleasing, grateful

gravis, e heavy, weighty, serious; venerable; pregnant

graviter *adv.* heavily, violently, greatly

gressus, ūs *m.* step, walk, course, gait

Grȳnēus, a, um of Grynium, a town in Asia Minor, with an oracle of Apollo

gurges, itis *m.* whirlpool, abyss, gulf

guttur, uris *n.* throat, gullet

H

habēna, ae *f.* rein, curb, check

haereō, ēre, haesī, haesus stick (to), cling (to) (+ *dat.*)

hālitus, ūs *m.* breath, exhalation

Hammōn, ōnis *m.* Hammon (or Ammon), god of North Africa, famous for his oracle and identified by the Romans with Jupiter

harēna, ae *f.* sand, beach

hasta, ae *f.* spear, lance, dart

hauriō, īre, hausī, haustus drain, drink (in)

hebetō (1) blunt, dull, dim, weaken

Hector, oris, *acc.* **ora** *m.* Trojan leader, son of Priam and Hecuba

hērēs, ēdis *m.* heir, successor

hērōs, ōis *m.* hero, mighty warrior

Hesperia, ae *f.* Hesperia, Italy; lit., the western place

hībernus, a, um wintry, of the winter, stormy

hiems, emis *f.* winter, storm

homō, inis *m. (f.)* man, mortal, human

hōra, ae *f.* hour, season, time

horrendus, a, um horrifying, dire, awesome

horreō, ēre, uī bristle, shudder, tremble, quake

horrēscō, ere, horruī shudder, tremble

horror, ōris *m.* horror, terror, shudder(ing)

hospes, itis *m. (f.)* guest, host, stranger

hospitium, (i)ī *n.* hospitality, welcome

hostis, is *m. (f.)* enemy, foe, stranger

hūmānus, a, um of man, human

humus, ī *f.* ground, soil, earth

hymenaeus, ī *m.* wedding (hymn), so called after Hymen, god of marriage

I

iaceō, ēre, uī, itus lie (low, outspread)

iactō (1) toss, buffet, vaunt, boast, utter

iaculor, ārī, ātus hurl, throw, fling

iānitor, ōris *m.* doorkeeper

Iarbās, ae *m.* African chieftain, one of Dido's suitors

iaspis, idis *f.* jasper, a semiprecious stone

ibi *adv.* there, then

ibīdem in the same place

ignārus, a, um ignorant, unaware, inexperienced; unknown, strange

ignāvus, a, um lazy, idle

igneus, a, um fiery, flaming

ignōbilis, e inglorious, common, lowly

ignōtus, a, um unknown, strange

Īliacus, a um Trojan, Ilian

Īlias, adis *f.* Trojan woman

Īlioneus, eī *m.* Trojan leader

Īlium, (i)ī *n.* Troy, Ilium, a city of Asia Minor

illīc *adv.* there, at that place

illūc *adv.* there, thither, to that place

imāgō, inis *f.* likeness, image, ghost, soul, form, picture

imber, bris *m.* rain, flood, storm, water

immemor, oris unmindful, heedless, forgetful

immēnsus, a, um boundless, measureless, immense, immeasurable

immineō, ēre menace (+ *dat.*), hang over, threaten

immītis, e fierce, cruel

immittō, ere, mīsī, missus let in, send in (to), loose(n), give freely (+ *dat.*)

immōtus, a, um unmoved, immovable, unshaken

impellō, ere, pulī, pulsus strike (against), drive, force, impel

impius, a, um unholy, impious, disloyal, wicked, accursed

implicō, āre, āvī (uī), ātus (itus) entwine

impōnō, ere, posuī, positus place upon, set to, impose (+ *dat.*), establish

imprimō, ere, pressī, pressus press (upon), imprint

impūne *adv.* unpunished, with impunity

inānis, e empty, idle, useless, vain

incēdo, ere, cessī, cessus walk (proudly), stride, march, go (majestically)

incendium, (i)ī *n.* a burning, fire, blaze, conflagration

incendō, ere, ī, ēnsus inflame, kindle, burn

inceptum, ī *n.* beginning, undertaking, purpose

incertus, a, um uncertain, doubtful, wavering

incipiō, ere, cēpī, ceptus begin, undertake

inclēmentia, ae *f.* cruelty, harshness

inclūdō, ere, sī, sus (en)close, confine

inclutus, a, um famous, renowned

incolumis, e safe, unharmed, intact

increpō, āre, uī, itus reprove, chide

incubō, āre, uī (āvī), itus (ātus) recline, lie upon, brood over (+ *dat.*)

incumbō, ere, cubuī, cubitus lean upon, urge on, brood over, lower (over), lie upon, hang over (+ *dat.*)

incutiō, ere, cussī, cussus strike (into) (+ *dat.*)

inde *adv.* thence, afterward, thereupon

indignor, ārī, ātus be angry, chafe; deem unworthy, despise

indignus, a, um undeserved, unworthy

indomitus, a, um uncontrolled, ungoverned

induō, ere, uī, ūtus don, clothe, put on

īnfandus, a, um unspeakable, accursed

īnfectus, a, um not done, false

īnfēnsus, a, um hostile, bitter

īnferō, ferre, tulī, lātus bear (in, into), bring (to), present

īnfēstus, a, um hostile, threatening

īnfīgō, ere, xī, xus fix, pierce, fasten (on), impale

informis, e shapeless, hideous

ingemō, ere, uī groan, roar, lament

ingredior, ī, gressus advance, enter, proceed, step, stride

inhumātus, a, um unburied

inimīcus, a, um hostile, enemy, unfriendly

inīquus, a, um unfair, unjust, hostile

iniūria, ae *f.* wrong, insult, injustice, injury

inlābor, ī, lāpsus glide in(to) (+ *dat.*)

inlīdō, ere, sī, sus dash against (into) (+ *dat.*)

innūptus, a, um unmarried, virgin

inops, opis needy, destitute, bereft (of)

inremeābilis, e from which there is no return, irretraceable

inrītō (1) vex, enrage, provoke

īnsānia, ae *f.* madness, frenzy, folly

īnsequor, ī, secūtus follow, pursue

īnsidiae, ārum *f.* snare, ambush, treachery

īnsīdō, ere, sēdī, sessus sit in (on), occupy

īnsignis, e distinguished, marked, splendid

īnsinuō (1) wind, creep, coil

īnsomnium, (i)ī *n.* dream, vision in sleep

īnsonō, āre, uī (re)sound, roar, echo

īnspiciō, ere, spexī, spectus look into

īnstar *n. indecl.* likeness, dignity, image (+ *gen.*)

īnstō, āre, stitī urge on, press on (+ *dat.*)

īnsula, ae *f.* island

īnsuper *adv.* above, besides

intentō (1) threaten, aim, stretch, extend

intereā *adv.* meanwhile, (in the) meantime

interpres, etis *m.* (*f.*) interpreter, agent

intorqueō, ēre, rsī, rtus hurl (against) (+ *dat.*)

intrō (1) enter, penetrate

intrōgredīor, ī, gressus to step in, enter

intus *adv.* within, inside

inultus, a, um unavenged, unpunished

invādō, ere, sī, sus attack, address

invehō, ere, ēxī, ectus carry in, convey

invictus, a, um unconquered, invincible

invidia, ae *f.* grudge, envy, jealousy

invīsus, a, um hateful, hated, odious

invius, a, um pathless, trackless

Īris, (id)is *f.* goddess of the rainbow, messenger of Juno

iste, ta, tud that (of yours)

istinc from there (where you are)

ita *adv.* thus, so

Italus, a, um Italian, of Italy

iter, itineris *n.* way, road, journey, route

iuba, ae *f.* mane, crest

iūdicium, (i)ī *n.* decision, judgment

iugum, ī *n.* yoke, (mountain) ridge

Iūlus, ī *m.* Ascanius, son of Aeneas

iungō, ere, iūnxī, iūnctus join, unite, yoke

iūrō (1) take oath, swear, conspire

iūs, iūris *n.* right, law, decree, justice

iussum, ī *n.* order, command, behest

iussus, ūs *m.* command, order, behest

iūstitia, ae *f.* justice, equity, righteousness, uprightness

iūstus, a, um just, fair, right(eous)

iuvenis, is *m.* (*f.*) youth, young (man or woman)

iuventūs, ūtis *f.* youth, (group of) young men

iuvō, āre, iūvī, iūtus help, please

iuxtā *adv.* close; (+ *acc.*) close to, next to

K

Karthāgō, inis *f.* Carthage, great commercial city in North Africa, rival of Rome

L

Lacaenus, a, um Spartan, Lacedaemonian

lacus, ūs *m.* lake, marsh

laedō, ere, sī, sus strike, hurt, offend, thwart

laena, ae *f.* (woolen) mantle, cloak

laetor, ārī, ātus rejoice, exult

laevus, a, um left, foolish, unlucky

lambō, ere lick, lap

lāmenta, ōrum *n.* lamentation, shriek

Lāocoōn, ontis *m.* Trojan priest of Neptune

lāpsus, ūs *m.* gliding, rolling, sinking

largus, a, um abundant, copious

lātē *adv.* widely, far and wide

latebra, ae *f.* hiding place, cavern, lair

lateō, ēre, uī lie hidden, hide, lurk, escape the notice (of)

Latīnus, a, um Latin, of Latium

Latīnus, ī *m.* early king of Italy whose daughter, Lavinia, married Aeneas

Latium, (i)ī *n.* Latium, district of central Italy around Rome

lātrātus, ūs *m.* bark(ing), howl(ing)

latrō (1) bark, howl, bay

lātus, a, um broad, wide, spacious

latus, eris *n.* side, flank

laudō (1) praise

Laurēns, entis of Laurentum, a city near Rome

laus, laudis *f.* glory, praise, merit

Lāvīn(i)us, a, um Lavinian, of Lavinium, an early Italian city

laxō (1) loosen, free, open, release

laxus, a, um loose, open, lax, free

legō, ere, lēgī, lēctus choose, collect, select, gather

Lēnaeus, a, um Lenaean, Bacchic, of Bacchus, god of wine

lēniō, īre, īvī (iī), ītus soothe, calm, soften

lētum, ī *n.* death, destruction, ruin

levis, e light, unsubstantial, slight, swift

levō (1) lift, lighten, raise, relieve

lēx, lēgis *f.* law, jurisdiction, regulation, decree

lībō (1) pour (as a libation), offer

Libya, ae *f.* region of North Africa

Libycus, a, um Libyan, of Libya, a region of North Africa

licet, ēre, uit, itum it is permitted

lignum, ī *n.* wood, timber
ligō (1) bind, tie, fasten
līlium, (i)ī *n.* lily
līmus, ī *m.* slime, mud, mire
lingua, ae *f.* tongue, language
linquō, ere, līquī, lictus leave,
  desert
līquēns, entis liquid, flowing
līvidus, a, um blue, dark, livid
locō (1) place, locate, establish, lay
longaevus, a, um aged, very old
longē *adv.* far (off, from), at a
  distance, (from) afar
loquor, ī, locūtus speak, say, tell,
  talk
lōrum, ī *n.* thong, leather strap, rein
luctor, ārī, ātus struggle, wrestle
lūctus, ūs *m.* grief, mourning,
  sorrow
lūdō, ere, sī, sus play with,
  deceive, mock
lūna, ae *f.* moon, moonlight
luō, ere, ī atone for
lūstrō (1) purify, survey, traverse
luxus, ūs *m.* luxury, splendor,
  excess
Lycia, ae *f.* country of Asia Minor
Lycius, a, um Lycian, of Lycia, a
  country of Asia Minor
lympha, ae *f.* water

M

māchina, ae *f.* machine, engine,
  device
mactō (1) sacrifice, slaughter, kill;
  honor through sacrifice
madeō, ēre, uī drip, be wet, reek
Maeonius, a, um Maeonian,
  Lydian, Asiatic

maereō, ēre mourn, grieve, pine
  (for)
maestus, a, um sad, mournful,
  gloomy
māgālia, ium *n.* huts, hovels
magis *adv.* more, rather
magister, trī *m.* master, pilot
magistrātus, ūs *m.* magistrate,
  officer
magnanimus, a, um great-souled
malum, ī *n.* evil thing, misfortune,
  disaster, trouble
mandātum, ī *n.* command,
  mandate, charge, behest, order
Mānēs (or **mānēs**), **ium** *m.* (souls
  of) the dead, Hades
manifestus, a, um clear, manifest
Mārcellus, ī *m.* 1. Marcus
  Claudius Marcellus, d. 208 BCE;
  famous Roman consul, served in
  both 1st and 2nd Punic Wars;
  2. Marcus Claudius Marcellus,
  42–23 BCE; son of Octavia (sister
  of Augustus) and first husband of
  Augustus' daughter Julia
marmor, oris *n.* marble
Marpēs(s)ius, a, um of
  Marpe(s)sus, a mountain on
  the island of Paros famous for
  its white marble
mātūrō (1) hasten, speed; ripen
Maurūsius, a, um Moorish
meātus, ūs *m.* course, path,
  motion
medicō (1) drug, medicate
meditor, ārī, ātus meditate, design,
  consider, think over, practice
medium, (i)ī *n.* middle, midst,
  center

mel, mellis *n.* honey

melior, ius better, superior, preferable

membrum, ī *n.* member, limb, (part of) body, part

meminī, isse remember, recall (+ *gen.*)

memor, oris remembering, mindful, unforgetting (+ *gen.*)

memorābilis, e memorable, glorious

memorō (1) (re)call, recount, relate

mēnsis, is *m.* month

mentum, ī *n.* chin, beard

mereō, ēre, uī, itus deserve, earn, merit

meritum, ī *n.* reward, service, merit

metuō, ere, uī fear, dread

metus, ūs *m.* fear, anxiety, dread, fright

micō, āre, uī quiver, flash, dart

mīlle; *pl.* **mīlia, ium** *n.* thousand

minister, trī *m.* attendant, servant

ministrō (1) tend, serve, supply

minor, ārī, ātus tower (over); threaten (+ *dat.*)

minores, um *m.* descendants; *lit.* smaller or younger ones (comparative of **parvus**)

minus *adv.* less

mīrābilis, e wonderful, marvelous

mīror, ārī, ātus wonder (at), admire

misceō, ēre, uī, mixtus confuse, mix, mingle, stir (up)

miserābilis, e miserable, wretched, pitiable

misereor, ērī, itus pity, commiserate (+ *gen.*)

mitra, ae *f.* mitre, cap, turban

Mnēstheus, eī (**eos**), *acc.* **ea** *m.* Trojan leader

mōbilitās, ātis *f.* activity, motion, speed

modus, ī *m.* manner, measure, limit, method

mōlēs, is *f.* mass, burden, heap, structure; difficulty

mōlior, īrī, ītus undertake, (strive to) accomplish, do, work, effect, make, prepare, attempt

molliō, īre, īvī (**iī**), **ītus** soothe, tame

mollis, e soft, yielding, easy, mild, tender

molliter *adv.* softly, gently, gracefully

monitum, ī *n.* advice, warning

monitus, ūs *m.* advice, warning

mōnstrō (1) point out, show, teach

mōnstrum, ī *n.* prodigy, portent, monster

mora, ae *f.* delay, hesitation, hindrance

moribundus, a, um dying, about to die

morior, ī, mortuus die, perish

moror, ārī, ātus delay, tarry, hinder, hesitate

morsus, ūs *m.* bite, biting, jaws, fangs

mortālis, is *m.* mortal, man, human, earthly

mōs, mōris *m.* custom, ritual, manner, usage

mōtus, ūs *m.* movement, emotion

mox *adv.* soon, presently

mūgītus, ūs *m.* bellow(ing), roar

mulceō, ēre, lsī, lsus calm,
soothe

multiplex, icis manifold, multiple

mūrex, icis *m.* purple (dye),
crimson, scarlet

murmur, uris *n.* murmur, roar,
rumble

mūrus, ī *m.* (city) wall,
battlement, rampart

Mūsa, ae *f.* Muse, patron goddess
of the liberal arts

mūtō (1) (ex)change, transform,
alter

Mycēnae, ārum *f.* city of central
Greece, home of Agamemnon,
leader of the Greek expedition
against Troy

N

nāvigō (1) (set) sail, navigate

nāvita, ae *m.* sailor, boatman

nebula, ae *f.* cloud, mist, fog

necdum *adv.* not yet, nor yet

nectar, aris *n.* nectar

nectō, ere, nex(u)ī, nexus bind,
fasten, weave

nefandus, a, um unspeakable,
unutterable

nefās *n. indecl.* impiety,
unspeakable thing, crime

negō (1) deny, refuse, say no
(not)

nemus, oris *n.* grove, wood,
forest

nepōs, ōtis *m.* grandson;
descendant

Neptūnus, ī *m.* Neptune, god of
the sea

nēquīquam *adv.* in vain, uselessly,
idly

nesciō, īre, īvī (iī) not know,
know not, be ignorant

neu, nēve and (that) not, and lest

nī, nisi if not, unless, except

nihil, nīl nothing, not at all

nimbōsus, a, um stormy, rainy

nimbus, ī *m.* rainstorm, (storm)
cloud

nimium *adv.* too (much), too
great(ly), excessively

nitēns, entis gleaming, bright,
shining

nō (1) swim, float

nocturnus, a, um of the night,
nocturnal

nōdus, ī *m.* knot, node; fold, coil

Nomas, adis *m.* tribe of North
Africa

nōndum *adv.* not yet

nōtus, a, um (well) known, familiar

Notus, ī *m.* (south) wind

novitās, ātis *f.* newness, novelty

novō (1) renew, make (new),
build, alter

noxa, ae *f.* crime, fault, hurt, harm

nūbēs, is *f.* cloud, fog, mist

nūbila, ōrum *n.* clouds,
cloudiness

nūbilum, ī *n.* cloud, cloudiness

numerus, ī *m.* number, multitude

numquam *adv.* never, at no time

nuntia, ae *f.* messenger

nuntius, (i)ī *m.* messenger,
message

nūsquam *adv.* nowhere, never

nūtrīmentum, ī *n.* food, fuel, nourishment

Nympha (or **nympha**), **ae** *f.* nymph, a minor divinity of the forests, waters, etc., appearing to humans as a beautiful maiden

O

ob on account of (+ *acc.*)

obdūcō, ere, dūxī, ductus draw over

obiciō, ere, iēcī, iectus present, place before

obiectus, ūs *m.* projection, hang, overhang

obitus, ūs *m.* death, downfall, ruin

oblīviscor, ī, lītus forget (+ *gen.*)

obmūtēscō, ere, tuī be dumb, stand speechless

obnītor, ī, sus (nixus) push against, strive, struggle

oborior, īrī, ortus (a)rise, spring up

obruō, ere, uī, utus overwhelm, crush

obscūrus, a, um dark, shadowy, gloomy, dim, obscure

obstipēscō, ere, stipuī be dazed, stand agape

obtundō, ere, tudī, tūsus (tūnsus) blunt, weaken, exhaust, make dull

obvius, a, um in the way, meeting, to meet (+ *dat.*)

occidō, ere, occidī, occāsus fall, perish, end, die

occubō, āre lie prostrate, lie dead

occultō (1) hide, conceal, secrete

occumbō, ere, cubuī, cubitus fall (in death)

occupō (1) seize (beforehand), occupy

ōcior, ius swifter, quicker; very swift

ōdī, isse hate, detest, loathe

Oenōtrus, a, um Oenotrian, from Oenotria in southern Italy

offa, ae *f.* morsel, cake

offerō, ferre, obtulī, oblātus present

officium, ī *n.* service, kindness, favor, courtesy

Oīleus, eī *m.* Greek king, father of Ajax

ōlim *adv.* (at) some time, once

Olympus, ī *m.* high Greek mountain, home of the gods; heaven

ōmen, inis *n.* portent, omen, sign

omnīnō *adv.* altogether, completely, utterly

omnipotēns, entis almighty, all-powerful, omnipotent

onerō (1) load, burden

onus, eris *n.* burden, load

operiō, īre, uī, rtus cover, hide

opīmus, a, um rich, splendid, sumptuous; **spolia opīma** "spoils of honor," won when a Roman general with his own hand slew the general of the enemy

oppetō, ere, īvī (iī), ītus encounter, meet (death)

opprimō, ere, pressī, pressus overwhelm, crush

ops, opis *f.* help, resources, power, wealth

optimus, a, um best, finest
  (superl. of **bonus, a, um**)
optō (1) choose, desire, hope (for)
opus, eris *n.* work, task, toil, deed
orbis, is *m.* circle, fold, coil, orb,
  revolution, earth
Orcus, ī *m.* Hades, (god of) the
  lower world
orgia, ōrum *n.* mystic rites, rituals
Ōrīōn, ōnis *m.* the storm-bringing
  constellation, named for a famous
  hunter transported to heaven
ōrō (1) beseech, pray (for), entreat,
  plead, argue
Orontēs, is (ī) *m.* comrade of
  Aeneas
os, ossis *n.* bone
ostendō, ere, ī, ntus show, display,
  promise
ōstium, (i)ī *n.* mouth, entrance;
  harbor
ōtium, (i)ī *n.* leisure, idleness, quiet

P
paeniteō, ēre, uī repent, be sorry
Pallas, adis *f.* Minerva, goddess
  of wisdom and the arts
palma, ae *f.* palm, hand
palūs, ūdis *f.* swamp, marsh
pandō, ere, ī, passus spread,
  open, loosen
Parcae, ārum *f.* the Fates
**parcō, ere, pepercī (parsī),
  parsus** spare (+ *dat.*)
pāreō, ēre, uī, itus obey, yield
  (+ *dat.*)
pariō, ere, peperī, partus (re)
  produce, gain, acquire, give
  birth to

Paris, idis *m.* Trojan prince, son
  of Priam, took Helen from her
  husband Menelaus and thus
  caused the Trojan War
pariter *adv.* equally, side by side,
  alike
partior, īrī, ītus distribute, divide
parum *adv.* slightly, too little, not
parvulus, a, um tiny, very small,
  little
parvus, a, um small, little
pascor, ī, pāstus feed, graze
passim *adv.* everywhere, all about
patior, ī, passus suffer, endure,
  allow
patria, ae *f.* homeland, country
patruus, ī *m.* paternal uncle
paucus, a, um little, few, light,
  scanty
pavor, ōris *m.* terror, shuddering,
  alarm
pāx, pācis *f.* peace, favor, grace,
  repose, quiet
pecus, oris *n.* flock, herd, swarm
pecus, udis *f.* animal (of the flock)
pedes, itis *m.* foot soldier, infantry;
  foot-traveller; (person) on foot
penātēs, ium *m.* household gods
pendeō, ēre, pependī hang,
  depend
penetrālis, e inmost, interior
penitus *adv.* deep within, deeply,
  wholly
penna, ae *f.* wing, feather
peragō, ere, ēgī, āctus
  accomplish, finish, traverse
pereō, īre, iī (īvī), itus perish, die
pererrō (1) wander through,
  traverse

perficiō, ere, fēcī, fectus finish, make

perfidus, a, um treacherous, perfidious

perflō (1) blow (over, through)

perfundō, ere, fūdī, fūsus soak, drench

Pergama, ōrum *n.* (citadel of) Troy

perhibeō, ēre, uī, itus present, say

perlābor, ī, lāpsus glide over

permittō, ere, mīsī, missus entrust, allow

pernīx, īcis active, nimble, swift

personō, āre, uī, itus sound through, make (re)sound

Phoenissa, ae *f.* Phoenician (woman), Dido

Phrygius, a, um Phrygian, Trojan

pietās, ātis *f.* loyalty, devotion, (sense of) duty, righteousness

piget, ēre, uit it displeases

pingō, ere, pīnxī, pictus paint, embroider

pinguis, e fat, fertile, rich

Pīrithoüs, ī *m.* Greek hero who descended to Hades with his friend Theseus to carry off Proserpina

placidus, a, um peaceful, calm, quiet

plācō (1) calm, quiet

plangor, ōris *m.* clamor, wailing, beating (of the breast), shriek

planta, ae *f.* heel; sole of foot

plēnus, a, um full, complete, swelling, filled

plūma, ae *f.* feather, plume

Poenus, a, um Phoenician, Carthaginian

polus, ī *m.* pole, sky, heaven

pondus, eris *n.* weight, burden

pōne *adv.* behind, after

pontus, ī *m.* sea, waves

populō (1) devastate, plunder, ravage

populus, ī *m.* people, nation, crowd

porta, ae *f.* door, gate, entrance, exit, opening

portitor, ōris *m.* ferryman

portō (1) carry, bear, take, convey, bring

post after, behind (+ *acc.*); *adv.* afterward, next

posthabeō, ēre, uī, itus place after, esteem less

postquam after (that), when

potēns, entis powerful, ruling (+ *gen.*), mighty

potior, īrī, ītus possess, gain (+ *abl.*)

potior, ius preferable, better

praeceptum, ī *n.* advice, instruction

praeda, ae *f.* booty, spoils, prey

praemetuō, ere fear beforehand

praeruptus, a, um steep, towering

praesēns, entis present, instant

praesentiō, īre, sēnsī, sēnsus perceive first, suspect

praesēpe, is *n.* stall, hive

praestāns, antis excellent, superior, surpassing

praestō, āre, stitī, status (stitus) excel, be better, surpass

praetendō, ere, ī, ntus hold before, use as screen; stretch before, extend

praetereā *adv.* besides, also, furthermore, hereafter

praeterlābor, ī, lāpsus glide by

praetexō, ere, uī, xtus fringe, cloak

prāvum, ī *n.* wrong, perverse act

pre(he)ndō, ere, ī, nsus seize, grasp

premō, ere, pressī, pressus (re) press, control, overwhelm, crush

pretium, (i)ī *n.* price, reward, value

prex, precis *f.* (usually in pl.) prayer, entreaty, vow

prīmō *adv.* at first, in the beginning

prior, ius soon, former, first, prior

prīscus, a, um ancient, primitive

prīstinus, a, um ancient, former

prius *adv.* former(ly), sooner, first, before

prō instead of, on behalf of, for, before (+ *abl.*)

procāx, procācis bold, insolent, wanton

procella, ae *f.* blast, gale, gust

profor, ārī, ātus speak (out), say

profugus, a, um exiled, fugitive

profundus, a, um deep, profound, vast

prōgeniēs, ēī *f.* offspring, progeny

prōgignō, ere, genuī, genitus bring forth, bear

prohibeō, ēre, uī, itus keep away, prevent, prohibit

prōlēs, is *f.* progeny, offspring

prōmereor, ērī, itus deserve, render service, merit, earn

prōnuba, ae *f.* matron of honor, bride's attendant

prōnus, a, um leaning forward, headlong

propāgō, inis *f.* offshoot, offspring, descendant, posterity

properō (1) hasten, hurry, speed

propinquō (1) approach, draw near (+ *dat.*)

propior, ius nearer, closer

proprius, a, um one's own, permanent, special

propter on account of, near (+ *acc.*)

prōra, ae *f.* prow (of a ship)

prōsequor, ī, secūtus follow, attend, escort

Prōserpina, ae *f.* wife of Pluto and queen of the underworld

prōspectus, ūs *m.* view

prōspiciō, ere, spexī, spectus look out on, see

prōtinus *adv.* continuously, at once, immediately

pudor, ōris *m.* shame, modesty, honor

puella, ae *f.* girl

pugnus, ī *m.* fist

pulcher, chra, chrum beautiful, handsome, splendid, illustrious, noble

pulvis, pulveris *m.* dust

purpureus, a, um purple, crimson

pūrus, a, um pure, bright, clean, clear

putō (1) think, suppose, consider

Pygmaliōn, ōnis *m.* brother of Dido

Q

quā *adv.* where(by), wherever, in any (some) way

quālis, e (such) as, of what sort

quam *adv.* how, than, as

quamquam although, and yet, however

quandō when, since, if ever, because

quantus, a, um how great, how much, how many, as much (as)

quassō (1) shake, shatter, toss

quater four times

quatiō, ere, quassus shake, shatter

queō, quīre, īvī (iī), ītus be able, can

querēla, ae *f.* complaint, lament

queror, ī, questus complain, (be) wail

quia because, since

quīcumque, quaecumque, quodcumque whoever, whatever

quiēs, ētis *f.* quiet, rest, sleep, peace

quiēscō, ere, ēvī, ētus rest, calm, cease

quiētus, a, um quiet, serene, calm, peaceful

quīn that not, but that, why not, in fact

quippe *adv.* to be sure, surely, indeed, truly

Quirīnus, ī *m.* the deified Romulus, legendary founder of Rome, represented as god of war

quisquam, quaequam, quicquam any(one), any(thing)

quisquam, quicquam anyone, anything

quisquis, quidquid (quicquid) *indef. pron.;* **quisquis, quodquod** *indef. adj.* whoever, whatever

quōnam *adv.* whither, (to) where on earth

quoniam since, because

quoque *adv.* also, furthermore, even, too, likewise

quot as many as

quotiēns how often, as often as

R

rabidus, a, um raving, mad, frenzied

rabiēs, ēī *f.* rage, fury, frenzy, madness

radius, (i)ī *m.* rod. spoke, ray, compass

rāmus, ī *m.* branch, bough, limb

rapidus, a, um swift, snatching, whirling, consuming

rapiō, ere, uī, ptus snatch (up, away), seize, ravish; whirl

raptō (1) snatch, drag, carry off

raptum, ī *n.* plunder, prey, booty

rārus, a, um scattered, wide-meshed, far apart

ratis, is *f.* raft, ship, boat

raucus, a, um hoarse, sounding, clanging

rebellis, e rebellious, insurgent

recēdō, ere, cessī, cessus depart, withdraw

recēns, entis recent, fresh, new

recidīvus, a, um revived, renewed

recipiō, ere, cēpī, ceptus receive, accept, take back, recover
recubō (1) recline, lie
recūsō (1) refuse, decline, object
recutiō, ere, cussī, cussus strike (back), shake
redeō, īre, iī (īvī) itus return
redoleō, ēre, uī be fragrant, smell (of)
redūcō, ere, dūxī, ductus bring back, lead back
refugiō, ere, fūgī flee, retreat, recoil, shun
refulgeō, ēre, lsī gleam, shine, glitter
refundō, ere, fūdī, fūsus pour (back, out)
regiō, ōnis *f.* district, region, quarter
rēgnātor, ōris *m.* ruler, lord, director
rēgnō (1) rule, reign
regō, ere, rēxī, rēctus rule, guide, direct, control
re(l)liquiae, ārum *f.* remnants, relics, leavings, rest
repellō, ere, reppulī, repulsus drive back, repel, reject
reperiō, īre, repperī, repertus find (out)
repleō, ēre, ēvī, ētus fill, stuff
repōnō, ere, posuī, pos(i)tus replace, lay away, store (up), deposit, put (back, away)
resīdō, ere, sēdī sit down
resistō, ere, stitī stop, resist (+ *dat.*)
resolvō, ere, ī, solūtus loose(n), free, pay, unravel
resonō (1) (re)sound, roar

respiciō, ere, spexī, spectus look (back) at, regard
respondeō, ēre, ī, ōnsus answer; sympathize with
restō, āre, stitī remain, be left
resurgō, ere, surrēxī, surrēctus rise again
revīsō, ere revisit, see again, return to
revocō (1) recall, call back, retrace, restore
revolvō, ere, ī, volūtus roll over, revolve
rīma, ae *f.* crack, fissure
rīmōsus, a, um leaky, full of cracks
rīpa, ae *f.* bank, shore
rōbur, oris *n.* oak; strength
rogus, ī *m.* (or **rogum, ī** *n.*) funeral pyre
Rōma, ae *f.* Rome, a city and empire
Rōmānus, a, um Roman, of Rome
Rōmulus, a, um of Romulus, Roman
rōscidus, a, um dewy
roseus, a, um rosy, pink
rota, ae *f.* wheel; chariot
rudēns, entis *m.* rope, cable
ruīna, ae *f.* downfall, ruin
rūmor, ōris *m.* rumor, report, gossip
rumpō, ere, rūpī, ruptus break, burst (forth), utter
rūpēs, is *f.* rock, cliff, crag
rūrsus, um *adv.* again, anew, back(ward)
rūs, rūris *n.* country (district)

S

sacerdōs, dōtis *m. (f.)* priest(ess)

sacrō (1) hallow, consecrate, dedicate

saepe *adv.* often, frequently, again and again

saepiō, īre, psī, ptus hedge in, enclose

saeviō, īre, īvī (iī), ītus rage, storm, be fierce

saevus, a, um fierce, harsh, stern, cruel

sagitta, ae *f.* arrow

sal, salis *n. (m.)* salt (water), sea

saltem *adv.* at least, at any rate

saltus, ūs *m.* forest, glade, pasture; leap, bound, dancing

salum, ī *n.* sea, swell (of the sea)

salūs, ūtis *f.* safety, salvation, health

Samos, ī *f.* island of the Aegean, center of the worship of Juno

sānctus, a, um sacred, holy, revered

sanguineus, a, um bloody, blood-red

saniēs, ēī *f.* blood, gore

Sarpēdōn, onis *m.* Sarpedon, Lycian son of Jupiter and ally of the Trojans

sat(is) *adv.* enough, sufficient(ly)

satiō (1) satisfy, sate, satiate, glut

Sāturnia, ae *f.* Juno, daughter of Saturn, father of the gods

Sāturnius, a, um (born) of Saturn, father of Jupiter and Juno

saucius, a, um wounded, hurt

scaena, ae *f.* stage, background

Scaeus, a, um Scaean (referring to the name of a gate at Troy)

scandō, ere, ī, scānsus mount, climb

scelerātus, a, um criminal, wicked

scelus, eris *n.* crime, impiety

scēptrum, ī *n.* staff, scepter, power

scīlicet *adv.* of course, to be sure, doubtless

scindō, ere, scidī, scissus split, divide

scintilla, ae *f.* spark

sciō, īre, īvī (iī), ītus know (how), understand

scopulus, ī *m.* rock, cliff, crag

scūtum, ī *n.* shield

Scyllaeus, a, um of Scylla, a ravenous sea-monster, part woman and part sea creature, girdled with fierce dogs and destructive to mariners who attempted to sail past her cave situated on a narrow strait opposite the great whirlpool Charybdis

sēcessus, ūs *m.* inlet, recess

sēclūdō, ere, sī, sus shut off, seclude, part

secō, āre, uī, sectus cut, slice, cleave

sēcrētus, a, um remote, hidden, secret

secundus, a, um following, favorable, obedient

secūris, is *f.* axe

sedeō, ēre, sēdī, sessus sit (down), settle

sedīle, is *n.* seat, bench

sēmianimis, e half-dead, dying

sēmita, ae *f.* path

sēmivir, virī half-man, effeminate

senātus, ūs *m.* senate, council of elders

senectūs, ūtis *f.* old age

senior, ōris *m.* old (aged) man, sire

sententia, ae *f.* opinion, purpose, view, resolve

sentiō, īre, sēnsī, sēnsus feel, perceive

sentus, a, um rough, thorny

sepeliō, īre, īvī (iī), pultus bury, inter

septem seven

serēnus, a, um serene, calm, fair, clear

Serestus, ī *m.* Trojan leader

Sergestus, ī *m.* Trojan leader

sermō, ōnis *m.* conversation, speech

serō, ere, sēvī, satus sow, beget

serpēns, entis *m.* (*f.*) serpent, snake

serpō, ere, psī, pstus creep (on), crawl

sertum, ī *n.* wreath, garland

sībilus, a, um hissing, whirring

Sibylla, ae *f.* the Sibyl, an ancient Italian prophetess

Sīcania, ae *f.* Sicily, a large island south of Italy

siccō (1) dry, stanch

Siculus, a, um Sicilian, of Sicily, a large island south of Italy

Sīdonius, a, um of Sidon, a famous city of Phoenicia

signum, ī *n.* sign, signal, token, mark

sileō, ēre, uī be silent, be still

silex, icis *m.* (*f.*) flint, rock, crag

similis, e like, similar (+ *dat.* or *gen.*)

Simoīs, entis *m.* river near Troy

simulācrum, ī *n.* image, phantom, likeness, statue

simulō (1) pretend, imitate, feign

sīn if however, if on the contrary, but if

sine without (+ *abl.*)

singulī, ae, a each, one by one

sinō, ere, sīvī, situs permit, allow; desert

sinuō (1) fold, curve, twist, wind

sinus, ūs *m.* fold, bosom, bay, hollow, gulf

sistō, ere, stetī, status stand, stop, stay

situs, ūs *m.* position; neglect; decay

sīve, seu whether, or, either if, or if

socius, a, um allied, associated, friendly

sōl, sōlis *m.* sun; day; personified as **Sōl, Sōlis** *m.* sun-god

soleō, ēre, itus sum be accustomed

solium, (i)ī *n.* throne, seat

solum, ī *n.* ground, soil, earth

solvō, ere, ī, solūtus loose(n), release, break down, free, pay

Somnus, ī *m.* Sleep, Slumber personified as a divinity

sonitus, ūs *m.* sound, roar, crash, noise

sonō, āre, uī, itus (re)sound, roar

sonōrus, a, um roaring, howling

sopōrō (1) make drowsy, drug

sopōrus, a, um sleepy, causing slumber

soror, ōris *f.* sister

sors, rtis *f.* lot, destiny, portion, oracle, fate

spargō, ere, rsī, rsus scatter, sprinkle

Sparta, ae *f.* region of Greece, home of Helen and Menelaus

speciēs, ēī *f.* appearance, sight, aspect

spelunca, ae *f.* cave, cavern, grotto

spernō, ere, sprēvī, sprētus scorn, reject, despise

spērō (1) hope (for, to), expect, suppose

spēs, eī *f.* hope, expectation

spīra, ae *f.* fold, coil, spire

spīritus, ūs *m.* breath, spirit, life, soul

spīrō (1) breathe (forth), blow, quiver (i.e., with signs of life), live

spolium, (i)ī *n.* hide (of an animal); commonly, in the *n. pl.*, spoils, arms stripped from an enemy, plunder

spōns, spontis *f.* wish, will, desire

spūma, ae *f.* foam, froth, spray

spūmō (1) foam, froth, spray

squāleō, ēre, uī be rough, be filthy

squāmeus, a, um scaly

stabilis, e firm, stable, lasting

stāgnum, ī *n.* still waters, depth

statuō, ere, uī, ūtus set (up), found, establish

stēllātus, a, um starred, star-spangled

sternō, ere, strāvī, strātus lay low, spread, strew

Sthenelus, ī *m.* Greek leader

stimulō (1) spur, goad, prick, incite

stīpō (1) stuff, crowd, throng, stow

stirps, pis *f.* stock, lineage, race

strātum, ī *n.* bed, couch; pavement

strepitus, ūs *m.* uproar, noise

strīd(e)ō, ere (*or* ēre), **dī** grate, creak, whir, hiss, rustle, roar

strīdor, ōris *m.* noise, creaking, roar, grating, whirring

stringō, ere, strinxī, strictus graze

struō, ere, strūxī, strūctus build, plan, contrive

studium, (i)ī *n.* eagerness, desire, zeal, pursuit

stuppeus, a, um (of) flax or hemp (used in the production of rope)

Stygius, a, um Stygian, of the Styx, a river in Hades

subdūcō, ere, dūxī, ductus take away, remove, beach, bring out of water

subiciō, ere, iēcī, iectus place under (+ *dat.*), vanquish

subigō, ere, ēgī, āctus push, force; subdue

subitō *adv.* suddenly

subitus, a, um sudden, unexpected

subnectō, ere, nex(u)ī, nexus tie (beneath), fasten

subolēs, is *f.* offspring, progeny, child

subrigō, ere, surrēxī, rēctus
raise, rise

subsistō, ere, stitī halt, stop,
withstand, resist

subter beneath, below

subtrahō, ere, trāxī, tractus
withdraw

subvectō (1) bear, convey,
transport

subvolvō, ere, ī, volūtus roll up

sūdō (1) sweat, perspire

sufficiō, ere, fēcī, fectus supply,
suffuse; be sufficient

sulcus, ī *m.* furrow, trench, ditch

summergō (subm–), ere, rsī, rsus
sink, drown

summoveō, ēre, mōvī, mōtus
remove

sūmō, ere, mpsī, mptus take,
assume; (+ **poenam**) exact (a
penalty)

superbia, ae *f.* loftiness,
haughtiness, pride, arrogance

superbus, a, um proud, haughty

superēmineō, ēre tower above

superō (1) surmount, surpass,
overcome, survive

supīnus, a, um flat, upturned

supplex, icis *m.* (*f.*) suppliant; *adj.*
suppliant, humble

suprā above, over (+ *acc.*)

suscipiō, ere, cēpī, ceptus take up,
beget, bear, receive, catch (up)

suscitō (1) arouse, stir up, excite

suspendō, ere, ī, ēnsus suspend,
hang (up)

suspiciō, ere, spexī, spectus
look from beneath, suspect,
look up at

sūtilis, e sewn, with seams

Sȳchaeus, ī *m.* deceased husband
of Dido

Syrtis (or syrtis), is *f.* region of
quicksand on the northern coast
of Africa; sand bar, reef

T

tābeō, ēre drip, soak, melt, waste

tabula, ae *f.* plank, board

tacitus, a, um silent, noiseless,
secret, still

taeda, ae *f.* (bridal) torch,
pinewood torch

tam *adv.* so (much), such, as

tamen *adv.* nevertheless, however,
but

tangō, ere, tetigī, tāctus touch,
reach

tantum *adv.* so much, so great(ly),
only

Tartareus, a, um of or concerning
Tartarus, abode of the wicked
and impious in Hades

taurus, ī *m.* bull, ox, bullock

tegō, ere, tēxī, tēctus cover, hide,
protect

tēla, ae *f.* web, textile

temnō, ere scorn, disdain,
despise

temperō (1) control, restrain,
refrain, calm

tempestās, ātis *f.* tempest, storm;
time

templum, ī *n.* temple, sanctuary,
sacred space, shrine

temptō (1) try, test, seek, examine,
attempt

tenāx, ācis tenacious, holding (to)

Tenedos, ī *f.* small island near Troy

tenuis, e slight, thin, fine, delicate

ter three times

tergum, ī *n.* back, body, rear, hide (of an animal)

terō, ere, trīvī, trītus rub, wear, waste

terreō, ēre, uī, itus frighten, terrify

terrificō (1) frighten, terrify, alarm

territō (1) frighten, terrify, alarm

tertius, a, um third

testor, ārī, ātus call to witness, swear by, testify

thalamus, ī *m.* marriage chamber, bedroom

theātrum, ī *n.* theater

Thēseus, eī (eos), *acc.* **ea** *m.* mythical king of Athens, who, among his other exploits, descended to Hades with his friend Pirithoüs to carry off Proserpina.

Thyias, adis *f.* Bacchant, a woman devotee of the worship of Bacchus

thymum, ī *n.* thyme, a flowering plant

Tiberīnus, a, um of the Tiber, an Italian river on which Rome is situated

Tiberīnus, ī *m.* (god of) the Tiber, river on which Rome is situated

timeō, ēre, uī fear, dread, be anxious

timor, ōris *m.* fear, anxiety, dread

torqueō, ēre, rsī, rtus twist, sway, hurl, turn

torreō, ēre, uī, tostus parch, roast

torus, ī *m.* (banqueting, funeral) couch, bed

torvus, a, um fierce, grim, lowering

tot so many, as many

totidem as many, so many

totiēns so often, so many times

trabs (trabēs), trabis *f.* beam, timber, tree

trāiciō, ere, iēcī, iectus throw across, pierce

tranquillus, a, um tranquil, calm

trāns across, beyond (+ *acc.*)

trānsfīgō, ere, xī, xus pierce, transfix

trānsmittō, ere, mīsī, missus cross, send across

trānsportō (1) carry across, transport

tremefaciō, ere, fēcī, factus make tremble, appall, alarm

tremō, ere, uī tremble, quiver, shake

trepidus, a, um trembling, excited

trēs, tria three

tridēns, entis *m.* trident, symbol of Neptune as god of the sea

trietēricus, a, um triennial

trifaux, faucis three-throated

Trīnacrius, a, um Trinacrian, Sicilian

Trītōn, ōnis *m.* a minor sea-god known for his skill in blowing a conch (sea shell) as a trumpet

Trītōnis, idis *f.* Minerva, goddess of wisdom and the arts

Tritōnius, a, um Tritonian (an
epithet of Minerva)

triumphus, ī *m.* triumph, victory

Troiānus, a, um Trojan, of Troy

Trōius, a, um Trojan, of Troy

Trōs, Trōis *m.* Trojan

tueor, ērī, itus (tūtus) watch, look
at, protect, eye

tumeō, ēre, uī swell, be swollen

tumidus, a, um swollen, swelling

tumultus, ūs *m.* tumult, uprising,
clamor

tumulus, ī *m.* hill, mound, tomb

turba, ae *f.* mob, crowd

turbidus, a, um troubled,
agitated

turbō (1) throw into confusion,
agitate, confuse, shake, disturb

turbō, inis *m.* whirl(wind, pool),
storm

turpis, e shameful, disgraceful

turris, is *f.* tower, turret

tūtus, a, um protected, safe,
secure

Tȳdīdēs, ae *m.* son of Tydeus,
Diomedes, who fought against
Aeneas in single combat before
Troy and would have killed him
had Venus not spirited her son
away

Tyndaris, idis *f.* daughter of
Tyndarus, Helen

tyrannus, ī *m.* ruler, chieftain,
tyrant

Tyrrhēnus, a, um Tyrrhenian,
of Etruria, a district of
northwestern Italy

Tyrus (os), ī *f.* city of Phoenicia,
birthplace of Dido

U

ūber, eris *n.* udder, breast;
(symbol of) fertility

ulcīscor, ī, ultus avenge, punish

Ulixēs, is (eī, ī) *m.* Odysseus, the
wily Greek leader who is the
central character in Homer's
Odyssey (his name in Latin is
Ulixes, or Ulysses)

ulterior, ius farther, further,
beyond

ultimus, a, um last, final, farthest

ultrā more than (+ *acc.*); *adv.*
beyond, farther

ultrīx, īcis avenging, vengeful

ultrō *adv.* further, voluntarily

ululātus, ūs *m.* wail, shriek, howl,
shout

ululō (1) howl, wail, shout, shriek

ulva, ae *f.* sedge, marsh grass

umbrifer, era, erum shady

ūmēns, entis moist, dewy, damp

ūmidus, a, um moist, damp,
dewy

umquam *adv.* ever, at any time

ūnā *adv.* together, at the same
time

uncus, a, um curved, bent,
hooked

unde from where, from which
source

undique *adv.* everywhere, from all
sides

undo (1) swell, roll, wave

undōsus, a, um billowing, wavy

unguis, is *m.* nail, claw

urgeō, ēre, ursī drive, force, press

uterque, utraque, utrumque each
(of two), both

uterus, ī *m.* belly, womb

utinam *adv.* oh that!, I wish that!

ūtor, ī, ūsus use, employ (+ *abl.*)

uxōrius, a, um wife-ruled, uxorious

V

vadum, ī *n.* shallow(s), shoal, depth(s)

vagor, ārī, ātus wander, roam, rove

valeō, ēre, uī be strong, avail, be able, fare well

validus, a, um strong, mighty, sturdy

vallis, is *f.* valley, vale, dale

vānus, a, um vain, idle, empty, useless, false

varius, a, um varied, different, diverse, manifold

vectō (1) convey, carry, bear

vehō, ere, vēxī, vectus carry, convey

vēlō (1) veil, cover, deck, clothe

vēlōx, ōcis swift, quick, rapid, fleet

velut(ī) (even) as, just as

venēnum, ī *n.* poison, venom, drug

venerābilis, e venerable, causing awe

Venus, eris *f.* goddess of love and beauty, love

vērō *adv.* truly, indeed, but

verrō, ere, ī, versus sweep (over)

versō (1) keep turning, roll, revolve

vertex, icis *m.* peak, summit, head, top; whirlpool

vertō, ere, ī, rsus (over)turn, (ex)change

vērum, ī *n.* truth, right, reality; *adv.* but

vērus, a, um true, real, genuine, honest

vēscor, ī use as food, feed upon, eat (+ *abl.*)

Vesta, ae *f.* goddess of the hearth

vester, tra, trum your(s), your own

vestīgium, (i)ī *n.* track, footprint, step, trace

vestis, is *f.* garment, cloth(ing), robe

vetō, āre, uī, itus forbid, prevent

vetus, eris old, aged, ancient, former

vibrō (1) quiver, vibrate, dart

victōria, ae *f.* victory, conquest, triumph

vigeō, ēre, uī flourish, be strong, thrive

vigil, īlis *m.* (*f.*) guard, watchman, sentinel; *adj.* wakeful, watchful, sleepless

vinc(u)lum, ī *n.* chain, bond, cable

vīnum, ī *n.* wine

virga, ae *f.* staff, wand, twig

virgō, inis *f.* girl, maid(en)

viridis, e green, fresh, vigorous

virtūs, ūtis *f.* manliness, excellence in battle, valor

vīsus, ūs *m.* sight, view, vision, aspect

vitta, ae *f.* fillet, garland, band

vīvus, a, um living, natural, alive

volitō (1) fly, speed, flit, flutter

volō (1) fly, move with speed

volūmen, inis *n.* fold, coil, roll

volūtō (1) revolve, turn (over), roll, ponder

vorō (1) swallow (up)

vulgus, ī *n. (m.)* crowd, throng, herd

vulnus, eris *n.* wound, deadly blow

vultus, ūs *m.* countenance, face, aspect

Z

Zephyrus, ī *m.* (west) wind